THE HOLY SACRIFICE OF THE MASS

BOOK OF THE HOLY CHILD (Grade One)

LIFE OF MY SAVIOR (Grade Two)

LIFE OF THE SOUL (Grade Three)

BEFORE CHRIST CAME (Grade Four)

THE VINE AND THE BRANCHES (Grade Five)

THE MISSAL (Grade Six)

HIGHWAY TO GOD (Grades Seven and Eight)

Accompanying this Series is the RELIGION IN LIFE CURRICULUM for grades one to six and PRACTICAL PROBLEMS IN RELIGION for grades seven and eight.

The Holy Sacrifice of The Mass

Prepared (in co-operation with a group of priests and sisters teaching in elementary schools)

IN THE CATECHETICAL INSTITUTE OF
MARQUETTE UNIVERSITY

George H. Mahowald, S.J., Ph.D., Chairman
Raphael N. Hamilton, S.J., Ph.D.
Gerard Smith, S.J., M.A.

By

EDWARD A. FITZPATRICK, PH.D.
Educational Director

ST. AUGUSTINE ACADEMY PRESS
HOMER GLEN, ILLINOIS

Nihil obstat:
  H. B. RIES,
    Censor librorum

Imprimatur:
  ✠ SAMUEL ALPHONSUS STRITCH,
    Archiepiscopus Milwaukiensis

June 24, 1936—July 28, 1937

This book was originally published in 1937 by The Bruce Publishing Company.
This edition retypeset in 2017 by St. Augustine Academy Press in imitation of
the 1937 edition, with the addition of a chapter (four) from the 1949 edition.
Several of the illustrations were replaced due to deterioration of the originals,
and many additional illustrations have been included.

Softcover ISBN: 978-1-64051-038-8
Hardcover ISBN: 978-1-64051-039-5

INTRODUCTION

To the Students:

We go to Mass to serve God, not merely to hear the music or to listen to the sermon. We go to Mass to give service to God in a great public act of worship. We go to Mass to pray with all other Catholics. We go to offer ourselves to God. By joining ourselves with Christ in the Mass our service to God is more pleasing and more worthy because of Christ. When we really participate in the Mass we surrender ourselves to God. We acknowledge we are His creatures.

All we have is His, and we have it as a privilege from Him. In surrendering ourselves to God, we want to give to Him what is His own.

This little book is written to help you as a lay person to make the Mass a real service of God. It shows you how men always desired to show their love of God, to praise Him, to be thankful to Him, and to ask His mercy and forgiveness for their sins. They did this by making many different kinds of offerings or sacrifices to God. They identified themselves with the Victim of the Sacrifice whether it was a lamb as in the Old Law among the Jews, or whether it is the Lamb of God, Christ Himself, as in the Mass.

There are a great many interesting things in this book for you to learn about sacrifices to God, about the Passion, Resurrection, and Ascension of our Lord, about the Missal and the way the Masses change from Sunday to Sunday and from season to season. Learn these things well. Memorize as many of the passages from the Mass and the Scriptures as you can. However, you must not forget that the main thing is to realize that in the Mass on every Sunday, as on every Holyday of Obligation and whenever else you go to Mass, you must join with Christ and offer up yourself. That will help make the Mass for you what it really is, the greatest prayer in the Church. Show in your attendance at Mass your love of the Most Holy Trinity, the Father, the Son, and the Holy Ghost.

CONTENTS

PART I
Foundations of the Mass

Chapter I

DO YOU TAKE PART IN THE SACRIFICE OF THE MASS?

The Most Solemn Moment of the Mass. "There is one part of the Mass which always makes me hold my breath and keep my eyes fixed on the priest," said a boy who had been attending Mass for five years. "While in the beginning of the Mass," he went on to say, "people are quiet and busy about their prayers, at this point everything takes on a great hush. A gentle ringing of a bell is a sort of beginning of it, then everything seems to become quieter and quieter, except for this gentle tinkling of a bell, and then one says, as he was taught in the early grades—it just seems to come out—*'My Lord and my God!'* "

The Consecration of the Mass. We know that the boy was speaking of the Consecration of the bread and the wine. It is, as Cardinal Newman says, a tremendous event. Men and women, boys and girls, might well hold their breath and a great hush fall over the congregation as the bread and wine is changed into the Body and Blood of Christ on the altar there before them. What a miracle!

This Is My Body. In the third grade we learned the words which the priest says at the time when, through the power of Christ, he changes the bread and wine into the Body and Blood of Christ. Over the host he says:

1

"Who the day before He suffered took bread into His holy and venerable hands, and with His eyes lifted up toward heaven, unto Thee, God, His almighty Father, giving thanks to Thee, blessed, broke and gave to His disciples, saying: Take and eat ye all of this, FOR THIS IS MY BODY."

He genuflects and adores It, and then elevates, that is, raises It above his head, so that the people also may adore.

At the time of the elevation it would be well for us to repeat the words of the Apostle Thomas, *"My Lord and my God."*

This Is the Blood of the New Testament. The priest then uncovers the chalice and takes it into his hands:

"In like manner, after He had supped, taking also this excellent chalice into His holy and venerable hands, and giving thanks to Thee, He blessed and gave to His disciples, saying: Take and drink ye all of this, FOR THIS IS THE CHALICE OF MY BLOOD, OF THE NEW AND ETERNAL TESTAMENT: THE MYSTERY OF FAITH: WHICH SHALL BE SHED FOR YOU AND FOR MANY UNTO THE REMISSION OF SINS.

"As often as ye shall do these things, ye shall do them in remembrance of Me."

The Last Supper. "Do this in remembrance of Me." These words carry our minds back to the first Holy Thursday. The twelve Apostles are there with Christ to celebrate the Jewish feast of the Passover. At that time these words were first spoken. Let us once more bring to our minds the picture of the Last Supper: Christ, His disciples, the meal.

The story as St. Matthew tells it briefly is as follows:

And while they were at supper, Jesus took bread, and blessed, and broke, and gave it to His disciples, and said: Take ye, and eat; this is My Body. And taking the chalice, He gave thanks and gave to them, saying: Drink ye all of this; for this is My blood of the New Testament, which shall be shed for many unto the remission of sins. (Matthew xxvi. 26-28.)

At the consecration the priest repeats the words of Christ:
"This is My Body. This is My Blood."

Melchisedech, the Priest of the Most High God.
The story of the priest Melchisedech also will come to
mind at this time, and the sacrifice he offered. He offered
bread and wine too. Melchisedech was the "priest of the

Most High God" at Salem. The first book of the Bible,
Genesis, tells about him. All we need recall now is the kind
of sacrifice he offered:

> But Melchisedech, the King of Salem, bringing forth bread
> and wine for he was priest of the most high God, blessed him
> [Abraham] . . . (Genesis xiv. 18.)

Non-Catholics Impressed by the Mass.   Non-
Catholics also who have attended Mass have been heard
to express somewhat the same feeling as that of the boy
whose words are given at the beginning of this chapter.
They are struck by the reverent quietness and attention
at the Mass. They are struck by what the youngster calls
"the great hush" at the Consecration of the bread and
wine which the gentle sound of the bell only seems to
make more solemn and more quiet. They have noticed
how everything leads up to this solemn moment and how
quickly the Mass is over after the Communion.

Non-Catholic Only a Spectator.   Impressive and
solemn as this is to a non-Catholic, it can never be so
impressive or solemn as it should be to you. The non-
Catholic is only a spectator. He cannot fully realize that
God Himself has come down on this very altar in front of
him. He does not realize that the priest of this sacrifice
on the altar is Christ Himself, or that He is also the Victim
offered to God the Father. We shall study these facts more
fully in this book.

You Are a Participant.   As for you, you are not a
spectator. You must take part in the sacrifice. You are a
participant. Only a little while before the Consecration,
the priest says, meaning you and every Catholic in the
church, "Brethren (i.e., Brothers), pray that my sacrifice
and *yours* may be acceptable to God the Father Almighty."

Have We Been Mere Spectators at Mass? We have often gone to Mass and been mere spectators. *We attend Mass,* we hear people say. We "hear" Mass, when we mean that we have listened. We have gone to Mass too and read our prayers, but we have not made the Mass itself *our* prayer. We have not lifted up our hearts to God with the priest.

Sacrifices Among the Hebrews. Men in all ages have made sacrifices to God. This was true in the olden times, particularly among the Hebrews, who preserved the knowledge of the one true God. These sacrifices will help us to understand the greatest of all sacrifices, the Sacrifice of the Mass. Sacrifice is in man's nature. He wants to please God. He wants to offer sacrifice to God as a penance for his own sins, or as a thanksgiving for the things he enjoys of God's creation. That seems true of men everywhere.

The First Mass. To appreciate how important the Mass is in our own lives and what it means to us, we must go back to the first Holy Thursday and Good Friday. Then Christ celebrated the Pasch of the Old Law and began (or instituted) there the sacrifice of the New Law. We shall then realize more fully the spirit of the Mass, and our part in it. We shall see that the Mass is a repetition of Calvary with the same Priest, Christ, and the same Victim, Christ.

The Liturgical Year and the Masses for Different Days. This study will show that the Mass changes from day to day, from Sunday to Sunday and from season to season. This makes it necessary that we learn something about what is called the Liturgical Year. It will also teach us how different the Mass is in its spirit during the year, even though the central part, the Canon, is the same always.

The Plan of This Book. This is, in short, the plan of this book—to study the following topics in the order given:

1. The Sacrifices of the Old Law.
2. The Last Supper, Calvary, and the New Sacrifice.
3. The Ordinary of the Mass (the unchanging parts).
4. The Liturgical Year.
5. The Individual Masses of Sundays and Holydays.

What Did I Learn from This Chapter?

1. What are the most solemn moments of the Mass?
2. What happens at the Consecration of the bread?
3. What happens at the Consecration of the wine?
4. Why do you think Cardinal Newman called the Mass a tremendous event? Do you think it is tremendous?
5. In your own words tell the story of the Last Supper.
6. Why does the Consecration mean more to you than to a non-Catholic?
7. What is necessary for a religious sacrifice?
8. Who was the Priest at the Last Supper (the first Mass)?
9. Who was the Priest on Calvary?
10. Who was the Victim at the Last Supper?
11. Who was the Victim on Calvary?
12. What is meant by the liturgical year?
13. Who is Melchisedech? Who is Thomas?

My Part

What did I do at the Consecration last Sunday?
- Did I read prayers at the Mass?
- Did I follow the Mass with the Missal?
- Did I say my beads?
- Did I listen carefully, watching the priest all the time?
- Did my mind wander off to other things?

Did I feel that I participated fully in the Mass?

What little or big sacrifices do you make (or have you made the past week or month)? For what purpose or purposes?

I shall do my best to be a participant in every Mass I attend.

I shall use my Missal every time I attend Mass.

I shall say the words of the Consecration along with the priest, and try to realize every time what a tremendous event the Mass really is.

Using the Missal

Find in your Missal:
- The Consecration of the bread.
- The Consecration of the wine.
- The *Orate Fratres* (Pray, brethren).

Be sure to use your Missal next Sunday.

Prayers

Learn by heart, if you do not know them exactly:
- The Consecration of the bread.
- The Consecration of the wine.
- The *Oratre Fratres* (Pray brethren).

Problems and Activities

Read the story of Da Vinci's "Last Supper." If possible, find a copy of the picture and bring it to class.

Read the story of Melchisedech in the Old Testament, and be prepared to tell it to the class.

Bring to class a liturgical or religious calendar. If none are available, write to a Catholic publisher for one. Look in your missal to see if there is a liturgical calendar there.

Be prepared in class to tell what you can learn from the liturgical calendar.

Every morning when you come to class go to the liturgical calendar to find out what you can about the day.

In any game that you play tell what the difference is between a participant and a spectator. Apply what you have said to your participation in the Mass.

Bible Passages

For the following passages:
1. Tell whether they are from the Old or the New Testament.
2. Find the passage in the Bible.

3. Who said the words?

4. When were they said? To whom?

a) "Take and eat; this is My Body."

b) "My Lord and my God."

c) "This is My Blood of the New Covenant."

d) "Do this in remembrance of Me."

Vocabulary

Consecration: from *consecrate*, to make holy, to set apart as sacred. It means that part of the Mass in which the bread and wine are changed into the Body and Blood of Christ.

Solemn: sacred, very quiet.

Chalice: a cup with a stand, especially the cup used to contain the wine in the Consecration of the Mass.

Remission: forgiveness, applied to sins.

Liturgical: relating to public worship, such as the Mass.

Spectator: A person who looks on.

Participant: A person who takes part, or joins in.

New Law: The law given by Christ and found in the New Testament and the teachings or tradition of the Church. The Old Law is the Law of Moses and the Old Testament.

New Covenant: The new arrangements made by Christ, contained in the New Testament and in the teachings or tradition of the Church. The Old Covenant is the covenant of the Old Testament. The New Law and the New Covenant have practically the same meaning.

Catechism (Christian Doctrine)*

• When and where are the bread and wine changed into the Body and Blood of Christ? (262)

• What is the first Mass? (263)

• When did Christ institute the Holy Eucharist? (239)

• Who were present when Christ instituted the Holy Eucharist? (240)

• How did our Lord institute the Holy Eucharist? (241)

---

* The numbers in parentheses following the Catechism questions refer to the numbers preceding the questions at the back of this book.

Chapter II

THE SACRIFICES MEN OFFERED GOD

Sacrifice of the Mass and Plan of Redemption. In order really to understand the Mass, we must know about God's plan for the redemption or salvation of man. The Mass is the result of that plan. When man fell into sin in the Garden of Eden, God promised that a Redeemer would come from the sons of Eve. God said to the devil, who had taken on the form of a serpent:

> "I will put enmity between thee and the woman and thy seed and her seed. She shall crush thy head, and thou shalt lie in wait for her heel."

Christ came to earth to save men because of that promise of God in the Garden of Eden. The Last Supper and the Crucifixion were a complete satisfaction to God the Father by Christ for the sin of Adam. On the first Holy Thursday Jesus offered the first Mass. He commanded that the Apostles should repeat what He had done, saying: "Do this in remembrance of Me." Thus Jesus gave us the Mass, the great center of Catholic worship. We shall emphasize this relation later.

Sacrifices to God. Men everywhere have tried to express their worship of God by giving up or offering something of their own to Him. Men everywhere have offered up animals to God—sheep, oxen—and even birds. They have in some places offered up their own children to God.

9

They have sacrificed other things, too. They made these offerings sometimes because they were sorry for their sins and desired God's forgiveness. They made these offerings or sacrifices, too, because they wished to acknowledge that God was their Creator and that they were His creatures. They did it to praise God or to give thanksgiving to God. In some way the person identified himself with his offering. He was giving something of his own—something that belonged to him. In this way, he asked for forgiveness of his sins, or expressed his thanksgiving, his praise, his love of his Creator, and his willingness to serve. These sacrifices were offered by a special group of men, selected for this purpose, the priests, at a special place—an altar in the temple or church, or on the hillside.

Four Elements in Sacrifice. It will be noted in this description of the sacrifices or offerings which men offered to God that there are four elements:

1. A victim—an animal or whatever is offered up to God.
2. A person who offered the sacrifice—the priest.
3. An altar—or place of sacrifice.
4. It should be noted, too, that the purpose was to satisfy God for our sins, to give Him praise or thanksgiving, or to ask Him for something (petition). In other words, the purpose was to acknowledge God as Creator and Lord of all things.

The people and the priest identified themselves with the victim offered. With the external or outward acts they joined their minds and hearts and souls.

God Teaches the Hebrews. What we have just said is true generally of mankind. We are, however, interested especially in the sacrifices or offerings or oblations made to God by the Jewish people, His chosen people. These sacrifices, or oblations, which means the same thing, were commanded by God Himself. He told or revealed to the Hebrews how they should worship Him. The manner of making the offering, the victims or offerings or oblations that were to be made, who was to offer them, are told in the early books of the Old Testament of the Holy Bible. They are found especially in the books of Moses: The Book of Genesis, The Book of Exodus, The Book of Leviticus, The Book of Numbers. Look at the Holy Bible at home or in the classroom and find these books in the Old Testament at its beginning.

An Example: The Jewish Pasch. To show what these rites, or rules or ways of offering sacrifice were, we quote from the Book of Exodus, Chapter 12, Verses 1 to 18, what is said of the feast of the Pasch, or Passover, which is the feast which Christ was keeping on the first Holy Thursday night. The reason for the feast is given fully in the passage quoted below:

1. And the Lord said to Moses and Aaron in the land of Egypt:

2. This month shall be to you the beginning of months: it shall be the first in the months of the year.

3. Speak ye to the whole assembly of the children of Israel, and say to them: On the tenth day of this month let every man take a lamb by their families and houses.

4. But if the number be less than may suffice to eat the lamb, he shall take unto him his neighbor that joineth to his house, according to the number of souls which may be enough to eat the lamb.

5. And it shall be a lamb without blemish, a male, of one year: according to which rite also you shall take a kid.

6. And you shall keep it until the fourteenth day of this month: and the whole multitude of the children of Israel shall sacrifice it in the evening.

7. And they shall take the blood thereof, and put it upon both the side posts, and on the upper door posts of the houses, wherein they shall eat it.

Hebrews celebrating the first Pasch.

8. And they shall eat the flesh that night roasted at the fire, and unleavened bread* with wild lettuce.

9. You shall not eat thereof any thing raw, nor boiled in water, but only roasted at the fire: you shall eat the head with the feet and entrails thereof.

10. Neither shall there remain any thing of it until morning. If there be any thing left, you shall burn it with fire.

11. And thus you shall eat it: you shall gird your reins, and you shall have shoes on your feet, holding staves in your hands, and you shall eat in haste: for it is the Phase (that is, the Passage) of the Lord.

12. And I will pass through the land of Egypt that night, and will kill every firstborn in the land of Egypt both man and beast; and against all the gods of Egypt I will execute judgments: I *am* the Lord.

13. And the blood shall be unto you for a sign in the houses where you shall be: and I shall see the blood and shall pass over you: and the plague shall not be upon you to destroy you, when I shall strike the land of Egypt.

14. And this day shall be for a memorial to you: and you shall keep it a feast to the Lord in your generations with an everlasting observance.

15. Seven days shall you eat unleavened bread: in the first day there shall be no leaven in your houses: whosoever shall eat any thing leavened, from the first day until the seventh day, that soul shall perish out of Israel.

16. The first day shall be holy and solemn, and the seventh day shall be kept with the like solemnity: you shall do no work in them, except those things that belong to eating.

17. And you shall observe *the feast* of the unleavened bread: for in this same day I will bring forth your army out of the land of Egypt, and you shall keep this day in your generations by a perpetual observance.

18. The first month, the fourteenth day of the month in the evening, you shall eat unleavened bread, until the one and twentieth day of the same month in the evening.

---

*   Unleavened bread is bread made without yeast. Leaven is any material such as yeast which causes fermentation, and thus raises dough. The Host in the Sacrament of the Holy Eucharist is made of unleavened bread.

19. Seven days there shall not be found any leaven in your houses: he that shall eat leavened bread, his soul shall perish out of the assembly of Israel, whether he be a stranger or born in the land.

20. You shall not eat any thing leavened: in all your habitations you shall eat unleavened bread.

21. And Moses called all the ancients of the children of Israel, and said to them: Go take a lamb by your families, and sacrifice the Phase.

22. And dip a bunch of hyssop* in the blood that is at the door, and sprinkle the transom of the door therewith, and both the door cheeks: let none of you go out of the door of his house till morning.

23. For the Lord will pass through striking the Egyptians: and when He shall see the blood on the transom, and on both the posts, He will pass over the door of the house, and not suffer the destroyer to come into your houses and to hurt *you*.

24. Thou shalt keep this thing as a law for thee and thy children forever.

25. And when you have entered into the land which the Lord will give you as He hath promised, you shall observe these ceremonies.

26. And when your children shall say to you: What is the meaning of this service?

27. You shall say to them: It is the victim of the passage of the Lord, when He passed over the houses of the children of Israel in Egypt, striking the Egyptians, and saving our houses. And the people bowing themselves, adored.

28. And the children of Israel going forth did as the Lord had commanded Moses and Aaron.

Two Kinds of Sacrifices. The sacrifices which God commanded the Jews to offer fall into two main classes:

1. Bloody sacrifices.
2. Unbloody sacrifices.

---

* A fragrant bushy plant.

Bloody Sacrifices. The bloody sacrifices of the Old Testament included the blood of sheep, goats, oxen, and doves. The blood was the source of life of animals, and in offering it the individuals acknowledged the Lordship of God over not only the victim offered but over the persons who offered it, or for whom it was offered. Among the Hebrews the chief of the bloody sacrifices was the Holocaust, that is, an offering completely burned up. This was offered every day, morning and evening. Often the victim was slain, and the blood poured out. The entire victim was burned. It was the great *public act* of worship to God.

In some of the sacrifices, especially the peace offering, expressing praise and thanksgiving to God, there was a sacred banquet, or meal, when certain parts were eaten by the person who gave the offering, by the priest and by the poor. In the Mass the Holy Communion is the Sacred Banquet. It is an important part of the sacrifice. Whenever we participate in the Sacrifice of the Mass we should plan to receive Holy Communion. This really completes our part in it.

Bloody Sacrifices: Abel and Abraham. One example of the offering of animals goes back to the very beginnings of the history of man. Abel, the shepherd, gave to the Lord God the firstlings, i.e., the firstborn, of his flock and God was pleased. This is what the book of Genesis (Chapter IV, verse 4) says:

> Abel also offered of the firstlings of his flock, and of their fat: and the Lord had respect to Abel, and his offerings.

Another example which is mentioned in the prayer of the Mass is the sacrifice of Abraham. This is told in the following words in the Book of Genesis:

Abraham is willing to sacrifice his only son
in obedience to God.

1. After these things God tempted Abraham and said to him: Abraham, Abraham. And he answered: Here I am.

2. He said to him: Take thy only begotten son Isaac, whom thou lovest, and go into the land of vision: and there thou shalt offer him for an holocaust upon one of the mountains which I will show thee.

3. So Abraham rising up in the night, saddled his ass: and took with him two young men and Isaac his son: and when he had cut wood for the holocaust he went his way to the place which God had commanded him.

4. And on the third day, lifting up his eyes, he saw the place afar off.

5. And he said to his young men: Stay you here with the ass: I and the boy will go with speed as far as yonder, and after we have worshiped, will return to you.

6. And he took the wood for the holocaust, and laid it upon Isaac his son: and he himself carried in his hands fire and a sword. And as they two went on together,

7. Isaac said to his father: My father. And he answered: What wilt thou son? Behold, saith he, fire and wood: where is the victim of the holocaust?

8. And Abraham said: God will provide himself a victim for an holocaust, my son. So they went on together.

9. And they came to the place which God had shown him, where he built an altar, and laid the wood in order upon it: and when he had bound Isaac his son, he laid him on the altar upon the pile of wood.

10. And he put forth his hand and took the sword, to sacrifice his son.

11. And behold an angel of the Lord from heaven called to him, saying: Abraham, Abraham. And he answered: Here I am.

12. And he said to him: Lay not thy hands upon the boy, neither do thou anything to him: now I know that thou fearest God, and hast not spared thy only begotten son for my sake.

13. Abraham lifted up his eyes, and saw behind his back a ram against the briers sticking fast by the horns, which he took and offered for a holocaust instead of his son.

14. And he called the name of that place, The Lord seeth. Whereupon even to this day it is said: In the mountain the Lord will see.

15. And the angel of the Lord called to Abraham a second time from heaven, saying:

16. By my own self have I sworn, saith the Lord: because thou hast done this thing, and hast not spared thy only begotten son for my sake:

17. I will bless thee, and I will multiply thy seed as the stars of heaven, and as the sand that is by the sea shore: thy seed shall possess the gates of their enemies.

18. *And in thy seed shall all the nations of the earth be blessed, because thou hast obeyed my voice.*

(Genesis xxii. 1-18.)

Unbloody Sacrifice: Sacrifice of Melchisedech.
In the history of the Hebrews in their relations with God, the character of Melchisedech, the high priest of God, stands out. In the offering which Melchisedech made to God we see the first anticipation or *type* of what happened centuries later on the first Holy Thursday night. After Abraham won his victory over the four kings, he was blessed by Melchisedech. This is how the story is told in the Book of Genesis:

18. But Melchisedech the king of Salem, bringing forth bread and wine, for he was the priest of the most high God.

19. Blessed him, and said: Blessed be Abram by the most high God, who created heaven and earth.

20. And blessed be the most high God, by whose protection the enemies are in thy hands. And he gave him the tithes* of all.

21. And the king of Sodom said to Abram: Give me the persons, and the rest take to thyself.

22. And he answered him: I lift up my hand to the Lord God the most high, the possessor of heaven and earth,

23. That from the very woof thread unto the shoe latchet, I will not take of any things that are thine, lest thou say I have enriched Abram:

---

*   This was the tax or donation to the church. This amounted to one tenth of what a man produced. The Jews of those days were farmers. *Tithe* means *one tenth.*

Some of the Hebrew prophets. Above are the prophets Joshua, Jeremias, Jonas, Isaias and Habbacuc. Below are Micheas, Aggeus, Malachias, and Zacharias. These men told much of the Saviour who was to come.

24. Except such things as the young men have eaten, and the shares of the men that came with me, Aner, Escol and Mambre: these shall take their shares.

(Genesis xiv. 18-24.)

Prophecy of Malachias. Malachias, the last of the Hebrew prophets, lived about four hundred years before Christ was born. He wrote one of the shortest books in the Old Testament. It has four brief chapters. In it he foretells or prophesies the coming of Christ and the "clean oblation or sacrifice of the New Testament." He said God was displeased with the impure sacrifices which the Jewish priests had been offering. To them Malachias reports God as saying, "I have no pleasure in you, and I will not receive a gift of your hand." The Lord of Hosts continues:

For from the rising of the sun even to the going down, My name is great among the Gentiles, and in every place there is sacrifice, and there is offered to My name a clean oblation, for My name is great among the Gentiles.

(Malachias i. 11.)

Memorize this Passage. This prophecy is fulfilled in the offering of the bread and wine—the Body and Blood of Christ—in the sacrifice of the Mass. This is truly a clean oblation—the purest offering that could be made, the Son of God. It is offered every day from the rising of the sun even to the going down thereof. Somewhere in the world, at all times, this sacrifice is offered. And truly is God's name great among the Gentiles—among all peoples.

Do You Give Yourself? By gifts or offerings we may serve God in many ways. Learned men, like St. Thomas Aquinas, point out three special ways.

We may give alms to our neighbor for the love of God. The value of this form of service depends upon

our intention. Why did we do it? Did we do it for God?
Almsgiving is one way to serve God by gift.

There is another way to serve God by gift. This way
is to give back or repay to God, through His Church and
the priests, part of our money or possessions which we
know come to us through God's grace. In olden days,
this amount was one tenth of a man's income or what he
received. This was called a *tithe*—which means one tenth.
The giving of tithes is a second form of service of God
by gift, and is based on our dependence on God. All we

have we owe to Him, and to show our dependence we pay tithes—or support the Church and the priests.

The third and highest form of service of God by gift is the Sacrifice which we have been studying. In the sacrifice we make a public gift-offering to God as a sign of our willingness to give—and to give ourselves. This act of self-surrender—of giving ourselves to God—is the highest form of service to God by gift—and the highest act of public worship. This is so in the Mass.

Summary and Conclusion. In the history of the Jews there are two things very wide apart that are, however, very closely related:

1. The promise of the Redeemer, the Messiah.

2. The prophecy of a "clean oblation."

It is in Christ that this promise is kept and that this prophecy is fulfilled.

In the fullness of time, that is, when God willed to do it, man was given this purest offering for his salvation. This was the perfect sacrifice, as we shall see, for man's sin, and for man to express to God his praise, thanksgiving, and love or adoration. He could ask for those things that were good for him through the same Christ who was offered up. He could expiate his sins, do penance for them. But to do this he must really join in the sacrifice. He must take part in it. He must offer himself up with the Victim of sacrifice. Well may we ask St. Paul's question:

13. For if the blood of goats and of oxen, and the ashes of an heifer being sprinkled, sanctify such as are defiled, to the cleansing of the flesh:

14. How much more shall the blood of Christ, who by the Holy Ghost offered Himself unspotted unto God, cleanse our conscience from dead works, to serve the living God?

(To the Hebrews ix. 13-14.)

What Did I Learn from This Chapter?

1. What is the plan of Redemption announced in the Garden of Eden?
2. What are the elements in a sacrifice to God?
3. For what purposes are sacrifices or offerings made to God?
4. What are the two principal classes of sacrifices?
5. Tell in your own words the story of the Jewish Passover.
6. Tell in your own words the story of the bloody sacrifice of Abraham.
7. Tell in your own words the story of the unbloody sacrifice of Melchisedech.
8. What was Malachias' prophecy? In what way was it fulfilled?
9. Who is: Abraham, Melchisedech, Abel, Malachias, Moses, St. Paul, the Messias?
10. What are the three forms of service to God by Gift? Which is the highest? Why?

My Part

1. After this, whenever I go to Mass, I shall remember that I can offer a much greater sacrifice to God than Abel, or Abraham, or Melchisedech made. I know, now, that it is a great favor or privilege for me to go to Mass and there to offer Jesus Christ Himself as a Victim for my sins. No wonder that those people who understand the Mass are eager to go as often as they can.

2. I shall do some good deeds during the week and offer them up in the Mass with the priest for my sins.

Memorize

1. The words of the angel of the Lord to Abraham after the sacrifice (Genesis xxii. 17-18).

2. The prophecy of Malachias (i. 11).

3. The question of St. Paul to the Hebrews (Hebrews ix. 13-14).

Problems and Activities

1. Repeat to the class the story of the Fall of our first parents, including the promise of a Redeemer.

2. In the Old Testament find the story of the god Moloch to show the class how people offered their own children to the gods. Do you know other stories of the same kind?

3. Show a picture of some Old Testament sacrifice and point out the four elements to be found. Tell also why the sacrifice was being offered.

4. From verse 8 of the quotations, tell whether the Israelites were mere spectators at the sacrifice of the lamb, or participants.

5. Find whether the following sacrifices were bloody or unbloody, and name what was offered:

    a) The sacrifice which Melchisedech made.
    b) The sacrifice which Abraham made.
    c) The sacrifice which Abel made to the Lord.
    d) The sacrifice which the Israelites had to make when they were leaving the land of Egypt.

Using the Missal

Find in your Missal:

a) The prayer which speaks of the sacrifices of Abel, Abraham, and Melchisedech.

b) The prayers in which the "clean oblation" is described in other words (right after the Consecration of the wine).

Did you use your Missal last Sunday?

Be sure to use your Missal next Sunday.

Bible Passages

For the following passages:

1. Tell whether they are from the Old or New Testament.
2. Name the Book from which they are taken.
3. Tell who said the words.
4. To whom were they spoken? When?

"Thou shalt keep this thing as a law for thee and thy children forever."

"I will bless thee, and I will multiply thy seed as the stars of heaven, and as the sand that is by the seashore: thy seed shall possess the gates of their enemies.

"And in thy seed shall all the nations of the earth be blessed, because thou hast obeyed my voice."

"...In every place there is sacrifice, and there is offered to My name a clean oblation for My name is great among the Gentiles."

Vocabulary

Enmity: hatred, such as the hatred of sin or the hatred of the devil.

Offerings: the animal or person or things (bread and wine) used in a sacrifice to God.

Sacrifice: the victim offered to God by the priest; the act itself.

Oblation: Offerings or Sacrifice or the victim offered to God. These three words have practically the same meaning.

Petition: a request or plea for something we wish.

Adoration: divine honor given to God; the highest praise, love, and respect. We give adoration to God in the Mass.

Priest: one who offers sacrifice to God.

Victim: the person or animal that is offered to God in a religious Sacrifice.

Unleavened: a bread in which a ferment such as yeast is not used.

Hyssop: a plant.

Holocaust: a burned offering to God especially as used among the Hebrews.

Gentiles: a term used by the Jews for people not Jews.

Catechism (Christian Doctrine)
- Did God abandon man after he fell into sin? (60)
- Who is the Redeemer? (61)
- What is a Sacrifice? (264)
- What is the Mass? (263)

"A prophet is come amongst us."
Yea, more than a prophet. God has visited His people.

Chapter III

THE FIRST MASS

Life of Christ Reviewed. Christ, the Messias, was born as the prophecies of the Old Testament had told, of Mary of the line of David, in Bethlehem in Judea. He is the Redeemer of the world. You know how He was born in a stable, and how the angels sang, "Glory to God in the Highest and peace on Earth among men of good will." You know, too, of the twelve years He lived the simple life in Nazareth with Mary, His mother, and His foster father, Joseph, and of His appearance in the temple with the doctors. Then the hidden life continues until He is thirty years old, when His public life begins, which lasts only three brief but crowded years. You have learned how He preached about the kingdom of God through parables, and how He taught men to repent or be sorry for their sins, to love God and to love their neighbors. You have learned, too, the wonderful miracles He performed. He changed water into wine. He multiplied seven loaves of bread and a few fishes so that He could feed a multitude and still have seven baskets of fragments remaining. He stilled the waves and the storms. He healed the sick, made the blind to see, and the lame to walk. He cleansed men of leprosy. He raised two men and a woman from the dead. Surely, as the Jews had said, "A prophet is come amongst us." Yea, more than a prophet. God has visited His people. "Is not this the Messias?" they asked—and it was.

Fall of Man and Salvation for All Men: Redemption. Thus the Fall of Man in the Garden of Paradise leads to the Crucifixion of the Son of God. The two events are directly related. The first one made the second one necessary. Through a man, Adam, the whole race of mankind was lost; through another Adam, Christ, all men everywhere could be saved. This is the Christian plan of redemption. The main events as they happened are:

1. Eve is tempted and eats the forbidden fruit.
2. Adam also disobeys God.
3. The promise of a Redeemer from the seed of Eve was made by God.
4. Adam and Eve are expelled from Paradise.
5. The Jewish prophecies of the Redeemer.
6. The birth of Christ fulfills the promise.
7. The Crucifixion of Christ.
8. The Resurrection of Christ.
9. The Ascension of Christ.
10. The Paraclete comes—The Church is born.

Christ's Love of Man. It is well to think over these wonderful three years of Christ's teaching. How He loved men! How He loved children! How He wished to serve them! How patiently He taught them! It is strange indeed that men should want to crucify and kill Him. But that is exactly what they wanted, and that is what they did. More even in His death than in His life, if that is possible, Christ showed His love for men. We are especially interested, in this chapter, in those two great days for human beings and their salvation—the day before His death and the day of His death.

Adam and Eve are driven out of Paradise,
but God promises to send a Saviour.

Wednesday in First Holy Week. Let us recall to our minds the great things that happened on the first Holy Thursday and Good Friday. This is the time of the first Mass and the first offering of the Body and Blood of Christ.

On Wednesday in the first Holy Week, Christ had foretold His crucifixion. He said to His disciples, "You know that after two days the Passover will be here; and the Son of Man will be delivered up and crucified." On this day Judas Iscariot went to the chief priests of the Jews to betray Jesus. The chief priests promised Judas thirty pieces of silver.

Holy Thursday. On Thursday the day began with the preparation for the Feast of the Pasch. The events of that day in detail are:

1. Jesus desires to eat the Pasch.
2. The Apostles strive for the first places.
3. Jesus washes the feet of His Apostles.
4. Jesus says He will be betrayed.
5. Judas leaves.
6. Jesus institutes the Holy Eucharist.
7. Jesus predicts the fall of Peter (first time).
8. The incident of the swords.
9. Jesus addresses His Apostles:
    A. Jesus strengthens His Apostles against the present trials.
    B. Jesus strengthens His Apostles against future trials:
        a) Abide in Me.
        b) Outward result of their abiding in Jesus.
        c) Effects of the coming of the Paraclete or Holy Ghost.
        d) Their sorrow shall turn to gladness.
        e) Prayer in the name of Jesus.
        f) The Apostles' confession of faith.
    C. The high priestly prayer of Jesus:
        a) Jesus prays for Himself.
        b) Jesus prays for His Apostles.
        c) Jesus prays for all believers.

10. Second prediction of Peter's fall.

11. The prayer and agony of Jesus.

12. Jesus is betrayed and taken.

13. Jesus before Annas. First denial of Peter.

14. Jesus before the Sanhedrin. (The Jewish Court.) Second and third denials of Peter.

15. Jesus is insulted and mocked.

Good Friday. It was a terrible night, but more terrible still were to be the events of the day called, strangely enough, Good Friday. The events for Good Friday are:

1. Jesus again before the Sanhedrin (Jewish court).

2. Despair of Judas.

3. Jesus before Pilate.

4. Jesus before Herod.

5. Jesus is led back to Pilate.

6. Jesus is crowned with thorns.

7. Jesus is sentenced to death.

8. Jesus carries the cross.

9. Jesus addresses the weeping women.

10. Jesus is crucified, and prays for His enemies.

11. The inscription. The division of His garments.

12. Jesus is mocked. His last words.

13. The Heart of Jesus is pierced.

14. Jesus is buried.

15. The sepulcher is sealed and guarded.

16. The women prepare spices and ointments.

Institution of the Mass. Now for some definite statements regarding the Last Supper. The Gospel account according to St. Matthew is as follows:

> But when it was evening, He sat down with his disciples. And whilst they were at supper, Jesus took bread, and blessed, and broke, and gave to His disciples, and said: Take ye, and eat; THIS IS MY BODY. And taking the chalice, He gave thanks, and gave to them saying: Drink ye all of this; for THIS IS MY BLOOD of the new testament, which shall be shed for many unto the remission

Christ institutes the First Mass with the words,
"This is My Body; This is My Blood."

of sins. And I say to you, I will not drink from henceforth of
this fruit of the vine, until that day when I shall drink it with you
new in the kingdom of My Father."

(Matthew xxvi. 20-29.)

The most important words in this Gospel account of
the Last Supper are these words of Christ: THIS IS MY BODY;
THIS IS MY BLOOD.

It will be seen that here is the source of the words in
the Mass. Notice especially that the change (transubstantiation)* from the bread and wine into the Body and Blood
actually took place at the Last Supper. What was seen was
the appearance of bread and wine. What was there was
the Body and Blood of Christ. That was really present.
Because this is a mystery, we call the separation of the
Body and Blood of Christ, His mystical death. His actual
death occurred on Good Friday, the next day. So in the
Mass we see our parish priest at the altar. But there is on
the altar the Mystical Christ making the offering. This is
a mystery which we believe, though the appearances are
not the reason we believe. Here is the mystical death of
Christ anticipating the actual death on Good Friday. And
because of Christ's own words—"Do this in remembrance
of Me"—it has happened in every Mass for two thousand
years since and will go on to the end of time.

Discourse Afterwards. In the wonderful talk, or
discourse, that followed, Christ said, among other very
important things:

Let not your heart be troubled. You believe in God, believe
also in Me. In My Father's house, there are many mansions. If
not, I would have told you: because I go to prepare a place for
you. And if I shall go and prepare a place for you, I will come

---

* Transubstantiation, a change from one thing or substance to
another thing or substance.

again, and will take you to Myself; that where I am, you also may be.

Jesus saith to him: I am the way, and the truth, and the life. No one cometh to the Father, but by Me.

If you love Me, keep My commandments.

Jesus answered and said to him: If any one love Me, he will keep My word, and My Father will love him, and We will come to him, and will make Our abode with him.

But the Paraclete, the Holy Ghost, whom the Father will send in My name, He will teach you all things, and bring all things to your mind, whatsoever I shall have said to you.

Peace I leave with you, peace I give unto you; not as the world giveth, do I give unto you. Let not your heart be troubled, nor let it be afraid.

(John xiv. 1-4, 6, 15, 23, 26-27.)

Christ knows that death awaits Him on the morrow. Notice especially His words of hope and consolation to His followers, "Let not your heart be troubled." Not only is there hope but there is a definite promise of heaven in His Father's mansions. It is through Christ only that we can come to the Father. He is our way to reach heaven. He is our Mediator with God the Father. He tells us, "I am the Way, the Truth, and the Light." He will send the Holy Ghost, and Christ shall live in the Church, and through it He will continue to give His grace—the fruits of the Redemption.

The Vine and the Branches. Christ continues His talk in that wonderful description of the Church under the image of the Vine and the Branches:

I am the true vine, and My Father is the husbandman.

Every branch in Me that beareth not fruit, He will take away; and every one that beareth fruit, He will purge it, that it may bring forth more fruit.

Now you are clean by reason of the word, which I have spoken to you.

Abide in Me, and I in you. As the branch cannot bear fruit
of itself, unless it abide in the vine, so neither can you, unless
you abide in Me.

I am the vine; you the branches: he that abideth in Me, and
I in him, the same beareth much fruit: for without Me you can
do nothing.

If anyone abide not in Me, he shall be cast forth as a branch,
and shall wither: and they shall gather him up, and cast him into
the fire, and he burneth.

This is My commandment, that you love one another as I
have loved you.

Greater love than this no man hath, that a man lay down his
life for his friends.   (John xv. 1-6, 12-13.)

We are the branches. We are all joined to Him. We,
therefore, must love one another as He has loved us. There
must be no separation from Him. This loving of all men in
communion with Christ we call the Mystical Body of Christ.
He is the Head. We are members of this Mystical Body just
as really as we are members of a nation, or a state, or a city.
We are all joined together with Christ. He is the Vine. We
are the Branches. That constitutes the Church.

And in a final quotation from this talk of Christ to His
disciples the fact is emphasized that He is our mediator in
heaven:

And in that day you shall not ask Me anything. Amen,
amen, I say to you: if you ask the Father anything in My name,
He will give it to you.

Hitherto, you have not asked anything in My name. Ask,
and you shall receive; that your joy may be full.

(John xvi. 23-24.)

Death on the Cross. Soon afterwards Christ was
betrayed. He was dragged before the Sanhedrin, the Jewish
court. He was sent from Pilate to Herod and back again.
He was scourged and mocked and crowned with thorns,

and finally condemned to death, although Pilate could "find no cause" for condemning Him. The crucifixion followed. The story is told in the Gospel according to St. Matthew, as follows:

> And after they had crucified Him, they divided His garments, casting lots; that it might be fulfilled which was spoken by the prophet, saying: They divided My garments among them, and upon My vesture they cast lots.
>
> And they sat and watched Him. And they put over His head His cause written: THIS IS JESUS, THE KING OF THE JEWS.
>
> Then were crucified with Him two thieves, one on the right hand and one on the left.
>
> And they that passed by, blasphemed Him, wagging their heads. And saying: Vah, Thou that destroyeth the temple of God, and in three days dost rebuild it; save Thy own self: If Thou be the Son of God, come down from the cross.
>
> In like manner also the chief priests, with the scribes and ancients, mocking, said: He saved others; Himself He cannot save. If He be the King of Israel, let Him now come down from the cross, and we will believe Him.
>
> He trusted in God; let Him now deliver Him, if He will have Him; for He said: I am the Son of God.
>
> And the selfsame thing the thieves also, that were crucified with Him, reproached Him with.
>
> Now from the sixth hour there was darkness over the whole earth, until the ninth hour.
>
> And about the ninth hour Jesus cried with a loud voice, saying: *Eli, Eli, lamma sabacthani?* That is, My God, My God, why hast thou forsaken Me?
>
> And some that stood there and heard, said: This man calleth Elias. And immediately one of them running took a sponge, and filled it with vinegar; and put it on a reed, and gave Him to drink. And the others said: Let be, let us see whether Elias will come to deliver Him.
>
> And Jesus again crying with a loud voice, yielded up the ghost.
>
> And behold the veil of the temple was rent from the top even to the bottom, and the earth quaked, and the rocks were

Jesus Christ, the Saviour whom God promised to
Adam and Eve, dies on the cross for men.

rent. And the graves were opened: and many bodies of the saints that had slept arose; and coming out of the tombs after His resurrection, came into the holy city, and appeared to many.

Now the centurion and they that were with him watching Jesus, having seen the earthquake, and the things that were done, were sore afraid, saying: *Indeed this was the Son of God.*

And there were many women afar off, who had followed Jesus from Galilee, ministering unto Him. Among whom was Mary Magdalene, and Mary, the mother of James and Joseph, and the mother of the sons of Zebedee.

And when it was evening, there came a certain rich man of Arimathea, named Joseph, who also himself was a disciple of Jesus. He went to Pilate, and asked the body of Jesus. Then Pilate commanded that the body should be delivered.

And Joseph, taking the body, wrapt it up *in a clean linen cloth.* And laid it in his own new monument, which he had hewed out in a rock. And he rolled a great stone to the door of the monument, and went his way. And there was there Mary Magdalene. and the other Mary, sitting over against the sepulcher.

(Matthew xxvii. 35-61.)

In the events of that Thursday and Friday, we have the first Mass and the Holy Eucharist instituted by Christ, Himself. He is the priest offering the sacrifice, or victim, to God the Father. He offers His own Body and Blood under the symbols of bread and wine. He Himself is the Victim. The High Priest, Christ, offering Himself, the Victim, in an outward manner made this a real sacrifice. It was, in fact, the Sacrifice of the Mass.

Sacrifice of the Mass and Sacrifice of the Cross. While the Sacrifice of the Cross and the Sacrifice of the Mass are the same sacrifice, there is a difference in the manner of the sacrifice. The Sacrifice of the Cross was a bloody sacrifice. On the cross, Christ was actually killed, or slain. His blood was shed. The Sacrifice of the Mass is an unbloody sacrifice. No blood is shed, nor is there a real death. There is a mystical death. Christ sitting in heaven at the right hand of God the Father can die no more. He died as the God-Man for our sins and that satisfied God's justice. In the Mass, the priest consecrates the bread and the wine separately. This separation of the Body and Blood represents Christ's death on the cross.

As sacrifices, the Sacrifice of the Mass and the Sacrifice of the Cross are the same. The priest is the same in both cases—Christ, our Blessed Lord. On Calvary Christ offered Himself. In the Mass, He offers Himself through the priest. The power which the priest exercises is the power of Christ, which is exercised in His name. The Victim is also the same—Jesus Christ. His Body and Blood are offered up to God the Father in the Mass. It was this same Body of Christ that was pierced and crucified on Calvary. It was His Blood that was shed. The Sacrifice of the Cross was offered to satisfy God's justice for the sins of men. It was to bring to men all the blessings and graces of God. It was also to honor and glorify God. These are exactly the purposes of the Sacrifice of the Mass. Both Sacrifices are ways of thanking God for His love and care of men and for the graces given to men.

What Did I Learn from This Chapter?

1. Tell briefly the facts of the life of Christ.
2. Tell in detail what happened to Christ on the first Holy Thursday.
3. Tell in detail what happened to Christ on the first Good Friday from midnight to the crucifixion.
4. When was the Mass instituted, that is, when was the first Mass said?
5. What is the Holy Eucharist?

6. When did Christ first give us the Holy Eucharist?
7. Tell what Christ said to the Apostles after the Last Supper.
8. Describe the Last Supper:
   a) Who was there?
   b) What Jewish feast day was it?
   c) Where was the place?
   d) What did Christ do?
   e) What did the persons present receive?
9. At the Last Supper:
   a) Who was the Priest?
   b) Who was the Victim offered?
   c) To whom was the Victim offered?
   d) What for?
10. At the Crucifixion:
   a) Who was the Priest?
   b) Who was the Victim offered?
   c) To whom was the Victim offered?
   d) What for?
11. What sentence in Christ's address or talk after the Last Supper shows that He was thinking of establishing or founding the Church?
12. Who is the Paraclete?

My Part

1. I shall keep in mind Christ's promise that in His "Father's house there are many mansions"; and that He will prepare a place for me. I shall try to deserve it.

2. I shall recall at the consecration of the Mass the events of the last two days of Christ's life on earth.

Prayers

Because of Christ's love of us, I shall often repeat our praise of Him, of His Heavenly Father, and of Mary and St. Joseph, in the "Divine Praises."

Blessed be God.

Blessed be His Holy Name.

Blessed be Jesus Christ true God and true Man.

Blessed be the name of Jesus.

Blessed be His Most Sacred Heart.

Blessed be Jesus in the Most Holy Sacrament of the Altar.

Blessed be the great Mother of God, Mary most holy.

Blessed be her holy and immaculate conception.

Blessed be the name of Mary, Virgin and Mother.

Blessed be St. Joseph, her most chaste spouse.

Blessed be God in His Angels and in His Saints.

I shall say them, too, whenever I hear anyone use God's name in vain.

Problems and Activities

1. Recalling what you have learned in the fifth grade, or at any other time, tell what you understand by Christ's discussion of the "Vine and the Branches."

2. What do these words of Christ mean to you: "In My Father's house there are many mansions. Were it not so, I should have told you, because I go to prepare a place for you"?

3. What will you do to earn it?

4. Bring to class pictures of the Crucifixion. Study the different pictures.

5. Tell, if you can, the name of the artist.

6. What is the Christian plan of Redemption?

7. What is the place of each of the following in the plan of Redemption:

> Adam's Fall
> Mary
> Christ's Crucifixion
> Christ's Resurrection
> Christ's Ascension
> The Paraclete
> The Church

Using the Missal

1. In the Ordinary of the Mass show the influence of Christ's words:

"I am the Way."

"No one cometh to the Father but through Me."

(See special study, p. 206.)

2. Did you use your Missal last Sunday?

3. I will use my Missal in participating in the Mass next Sunday.

4. Find out from your liturgical calendar or in your Missal, the names of any saints whose feast days are celebrated this week. Find out something about the saint. Does your Missal tell you anything about the saint or feast? What?

Bible Passages

For the following passages from the Bible:

1. Tell whether they are from the New or the Old Testament.
2. Tell the name of the book from which it is taken.
3. Tell who is the speaker.
4. Tell to whom he was speaking. When?
    a) "Is not this the Messias?"
    b) "Do this in remembrance of Me."
    c) "If you love Me, keep My commandments."
    d) In My Father's house there are many mansions. Were it not so, I should have told you, because I go to prepare a place for you."
    e) "This is My commandment, that you love one another as I have loved you."
    f) "Greater love than this no man has, that one lay down his life for his friends."
    g) "If you ask the Father anything in My name, He will give it you."
    h) Truly He was the Son of God."

Memorize

All the foregoing quotations.

The passage on the Vine and the Branches in the text.

Vocabulary

Agony: great pain or suffering such as Christ suffered in carrying the cross, and while He hung on the cross.

Sepulcher: a grave; a place where a person is buried, such as the place where the dead body of Christ was placed after He was taken down from the cross.

Sanhedrin: Jewish supreme council or court.

Transubstantiation: a change from one thing into another. This word is used especially of the change of the bread and wine into the Body and Blood of Christ in the Mass.

Mansions: beautiful or magnificent homes.

Blaspheme: to speak evil of God.

Commemoration: to do something to recall to mind an event or person; remembrance. When the priest says the Mass he recalls the events of the first Holy Thursday. This is a commemoration.

Catechism (Christian Doctrine)

- Did God abandon man after he fell into sin? (60)
- Who is the Redeemer? (61)
- What do you believe of Jesus Christ? (62)
- What do you mean by the Incarnation? (69)
- Did the Son of God become man immediately after the sin of our first parents? (72)
- On what day was Christ born? (75)
- How long did Christ live on earth? (76)
- What did Jesus Christ suffer? (78)
- On what day did Christ die? (79)
- Why do you call that day "good" on which Christ died so sorrowful a death? (80)
- Where did Christ die? (81)
- How did Christ die? (82)
- Why did Christ suffer and die? (83)
- What is the Holy Eucharist? (238)
- When did Christ institute the Holy Eucharist? (239)

- Who were present when our Lord instituted the Holy Eucharist? (240)
- How did our Lord institute the Holy Eucharist? (241)
- What happened when our Lord said, "This is My body; this is My blood"? (242)
- What is this change of the bread and wine into the body and blood of our Lord called? (246)
- When and where are the bread and wine changed into the body and blood of Christ? (262)
- What is the Mass? (263)
- Is the Mass the same sacrifice as that of the Cross? (265)
- How is the Mass the same sacrifice as that of the Cross? (266)
- What were the ends for which the sacrifice of the Cross were offered? (267)
- Is there any difference between the sacrifice of the Cross and the sacrifice of the Mass? (268)

Chapter IV

THE MASS, THE PRIESTHOOD, AND THE CHURCH

The Jewish Sacrifice on Passover

"Do this in remembrance of Me."

These are the words of Jesus Christ on the first Holy Thursday night. It was Jesus' last supper before His Crucifixion the next day. He was speaking to the Apostles who had come up with Him to Jerusalem to celebrate the great Jewish feast of the Passover, often called the *Pasch*. It was a bloody sacrifice of a lamb and a kid "and," says the Old Testament, "they shall eat the flesh that night roasted at the fire, and unleavened bread with wild lettuce." The blood was to be sprinkled on the transom of the door and on both door posts. The blood on the door would identify the houses of the Jews. These houses the Lord would pass over, and not permit the destroyer to come into them and hurt those living in them. In passing over the land, the Lord struck only the Egyptians. "And this day shall be for a memorial to you: and you shall keep it a feast to the Lord in your generations with an everlasting observance." Moses in telling this to the Jews, said it simply: "Thou shalt keep this thing as a law for thee and thy children forever."

Christ Institutes the Sacrifice of the New Law on Passover. On that very night echoing almost the words to the Jews, "this day shall be for a memorial to you," Jesus told the Apostles under the New Covenant, "Do this for a commemoration of Me." On that night, around AD 33, Christ offered the first sacrifice of the New Covenant which was to end or culminate in His death on the Cross the next day. The unbloody sacrifice in which the bread and wine was made the Body and Blood of Christ occurred on Thursday evening. The bloody sacrifice was on the Cross the next day. When Jesus suffered for three hours His dying agony, His blood was spilled as His hands and feet were pierced by the nails, and His side by the soldier's spear. The unbloody sacrifice of the bread and wine changed into the Body and Blood of Jesus, and the bloody sacrifice of His body and blood on the Cross are one.

The Priest and Victim on Holy Thursday and on Calvary. The sacrifice of the first Holy Thursday evening, which was the first Mass, was the same sacrifice as the one on the Cross on the first Good Friday. In a sacrifice there must be a victim offered to God, and there must be a person offering up the victim to God. We call persons who offer up sacrifices to God for themselves and for the people, priests. In the first Mass, Jesus was the Victim because it was His Body and Blood that were offered to God for the sins of men. Jesus Himself offered to God the bread and wine which became His Body and Blood to save or redeem mankind. He was, therefore, the priest—the High Priest.

In the sacrifice on Calvary it is unmistakably clear that Jesus is the victim. We see Him nailed to the Cross, we hear His words of agony and we see Him die. He was, as the Catechism says, physically slain. He was, too, the priest. It was Jesus who prophesied what was to happen,

Christ is mystically present in every Mass,
offering His own body and blood through the ordained priest.

and knowing what was to come, He consented to it, and did nothing to prevent it. And addressing God the Father, He said, "Not My will, but thine be done." The offering was made in both cases for the sins of men—that they might have Life or grace and have it more abundantly.

Christ Is the High Priest in the Mass.

"Do this in remembrance of Me."

What is meant by the word "*this*" in this sentence? It is the changing of the bread and wine into the Body and Blood of Christ. Only the power of Christ could do this. He must be present in every Mass as the High Priest. We say He is mystically present in every Mass, offering to God, the Father, His own body and blood through the ordained priest. He is the principal priest. To make clear what is happening in the Mass, we have a human being, called a priest, to make the offering and who, through the Power of Christ, can change the water and wine into the Body of Christ. And so the *Victim*, Jesus, is present again on our altars after the words of Jesus which the priest repeats: "This is My Body. This is My Blood."

Conferring the Priesthood on the Apostles. The power to change the bread and wine into the Body and Blood of Christ was given to the Apostles on that first Holy Thursday night. *Jesus was not merely issuing a command; He was giving to these men,* and to their successors as we shall see, the *Power* to carry out His command. This was the first ordination of priests in the Roman Catholic Church. This was the beginning, or institution, of the Sacrament of Holy Orders.

Granting Another Supernatural Power—To Forgive Sins. How wonderfully Christ thought of these priests to whom He had given this supernatural power to change the bread and wine into His Body and Blood is shown by another power He gave them. After Jesus died on the cross and rose again gloriously from the dead on Easter, He remained on earth forty days until the Ascension. After His resurrection He met first Mary Magdalene; He told her to go and tell the disciples what she had seen. She did. Then the Gospel according to St. John continues:

> Now when it was late that same day, the first of the week, and the doors were shut, where the disciples were gathered together, for fear of the Jews, Jesus came in and stood in the midst and said to them: Peace be to you. And when He had said this, He showed them His hands and His side. The disciples therefore were glad, when they saw the Lord. He therefore said to them again: Peace be to you. As the Father hath sent Me, I also send you. When He had said this, He breathed upon them; and He said to them: Receive ye the Holy Ghost. Whose sins you shall forgive, they are forgiven them; and whose sins you shall retain, they are retained."
>
> (St. John xx. 19-23.)

Respect and Honor for Bishops and Priests. These were some of the great powers given to the representatives of Christ on earth: the supernatural power to change, through the power of Jesus Christ, the bread and wine into the Body and Blood of Christ, and the supernatural power to forgive or retain sins, through the power of Christ. It is no wonder, then, that Catholics pay so much reverence and honor to these representatives of Christ. When we pay respect to them we are really paying respect to Christ, for as Christ said, "without Me you can do nothing."

The Catholic Priesthood. Jesus Christ is the High Priest, the principal priest at every Mass. He offers to His Heavenly Father, *through* the ordained priest, His own Body and Blood. The priest is a man who wanted to give his life to serving God at His altar by saying Mass, forgiving sin, and helping people in the sacred ministry. He has a reputation for excellent character and has spent years in training in school, college, and seminaries for this great work. To be ordained as a priest, he must be called to the priesthood by his Bishop. The sacrament by which a man, called by his Bishop, becomes a priest is *Holy Orders*. This sacrament gives the soul a special mark or character, which means a special sharing in the priesthood of Christ.

As we have seen, every Catholic assisting at Mass participates in offering the sacrifice of the Mass. The words of the priest in the Mass when he says that he offers my sacrifice and *yours*, show this. The priests share in this priesthood of Christ in a special manner. The Bishops share it fully. We, you and I, share in it to some degree. Always remember that when you go to Mass. You are not a spectator, you are a participant in the Sacrifice of the Holy Mass.

Christ's Promise to Be With the Church "All Days." The power that was given to the Apostles was clearly not given to the Apostles to be exercised only for the people who happened to live at that time. Jesus died to save all men. Just before His Ascension, Christ gave them the power to forgive sins. In the text in the Gospel according to St. Matthew, the statement that was quoted above from St. John is given more fully:

> "All power is given to me in heaven and in earth. Going therefore, teach ye all nations; baptizing them in the name of the Father, and of the Son, and of the Holy Ghost. Teaching them to observe all things whatsoever I have commanded you; and behold I am with you all days, even unto the consummation of the world."
>
> (St. Matthew xxviii. 18-20.)

So with Christ present with His Church even to the end of time, His power could be continued to the end of time. Malachias' prophecy would then be fulfilled.

"For from the rising of the sun even to the going down, My name is great among the Gentiles, and in every place there is sacrifice, and there is offered to My name a clean oblation, for My name is great among the Gentiles." (Malachias i. 11.)

Continuing the Priesthood. How was this priesthood which was conferred on or given to the Apostles to be continued? The answer is found in what happened. In the Acts of the Apostles we read that the Apostles conferred the sacrament on Paul and Barnabas. We read:

And as they were ministering to the Lord, and fasting, the Holy Ghost said to them: "Separate Me Saul and Barnabas, for the work whereunto I have taken them." Then they, fasting and praying, and imposing their hands upon them, sent them away."
(Acts xiii. 2-3.)

And so Paul made Timothy a Bishop:

"For which cause I admonish thee, that thou stir up the grace of God which is in thee, by the imposition of my hands."
(II Timothy i. 6.)

Christ on the first Holy Thursday night spoke from His heart great words to His Apostles. He began giving them words of comfort. He began, "Father, the hour has come," and then continued:

"Glorify Thy Son, that Thy Son may glorify Thee. As Thou hast given Him power over all flesh, that He may give eternal life to all whom Thou hast given Him. Now this is eternal life: that they may know Thee, the only true God, and Jesus Christ, whom Thou hast sent. I have glorified Thee on the earth; I have finished the work which Thou gavest Me to do. And now glorify Thou me, O Father, with Thyself, with the glory which I had, before the world was, with Thee."
(St. John xvii. 2-5.)

He prayed for the disciples, "those whom Thou hast given Me" and then a direct prayer to the Father:

> "Holy Father, keep them in Thy name whom Thou hast given Me; that they may be one, as we also are. While I was with them, I kept them in Thy name. Those whom thou gavest Me have I kept; and none of them is lost, but the son of perdition, that the Scripture may be fulfilled."
>
> (St. John xvii. 12-13.)

Christ came to bring everlasting life to all men, a life of grace on earth and a life of glory in Heaven. He prayed for His Apostles and all men that God might keep all of them. That is the purpose of His sacrifice.

The Church of Christ. Christ died not only for the Apostles but for all men. He wanted to secure for them everlasting life. He made the Apostles, Bishops, or priests. In their own day they appointed their successors and new priests who could change, through the power of Christ, the substance of the bread and wine into the Body and Blood of Christ who could forgive sins. The succession of Bishops and priests goes back to the Apostles themselves. The priests and Bishops were to make all men disciples, to teach them all the truths Christ had taught them. He was to be united with them, as He and the Father were united. He was the vine and they were the branches. And what can all these people united to Christ and served by His priesthood be but the Church of Christ? They are united together by their belief and their service and they are bound to Christ as their head. St. Paul always used this image of the Body as expressing the relation between Christians and Christ: Christ is the head, they are the members of the body. All Christians related to Christ are called the Mystical Body of Christ. This is another way of describing the Church.

Membership in this Body is by means of Baptism. All members participate in the same sacrifice and receive the same sacraments. They have the same faith, believing in the truths which the Church teaches. This great congregation of baptized persons are under the authority of the Pope, the Vicar of Christ on Earth, and the Bishops who are in communion or joined with Him in ruling the Church.

The Holy Ghost. Christ told the disciples to wait, for He would send them the Paraclete or Advocate who would come to them and remind them of all things He had told them and teach them all things that they would need to know. Christ would stay with the Apostles and their successors forever and so would the Paraclete or Advocate. Christ Himself had said: "I will be with you all days even unto the consummation of the world." He said regarding the Holy Ghost, who is also called the Holy Spirit, the Paraclete or the Advocate, that

> "And I will ask the Father, and He will give you another Paraclete, that He may abide with you forever. The Spirit of truth, whom the world cannot receive, because it seeth Him not, nor knoweth Him; but you shall know Him, because He shall abide with you, and shall be in you. . . . But the Paraclete, the Holy Ghost, whom the Father will send in My name, He will teach you all things, and bring all things to your mind whatsoever I shall have said to you."
>
> (John xiv. 16-17, 26.)

> "...for if I go not, the Paraclete will not come to you; but if I go, I will send Him to you . . . but when He, the spirit of truth, is come, He will teach you all truth." (John xvi. 7, 13.)

Pentecost and the Beginning of the Church. The Holy Ghost dwells in the Church and will remain with it forever. We often read of the "indwelling of the Holy Ghost" in the Church. By this is meant that he is part of the Church and in accordance with Christ's promise he will

The Descent of the Holy Spirit marks
the Birthday of the Church.

remain in it, or dwell in it for all time. The Holy Ghost did come upon the Apostles in their upper room in the house in Jerusalem, forty days after Christ ascended into heaven. All twelve (including Matthias, in Judas' place) and Mary were gathered in the room; then a violent wind arose and filled the house. But let us read the story as it is told in the Acts of the Apostles:

> And when the days of Pentecost were accomplished, they were all together in one place: And suddenly there came a sound from heaven, as of a mighty wind coming, and it filled the whole house where they were sitting. And there appeared to them parted tongues as it were of fire, and it sat upon every one of them: And they were all filled with the Holy Ghost, and they began to speak with divers tongues, according as the Holy Ghost gave them to speak.   (Acts of Apostles ii. 1-4.)

With the presence of the Holy Ghost we have the beginning of the Church of Christ. This has always been regarded as the birthday of the Roman Catholic Church. Christ had already provided for its visible head. Peter was to be that head—for Christ said to him: "Thou art Peter and upon this rock I shall build My Church and the gates of hell shall not prevail against it." Whenever a list of the Apostles is given in the New Testament, Peter is always named first. He was recognized as the visible head of the Church, the Pope, though Jesus Christ is always recognized as the invisible and supernatural head of the Church. There have been during the twenty Christian centuries more than two hundred and fifty successors of St. Peter. Pope Pius XII is the two hundred and sixty-second Pope.

Christ and the Church. It is this organization, the Roman Catholic Church, through which Christ works and ministers to men. Its sacraments are the channels of His grace. This is the way to heaven. He is the Way, the

Truth and the Life. Here is a world wide organization established by Christ himself, and made up in the first instance of His Apostles, guided by the Holy Ghost which carries out the command of Holy Thursday night, "Do this in remembrance of Me." In all the world, north and south, east and west, the clean oblation of Christ's Body and Blood is offered. It is only through such a world wide means that this memorial could serve all men. The language in which it is offered—this clean oblation— is determined by the Roman Catholic Church. The language is Latin in almost every part of the world. This is the main part of its Liturgy—the Mass.

What Did I Learn from This Chapter?

1. What is the Jewish feast of the Passover?
2. What happened on the Jewish Passover, in the last year of Christ's life?
3. How did the sacrifice on the first Holy Thursday differ from the sacrifice on the first Good Friday?
4. Tell who is the High Priest and who is the Victim in each of the following sacrifices:
    a) The Last Supper
    b) The Crucifixion
    c) The Mass said last Sunday
5. In the Mass of last Sunday in the Church you attend, tell who was:
    a) The principal priest
    b) The ordained priest offering the Mass
6. What supernatural power did Christ give the Apostles on Holy Thursday?
7. What other supernatural power did Christ give to the Apostles? Why do we honor and respect priests and bishops?
8. What persons have the priesthood fully?

9. What persons have the priesthood in a special manner but not fully?

10. To what extent does the Catholic lay person have the powers of the priesthood?

11. Did Jesus Christ give priestly powers to the Apostles for themselves only? Explain.

12. Does the power of the priests and bishops today in the Catholic Church go back to the Apostles? Explain.

13. Who made up the Church on the first Pentecost?

14. Who make up the Church to-day?

    a) What persons?

    b) How did they enter it?

    c) Who is the Head (invisible and visible) of the Church?

    d) Who rules the Church throughout the world?

    e) Do the members believe the same things?

    f) Do they make the same sacrifice to God?

    g) Do they have the same sacraments?

15. What are the various names given to the Holy Ghost?

16. What promise did Jesus Christ make regarding the Holy Ghost?

17. When was it fulfilled?

18. What is meant by the Holy Ghost "indwelling in the Church"? Tell what happened on Pentecost?

19. What promise did Christ make regarding Himself and the Church?

My Part

1. I shall tip my hat, or gently bow my head when a priest passes as a mark of respect.

2. I shall be more attentive and more reverent at Mass because of the important part I am to take in the Mass.

3. I shall always be reverent and more attentive at every Mass because Christ is the principal priest in every Mass.

Memorize: Passages from the Bible

1. "Do this in remembrance of Me"
2. The power to forgive sins: Matthew xxviii. 18-20
3. The Description of the First Pentecost:
    Acts of the Apostles ii. 1-4

Using the Missal

Read carefully by yourself
1. The Consecration of the Host
2. The Consecration of the Wine
3. The Communion Prayers from the Lord's Prayer to the Ablutions
4. The Priest's prayers after the *Ite Missa Est*

Vocabulary

Mystical: having a secret meaning or beyond ordinary human understanding; cannot be seen.

Such as, the mystical presence of Christ on the Altar in the Mass as the principal priest.

Principal: chief, main, or most important.

Christ is the principal priest at the Mass.

Ordination: the process by which a lay person becomes a priest; the Sacrament of Holy Orders.

Disciple: a follower of a leader; a believer in his doctrines. The Apostles were disciples; the three Marys were also disciples of Christ.

Apostles: leaders in a movement or missionaries of a movement.

Applied especially to the twelve disciples chosen by Christ to preach His Gospel to the whole world.

Minister: to serve or guide or help, or to act for.

Applied here especially to the services of a priest called the sacred ministry.

Holy Ghost: the third Person of the Blessed Trinity, called also the Holy Spirit, the Paraclete, the Advocate.

Perdition: hell; loss of one's soul.

Judas is the son of perdition referred to in the text.

Congregation: a small unit or all the people belonging to an organization, particularly a religious organization; e.g., the congregation of St. Rose's Church, or as in the text, all the people belonging to the Church of Christ.

Catechism (Christian Doctrine)

- •What is the Church? (115)
- •Who is the invisible head of the Church? (116)
- •Who is the visible head of the Church? (117)
- •Why is the Pope, the Bishop of Rome, the visible head of the Church? (118)
- •Who are the successors of the other Apostles? (119)
- •Why did Christ found the Church? (120)
- •Who sent the Holy Ghost upon the Apostles? (99)
- •Why did Christ send the Holy Ghost? (100)
- •Will the Holy Ghost abide with the Church forever? (101)
- •What is the Sacrament of Holy Orders? (278)
- •How should Christians look upon the priests of the Church? (280)
- •When did Christ give His priests the power to change bread and wine into His body and blood? (249)
- •How do you know that the priest has the power of absolving from the sins committed after Baptism? (189)

Chapter V

THE MASS OF THE CATECHUMENS AND THE MASS OF THE FAITHFUL

The First Mass: Its Essence. The Mass from the first Holy Thursday night, more than nineteen hundred years ago, until this very day has always been the same act. That act is the offering of the Body and Blood of Christ under the form, or species, of bread and wine. Go back for a minute to that first Holy Thursday. There is the table which serves as the altar. There is Christ Himself as High Priest. There is the bread and the wine. Christ takes the bread, blesses it, offers it to His Father and announces the transubstantiation, i.e., the change from one thing into something else: THIS IS MY BODY.

In like manner He takes the chalice full of wine, blesses it, offers it to God, the Father, and announces the transubstantiation: THIS IS MY BLOOD.

The Apostles then received their First Holy Communion.

The Same Today. This was the essence of the First Mass as told in the Gospels. This is the essence of the Mass today. In the course of the nineteen centuries, many additions have been made to the essential core— the Consecration—until it has developed into the form which we have today. The Church has added to the Consecration many beautiful prayers and many impressive ceremonies. The purpose of these is to help us realize the part we play in this greatest of all sacrifices.

A million people attended the Eucharistic Congress Mass
in Dublin in 1932.

We are not mere spectators, or lookers-on; we join with
the priest and Christ in the sacrifice.

Mass of the Catechumens. In the early centuries of
the Church, only the faithful could attend the Eucharistic
Sacrifice—the offering of the Body and Blood of Christ
under the form of bread and wine. Those who had not yet
become Christians, but who were undergoing instruction,
were called Catechumens. For them the service consisted
of prayers, psalms, and instruction. Before the Eucharistic
Sacrifice was offered, the Catechumens were dismissed.

There was then a part of the Mass before the Eucharistic
Sacrifice which the Catechumens attended, and there was
the Eucharistic Sacrifice and Banquet which only the
Faithful could attend. When these two parts of the Mass,
as we know it, were combined, this *first* part of the divine

service, consisting of prayers, psalms, and instruction intended for the Catechumens, came to be known as *The Mass of the Catechumens.*

Mass of the Faithful. The main part of the Mass, the offering of the Body and Blood of Christ under the form of bread and wine and the Banquet, or Communion, was intended in the early days only for the faithful, and this was called *The Mass of the Faithful.*

This is the very solemn part of the Mass. It is the part of the Mass we must hear if we are to satisfy or fulfill the obligation to hear Mass. It begins with the Offertory.

The Missal. Today these two parts are combined and constitute the Mass: The Mass of the Catechumens; The Mass of the Faithful.

The book containing the prayers of the Mass is called the *Missal.* It is the book the priest reads from at the Mass. It is written in *Latin.* It is also prepared in a form for you and me in which the Latin is given and the English translation right alongside of the Latin. Sometimes only the English translation is given. The Missal is the prayer book you should always use at Mass. You can read the prayers of the Mass with the priest. You and he and all present must join together in offering the Mass.

Two Main Divisions of the Mass, and the Parts. If you will take your Missal, you can list the prayers that are said at the Mass. After you have listed them on your paper or on the board in the schoolroom, your teacher will discuss with you where the divisions are made. The main division between the Mass of the Catechumens and the Mass of the Faithful comes after the Creed (*Credo*). If we marked the divisions of the Mass, your list would look like this:

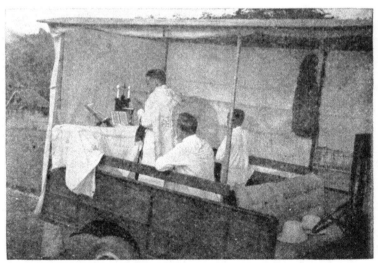

The missionaries say Mass wherever they can.
Yet it is the same Christ who comes, whether
there be many present or only a few.

THE MASS*

A. Mass of the Catechumens.

First Part: *Prayer*—from the *Asperges* to the Collect.
1. The Sprinkling of Holy Water.
2. The Sign of the Cross.
3. The Psalm, *Judica Me.*
4. Public Confession.
5. The Priest at the Altar.
5. The Introit.
7. The Kyrie.
8. The Gloria.

Second Part: *Instruction*—from the Collect to the Credo.

DOMINUS VOBISCUM—OREMUS.

1. The Collect or Prayer.
2. The Epistle, or sayings of the Prophets and Apostles.
3. The Gradual and Alleluia or Tract.
4. The Gospel, or words of our Lord.
5. The Sermon.
6. The Credo.

B. Mass of the Faithful.

Third Part: *Offertory*—from the Offering to the Preface.

DOMINUS VOBISCUM—OREMUS.

1. The Offering of Bread and Wine.
2. The Incensing of the Offerings and of the Faithful.
3. Washing of the Hands.
4. Prayer to the Most Holy Trinity.
5. The *Orate Fratres* and *Secret*, with the *Amen* ratifying the Offertory.

---

*   Printed for reference only.

Fourth Part: *Consecration*—from the Preface to the Lord's Prayer.

DOMINUS VOBISCUM—SURSUM CORDA.

1. The Preface to the Canon.
2. The Canon, or Rite of Consecration.
3. Remembrance of the Living.
4. Prayers Preparatory to the Consecration.
5. The Transubstantiation and Major Elevation.
6. Oblation of the Victim to God.
7. Remembrance of the Dead.
8. End of the Canon and Minor Elevation, with the *Amen* ratifying the prayers of the Canon.

Fifth Part: *Communion*—from the Lord's Prayer to the Ablutions.

OREMUS.

1. The Lord's Prayer and *Libera Nos*.
2. Breaking of the Host.
3. The *Agnus Dei*.
4. Prayers Preparatory to the Communion.
5. Receiving of the Body and Blood of our Lord, with the *Amen* of Association—formerly uttered by the Congregation.

Sixth Part: *Thanksgiving*—from the Communion to the end.

DOMINUS VOBISCUM—OREMUS.

1. Prayers during the Ablutions.
2. The Communion, Antiphon, and Postcommunion.
3. The *Ite Missa Est* and Blessing.
4. The Last Gospel.
5. Prayers at the Foot of the Altar (prayers after Mass).
6. Canticle of the Three Children (Thanksgiving after Mass).

| GOSPEL SIDE | ALTAR CENTER | EPISTLE SIDE |

ORDER OF MASS

I. Introductory Service

(Mass of Catechumens)
A. PRAYER PART (Giving)

2. Introit
5. Collect(s)

1. Prayers at foot of altar
3. Kyrie
4. Gloria

1. Epistle
2. Gradual

B. INSTRUCTION PART
(Receiving)
3. Prayer before Gospel
6. Nicene Creed

4. *Gospel*
5. *Sermon*

{ *Alleluia* *Tract* *Sequence* }

II. Eucharistic SACRIFICE
(Mass of Faithful)
A. OBLATION (Giving)
1. *Offertory verse*
2. Offering of bread
4. Offering of wine
6. Pray brethren
7. *Secret(s)*
8. Preface
9. Holy, Holy, Holy
(bell rings three times)
10. (Canon) Memento for Church, living, saints
11. Oblation prayer (bell)
12. Consecration
(bell rings six times)
13. Oblation prayer
14. Memento for dead, us sinners, all nature
15. Doxology and Amen

3. { Wine and water }
5. Lavabo

B. BANQUET (Receiving)
1. Our Father
2. The Peace of the Lord
3. Lamb of God
4. Priest's Communion
(bell rings three times)
5. Communion of people
6. First ablution
10. Dismissal
11. Blessing

7. 2nd ablution
8. *Comm. verse*
9. *Post-Comm.(s)*

12. Last Gospel

Parts in Italic vary. Parts underlined are sometimes left out. (Taken from the *St. Andrew's Missal*, courtesy of E. M. Lohmann Co.)

A picture of a Pontifical High Mass. Notice the bishop seated at the left.

Solemn High and Low Mass. The above list of divisions of the Mass is for the solemn high Mass. The solemn high Mass is sung by a priest attended by two assistants, a deacon and a subdeacon, assisted by a choir and a number of servers called acolytes, or altar boys. Incense is used. The high Mass is also sung by the priest, but he has no assistants except the servers, and incense is not used. The low Mass has a somewhat simpler ceremonial and the priest need be attended only by the altar boy. No part of a low Mass is sung. Incense is not used. The low Mass became general about the ninth century. We must briefly mention the principal kinds of Masses you will hear of. It should be remembered, however, that all Masses are essentially the same: the offering of the Body and Blood of Christ as a sacrifice to the Most Holy Trinity. But names are given to Masses according to the rank of the one saying them. They are named also according to the formality and ceremonies of the Mass. The Mass with the most ceremonies is the solemn high Mass, the next, the high Mass, and the other, the low Mass. Masses are also given names according to the purpose: e.g., for a person just married, a nuptial Mass, or a Mass for a dead person, a requiem Mass.

1. The *solemn high Mass* is the Mass sung by a priest. He is attended by two assistants, a deacon and a subdeacon, and assisted by a choir and a number of servers, called acolytes. Sometimes, one of the Masses on Sunday is of this type.

2. A *high Mass* is a Mass sung by one priest, attended only by the altar boys.

3. A *low Mass* is a Mass by one priest in which the prayers are recited, not sung. There is no choir.

4. A *pontifical Mass* is a solemn Mass of a bishop with some special ceremonies. This name is also given to a solemn Mass said by the pope.

5. A *nuptial Mass* is a Mass said with special ceremonies for those just married. This is done to bring special blessings upon the married couple. Nuptial Masses are not said during Lent or Advent.

6. A *requiem Mass* is a Mass said for persons who have died. It may be at the time of death or any time later, e.g., on an anniversary. The priest wears black vestments.

How You Should Take Part in the Mass. For such a great event as the Mass, in which God comes down to the altar of our parish churches and performs a great miracle for us, we should carefully prepare ourselves. You should do at least the following:

1. Be in your seat at Church at least five minutes before the Mass begins.

2. Have your Missal with you to be able to join your prayers with those of the priest and all Catholics.

3. Know what Sunday it is and have the Missal marked to be prepared to pray with the priest.

4. Growing out of "3" you will have given some thought, as you wait for the priest to enter, to the purpose of the Mass and of the feast of the day. This will put you in the spirit which the Catechism says you should have to listen to the Mass "with reverence, attention, and devotion."

5. During the Mass you will join the priest in praying the Mass. This will keep your interest in the Mass. You will be very respectful. You will not talk to your neighbor, or point to anything, or push or nudge him. You will, in short, show "every outward mark of respect and devotion" to Christ.

6. And to receive and enjoy *to the full* the benefits of the Mass, you should receive Communion every time you assist at Mass,* sacramentally, or at least spiritually, that is, by desire. This is the spirit of the Church. The preparation for Communion is, of course, an excellent preparation for the Mass itself—confession,

---

* Communion can, of course, be received only once a day.

Mass is said even in the air. This picture was taken on the
German zeppelin, the Hindenburg, on its first trip to America.

penitence (or grace maintained from a previous confession),*
and fasting.

Summary. The Mass has been the same sacrifice from
the first time it was offered on the first Holy Thursday night
when Christ was physically present, down through the ages
when it has been offered every day "from the rising of the
sun to the going down thereof," with Christ mystically
present as priest. The priest we see at the altar acts only
for Christ. This is most simply shown in his statements at
the Consecration: THIS IS MY BODY; THIS IS MY BLOOD.

The Mass said by Christ, on the first Holy Thursday
night, consisted of a sacrifice (the Consecration) and
a banquet (the Communion). In the course of time,

---

* It is not necessary to go to confession each time before receiving
Holy Communion, unless one has committed a mortal sin since the
last confession.

additional prayers and ceremonies were added, as we can see by examining any Missal.

The principal parts of the Mass—the Offertory, Consecration, and Communion—were attended in early days only by the faithful, i.e., baptized and believing Catholics. Those who wished to become Catholics and were being instructed came to the Church at the time of the Mass and recited prayers and received instruction. However, they were not permitted to be present at the principal parts. They were dismissed before the Offertory. The part of the service attended by the Catechumens came to be called "The Mass of the Catechumens." The part of the service attended by the faithful came to be called, "The Mass of the Faithful." Today we attend the entire Mass, consisting of the Mass of the Catechumens and the Mass of the Faithful. The Mass of the Catechumens is an excellent preparation for the more solemn Mass of the Faithful. Notice as you attend Mass next Sunday that the Mass of the Catechumens is said principally at the sides of the altar, and the Mass of the Faithful principally at the center of the altar.

What Did I Learn from This Chapter?

1. Of what did the Mass consist when Christ instituted it on the first Holy Thursday night?
2. What has been added to the Mass since Christ instituted it?
3. What part of the Mass must be heard to satisfy the law of the Church?
4. What are the names of the two main divisions of the Mass?
5. What prayer ends the Mass of the Catechumens?
6. What prayer begins the Mass of the Faithful?
7. What is the Missal? In what language is the Missal on the altar written?

8. What is a solemn high Mass? a low Mass?

9. What is a pontifical Mass?

10. What is a nuptial Mass? a requiem Mass?

11. What is the Latin word for "I believe"?

My Part

1. I shall be in Church five minutes before the Mass begins whenever I attend.

2. I shall always use my Missal in taking part in the Mass.

3. At Mass I shall always keep my mind on the priest and what he is doing, recalling the first Mass.

4. I shall remain in my seat until the priest has left the altar and is in the sacristy.

5. I shall try to prepare for Communion and receive Communion at all Masses I attend.

Problems and Activities

1. Find out what you can about the Catechumens.

2. Tell the class what you mean by a banquet and how all the guests take part. Apply this to Holy Communion.

3. Find out whether the priest says in the center of the altar or at the sides of it:

    a) the Mass of the Catechumens.

    b) the Mass of the Faithful.

4. Find out in your Church:

    a) When during the Mass the people stand.

    b) When they sit.

    c) When they kneel.

Using the Missal

1. Find in the Missal the Latin words *Ite, Missa est* (Go, the Mass is ended, or, Go, you are dismissed). Was there ever a dismissal at any other place in the Mass?

2. Find in the Missal the Creed (*Credo*, Latin for "I believe"). Do you notice any difference in your feelings and attitude in the Mass up to the Creed, and after (i.e., between the Mass of the Catechumens and the Mass of the Faithful)?

3. Listen next Sunday after the Gospel and Sermon so that you can hear the priest say "Credo." This is the first word of the Nicene Creed. It is almost the same as the Apostles' Creed which you know. You know when you hear this that the Mass of the Catechumens is coming to an end.

4. Are you using your Missal every time you attend Mass?

Vocabulary

Catechumens: in the early Church catechumens were people who were preparing to become Christians by receiving religious instruction and who had not yet been baptized.

Faithful: people who believe, the laity. You are a member of the faithful.

Pontifical: relating to a pontiff, or priest of high rank, such as a bishop.

Catechism (Christian Doctrine)
- What is the third commandment? (353)
- What are we commanded by the Third Commandment? (354)
- How are we to worship God on Sundays and holydays of obligation? (355)
- Why does the Church command us to keep the Sunday holy instead of the Sabbath? (357)
- How should we assist at Mass? (269)
- Which is the best manner of hearing Mass? (270)

Chapter VI

THE LITURGICAL YEAR AND THE MASS*

Every Mass is centered around the Consecration. This never changes. The identical words are spoken in the Consecration of every Mass that is said. But the character of the Mass we hear on Sundays and holydays changes from day to day. Some parts are omitted, some parts are changed from day to day, some parts change only at certain seasons of the year. It is natural for us to ask why there are these changeable parts.

Ordinary of the Mass. Let us first understand how these changing parts are made clear in the book we will use at Mass—the Missal. If you will take your Missal and examine it, you will find a large section called *The Ordinary of the Holy Mass* or just the Ordinary of the Mass. This contains those parts of the Mass which do not change, or which change only rarely.

If you will look through the Ordinary of the Mass, you will find the Consecration, i.e., the consecration of the bread and wine so that it becomes the Body and Blood of Christ. You will notice that it is part of what is called the "Canon of the Mass." Canon as used here means rule. It is prescribed. It must be said in this exact form. It includes those absolute essentials of the Mass which Christ included in the First Mass.

---

* This chapter should be a concrete study of the Missal itself. It would be well if the child follow closely the Missal used in the Mass by the priest. He should have, of course, his own Missal. The purpose of this chapter is information.

Proper of the Season. If you will look through your Missal you will find two sections called *The Proper of the Season* and *The Proper of the Saints.* You will notice that these parts are different for each Sunday and weekday. The Proper of the Season and the Proper of the Saints contain the changeable parts of the Mass. These are the parts of the Mass proper or set aside for each day. These parts together with the ordinary of the Mass make up the Mass for a particular day. In a complete Missal, the Masses for each day of the year are given. In the Missal on the altar from which the priest reads, all of the Masses are contained. There are also Missals prepared for lay people that contain just the Masses for Sundays and Holydays of obligation. These are called Sunday Missals.

Liturgical Year. In order to understand the changeable parts of the Mass, it is necessary that we know something about the *liturgical year.* This is the year as it is divided by the Church. It has its seasons, and its days are named after some great event in the Life of Christ, of Mary, or of the saints, or of the progress of the religious or liturgical season. A Feast is sometimes celebrated on the Sunday following it, and this is often referred to as a feast within the *octave* (eight days). The day before a feast is called the *vigil* of the feast. The vigils of some feasts are fast days, the vigil of Christmas, for example.

Through the liturgical year, we live again the events of the life of Christ and celebrate, "by Christ and with Christ, and in Christ," the mysteries of the redemption of man. And in this way, too, we honor the memory of saints.

Division of Liturgical Year. There is a division of the liturgical year based on the two principal events of the Life of Christ:

• The Birth of Christ or the Incarnation;

• The Passion, Death, and Resurrection of Christ.

The division of the liturgical year, or *cycles*, as they are called, centering around these events are:

1. The Christmas Cycle, or The Cycle of the Incarnation.

2. The Easter Cycle, or The Cycle of the Redemption.

In the celebration of these two great periods of the life of Christ, the Church has divided each cycle into three periods: a period of preparation, a period of the celebration proper, and a continuation (or prolongation) of the celebration for a number of weeks after.

Christmas Cycle. The Christmas Cycle or the Cycle of the Incarnation extends over about twelve Sundays. The liturgical year begins on the First Sunday in Advent. This is the fourth Sunday before Christmas. One might think the feast of Christ's Birth—Christmas itself— should be the beginning of the liturgical year, but we can see how very proper it is to prepare for that great event. We can recall to mind how for centuries the Jews looked forward to the coming of the Messias. During the four weeks of this Advent season we can look forward to His coming or advent.

The celebration of Christmas itself takes up two to three Sundays, ordinarily two. This period extends from December 24 to January 14. This celebrates the appearance of Christ in the world. It is a time of joy because Christ came from heaven and took the form of a human being and dwelt among us. This is also called the Epiphany season. "Epiphany" means appearance or manifestation.

The period after the Christmastide which continues the joyful celebration of Christmas includes from one to six Sundays. Instead of being called the Sundays after Christmas, they are called the Sundays after Epiphany.

CHRISTMAS CYCLE—MYSTERY OF THE INCARNATION

		Sundays
Preparation (Purple Vestments)	I. Advent (From first Sunday of Advent to December 24)	4
Celebration (White Vestments) [Christmas-Epiphany]	II. Christmastide (Dec. 24 to Jan. 14)	2
Prolongation (Green Vestments)	III. Time after the Epiphany (Jan. 14 to Septuagesima Sunday)	6

Easter Cycle. As in the Christmas Cycle, so in the Easter Cycle, the time is divided into three periods: first, preparation; second, the celebration proper; and third, the continuation of the celebration. As you know, Easter Sunday falls on a different date each year, but it is always between March 22 and April 25. It is determined by the position of the moon. Most Missals have calendars which give the date of Easter for many years to come. What is the date of the next Easter?

The preparation for Easter (the day of the Resurrection), lasts about nine weeks. This time of preparation is subdivided into three parts:

1. The first part of the period of preparation extends from the first Sunday after the close of the Christmas Cycle, called Septuagesima Sunday, to Ash Wednesday. This time itself is called Septuagesima and extends three weeks.

Before the printing press was invented,
Missals, like all books, were written by hand.
They were often beautifully decorated.
This picture shows a page of an old Missal.

Septuagesima means seventieth, though here it does not have any numerical significance. Lent, in Latin, is called *Quadragesima*, which means fortieth. The Sundays before it are called Quinquagesima (fiftieth), Sexagesima (sixtieth), and Septuagesima (seventieth), though, of course, there are only seven days between rather than ten.

2. The second part of the preparation includes four Sundays and is the first part of Lent.

3. The third part of the period of preparation includes the two Sundays in which Christ's passion is celebrated, extending to Easter, and is the second part of Lent.

The celebration of the Easter Cycle extends over seven Sundays, from the Resurrection of Christ Himself on Easter Sunday to Trinity Sunday. This period is called the Eastertide.

The rest of the liturgical year extends for at least 24 Sundays. It is named from the feast of Pentecost, and the Sundays are called the first or second Sunday after Pentecost, or whatever their number may be. These facts may be briefly summarized in the following chart:

EASTER CYCLE—MYSTERY OF THE REDEMPTION

		Sundays
Preparation (remote) (Purple Vestments)	I. Septuagesima (From Septuagesima to Ash Wednesday)	3
(near)	II. Lent (From Ash Wednesday to Passion Sunday)	4
(immediate)	III. Passiontide (From Passion Sunday to Easter)	2

Celebration	IV. Eastertide	7

(White and Red
    Vestments)
  [Easter-Pentecost]
	(Easter Sunday to
	    Trinity Sunday)	

Remaining Portion of Year
  (Green Vestments)
	V. Time after Pentecost
	    (Trinity Sunday to
	    Advent)
		24-28

Liturgical Colors. The color of the vestments which the priest wears shows the spirit of the seasons of the liturgical year as well as the spirit of particular feast days. Five colors are used ordinarily in the vestments of priests: white, green, purple (violet), red, and black. Other colors also used are gold and rose.

In general during the period of the celebration of the two main liturgical feasts, the Incarnation and the Resurrection, the priests wear *white* vestments on Sundays. During the period of preparation for these great feasts in both the Christmas and Easter cycle, the priests wear *purple* vestments on Sundays. In the period after the feasts in both cycles, the priests wear *green* vestments on Sundays.

Meaning of Liturgical Colors. Let us see what the meaning of these colors are in the liturgy of the Church.

White is the color of purity, of innocence, and of joy and glory. White is used, therefore, at the two central periods of celebration of the liturgical year, Christmas and Easter, and on all the feasts of our Lord. White is used, too, on the feast days of the Blessed Virgin—for example, the Annunciation, the Immaculate Conception, and the Assumption. It is used also on feasts of virgins, confessors, and saints who are not martyrs.

Purple is the color of sorrow, mourning, and penitence. Purple vestments are worn during the seasons in *preparation* for the two great feasts of the liturgical year, Advent and Lent. They are periods of *penitence*. By penance we prepare ourselves for the great feasts. This is true, too, for the vigils, or the preparation *the day before* for individual feasts. These are ordinarily days of penance. The vestments are purple, too, on such vigils.

Green is the color of hope. It is the color of the periods after Epiphany and after Pentecost. Green vestments are worn on most of the Sundays of the year.

Red is the sign of blood and of fire. It stands for bravery and courage. *Red* is used on the feasts of Pentecost to signify the "tongues of fire." It is used on the feasts of martyrs—and more particularly on the feasts of the Apostles except St. John—to signify blood. All the Apostles except St. John were martyred, that is, killed for the faith. It is used, too, on feasts of the Holy Cross.

Black is the sign of bitter grief and of death. Black vestments are used on Good Friday, and are used in Masses for the dead.

Gold and *rose* vestments are also worn. Gold vestments are worn in particular at the greatest feasts of the liturgical year on Christmas and Easter in place of white. Gold vestments *may* also be worn when green, white, or red vestments are ordinarily required.

Rose vestments may be worn on two Sundays—the third Sunday in Advent and the fourth Sunday in Lent.

The Missal—The Liturgical Book of the Mass. The Missal is one of the official books used in the liturgy of the Church. It is the book used in the Mass. It contains principally the Ordinary of the Mass and the different Masses said throughout the year. It is the book which the altar boy carries from the Epistle to the Gospel side of the altar when toward the end of the Mass of the Catechumens the priest is ready to read the Gospel.

Latin, the Liturgical Language. The Missal is written in Latin, which is the liturgical language. This is now a dead language, but it is kept because in a universal Church spread throughout the world among people of many languages, a common or universal language is necessary. It is not affected by the differences of nations, and the meaning of its words does not change as happens with English words, or French words, or other living languages. It helps to fix the form of the principal doctrines of the Church. It makes communication between the parts of the Church possible. It makes it very convenient for a priest to say Mass even in a foreign country.

Missal for the Laity. The little book we have containing the Masses is taken from this Missal that is used on the altar. Of course for our use it contains a translation. Some Missals for lay folk contain only the English, others have the English and Latin in columns alongside of each other. Some of them are simply "Sunday Missals" containing the Masses only for the Sundays and the holydays of obligation: Others are "Daily Missals," containing the Masses for every day in the year. Examine your Missal now to see which kind you have.

Does it have English only?

Does it have both Latin and English?

Is it a Sunday Missal?

Is it a Daily Missal?

Proper of the Season and the Ordinary of the Mass. We have seen that the Missal contains the *Ordinary* of the Mass—that is, the parts that are ordinarily (except for a few places) always the same. The Missal contains, too,

The Missal on the altar. The Missal stands on the epistle side
of the altar at the beginning and end of Mass.

the *Proper of the Season*. We have studied the liturgical
year, and we have noticed its division into two cycles,
the Christmas and Easter Cycles. These two principal
parts of the liturgical year are further subdivided into
three divisions. The Masses change with these seasons,
particularly in such parts as the Introit, Collect, Epistle,
Gospel, and some others. We notice it especially every

week as the priest reads the particular, or *proper*, Gospel for that Sunday. This is as we know the Proper of the Season. As the Missals for the laity are printed, we make up the Masses for a particular Sunday by adding at the proper place in the Ordinary of the Mass, the changeable parts proper to the day as given in the Proper of the Season.

Proper of the Season or Temporal Cycle. This cycle or sequence beginning with the first Sunday in Advent and extending to the twenty-fourth Sunday after Pentecost is called the Proper of the Time or the Temporal Cycle. The Masses in this cycle aim to show the life of our Lord in relation to the great mysteries of our religion.

Proper of the Saints, or Sanctoral Cycle. If we were to examine the Missal in detail, we would find a series of Masses devoted to the Blessed Virgin, the angels, the Apostles, martyrs, and other saints. This is called the Proper of the Saints or the Sanctoral Cycle. These feast days do not have any necessary relation to the Proper of the Season. The saint has a particular day assigned to him. It is ordinarily the day of his death. His feast day really celebrates the beginning of his entrance into eternal life. The Proper of the Saints begins with the feast that falls on November 29 and gives in order of time the other feasts of the year, the feasts of our Lady, and of angels and of the saints. Find these in your Daily Missal if you have one.

Common of the Saints. There is one other section of Masses that we should know. There are a good many saints who do not have a special or proper Mass of their own. In this section called the "Common of the Saints" are the Masses for these saints. If the individual is a martyr, there is a Mass for martyrs, and so for bishops, virgins, widows, and various other classes of saints.

Summary. The parts of the Missal which the laity are especially interested in are:
1. The Ordinary of the Mass.
2. The Proper of the Season.
and in a somewhat less degree in:
3. The Proper of the Saints.
4. The Common of the Saints.

There are two special Masses that the laity are interested in and sometimes attend: the Requiem Mass, that is, the Mass for the Dead, and a Nuptial Mass, a Mass for a couple married in the Church.

What Did I Learn from This Chapter?

1. What is the liturgical year?
2. What are its two principal divisions or cycles?
3. What are the three divisions of the Christmas Cycle?
4. What are the three divisions of the Easter Cycle?
5. Which belongs to the Easter Cycle? to the Christmas Cycle:
    a) The season of Advent
    b) Eastertide
    c) The season after Pentecost
    d) Christmastide
    e) Season after Epiphany
    f) Season of Lent
    g) Season of Septuagesima
    h) Passion time
6. Mark each of the seasons given in Question 5 to show what part of the cycle it is:
    a) Preparation (Prep)
    b) Celebration (Cel)
    c) Continuation (Con't)
7. What is the Missal?
8. In what language is the Missal on the altar written?
9. Why is the Missal written in this language?

10. What is the Ordinary of the Mass?
11. What is the Proper of the Season?
12. What other parts of the Missal will you need to join with the Ordinary of the Mass to make a complete Mass for Sunday?
13. What is the Canon of the Mass?
14. What is the vigil of a feast?
15. What are the feasts of our Lord?
16. What are the principal feasts of Mary?
17. What is the difference between the Proper of the Time and the Proper of the Saints? What other names do these propers have?
18. What is the Common of the Saints?
19. What are the colors of the vestments worn by priests saying Mass?
20. What is the meaning of each color?
21. What are the colors of the vestments worn during the seasons given in Question 5?
22. What is meant by vigil? octave?

My Part
1. I shall use my Missal every time I attend Mass.
2. I shall prepare my Missal each time before I go to Church.
3. Was I in my pew five minutes before Mass began last Sunday?
4. Do I remain in my seat until the priest has left the altar and is in the sanctuary?
5. I shall plan to go to Communion next Sunday.

Problems and Activities
1. Take an ordinary calendar and mark off the seasons of the Liturgical Year. Take a crayon and mark the season in preparation for each cycle in purple, the season of celebration in white (or gold), and the season for the continuation of the celebration in green.
2. If you have in your room the *Character Calendar*, use it each morning to get a thought which will guide you during the day.

3. Write a brief biography or sketch of the life of an important saint whose feast day occurs this month.

4. Select a patron saint for your grade.   Whom do you recommend? Why?

5. Make a list of the feasts of our Lord.

6. Make a list of the feasts of the Blessed Virgin Mary.

Using the Missal

1. On what pages in your Missal do you find:
   a) The Ordinary of the Mass
   b) The Proper of the Season

2. Find in your Missal in the Ordinary of the Mass:
   a) The Canon of the Mass
   b) The Consecration of the Host
   c) The Consecration of the Wine

3. Find in your Missal the Mass for:
   a) Palm Sunday
   b) The second Sunday after Pentecost
   c) The feast of the Immaculate Conception
   d) The feast of the Ascension
   e) Christmas
   f) Sexagesima Sunday
   g) Second Sunday after the Epiphany
   h) Pentecost Sunday
   i) Trinity Sunday
   j) Ash Wednesday

Which of these Masses did you find in the Proper of the Saints?

4. Find in the Proper of the Saints the Mass for the feast days of the following saints, giving the date:
   a) St. Andrew
   b) The Nativity of the Blessed Virgin Mary
   c) St. Stephen
   d) Assumption of the Blessed Virgin Mary
   e) Holy Apostles Peter and Paul
   f) Nativity of St. John the Baptist
   g) St. Gabriel

    h) Your patron saint

    i) The patron saint of your teacher

    j) The patron saint of your pastor

    k) The patron saint of your church

    l) The patron saint of our country

5. Find in your Missal the complete Mass for the last Sunday under the direction of your teacher.

6. Prepare your Missal for next Sunday's Mass.

    a) Find out what Sunday it is.

    b) Mark the Ordinary of the Mass.

    c) Mark the Proper for the Day.

Vocabulary

Canon: the part of the Mass that is fixed or cannot be changed which includes the Consecration.

Ordination: the act by which a person becomes a priest. The time when a priest receives the Sacrament of Holy Orders.

Proper: that which especially belongs to a day or a person. The proper of the Mass is the part of the Mass especially set aside for that day.

Epiphany: the appearance or Manifestation of Christ, the Son of God, in the world, especially the annual celebration of the day the three Kings visited the Christ Child.

Pentecost: the day the Holy Ghost descended on the Apostles. The day on which this event is celebrated each year; the birthday of the church.

Martyrs: persons who willingly suffer death as a penalty for refusing to renounce their religion or any part of it; persons who are killed or die for a cause.

Chapter VII

THE PRIEST PREPARES FOR MASS*

As a part of our preparation for entering fully into the spirit of the Mass and cooperating and participating with the priest and Christ in the Sacrifice, we should know more about the altar and about the vestments which the priest wears while offering the Mass. This is given as information to help make the devotion of the Mass more clear.

Christ, the High Priest. Just as the sacrifice of the Old Law required a priest, so does the sacrifice of the New Law. The priest at the Last Supper was Christ Himself. The priest in every Mass is Christ Himself. Just as He personally offered Himself as the Victim on the first Holy Thursday so He does in a mystical manner in every Mass. The Mystical Christ is the High Priest in every Mass. The priest saying the Mass acts as Christ's representative and ours. Christ is the head of His Mystical Body. The Mystical Body includes you and me and every baptized person. It includes your mother and father, it includes all the other boys or girls in your class and in your school. It includes everybody in Church on Sunday. We all must join with Christ in the offering of the Mass.

Great Privilege of the Catholic Priesthood. The priest being ordained a priest by a bishop who traces his

---

* It is imperative if this chapter be effective that the priest should vest before the class and say the prayers. This, of course, may be done in the sacristy. It is essential, too, that the children be taken to the altar (reverently) and shown the altar and all that is on it when Mass is about to begin.

power directly to the Apostles and to Christ, has the great privilege of saying the Mass. By the authority and power of Christ, the priest will be able to offer Christ Himself to the Most Holy Trinity. After the Consecration Christ Himself will be truly present (the Real Presence) on the altar. For the great privilege of being the instrument through whom Christ works directly, the priest, in great humility, prepares himself carefully and prayerfully for his part in the Sacrifice of the Holy Mass.

Your pastor, either in the sacristy of the church or in your classroom, will go through the ceremonies and the prayers which he follows in putting on his vestments. What he will do and what he will tell you may be briefly told in the following notes:

> The priest enters the sacristy in the ordinary black cassock in which we so often see him. It is the garment he ordinarily wears about the school.
>
> The priest washes his hands, and asks God for the grace of purity. He says the following prayer: "Give virtue, O Lord, unto my hands, that every stain may be wiped away: so that I may be enabled to serve Thee without defilement of mind or body."

Vessels and Other Things Used in Mass. After he washes his hands he prepares the vessels and other things he will need in the Sacrifice of the Mass. These are described below.

> First he prepares the *chalice,* which is the cup in which the wine and the water are placed during the Sacrifice of the Mass. This cup is made either of silver with the inside gold-plated, or it may be made entirely of gold.
>
> On the top of the chalice he places a folded linen cloth, called the *purificator,* with which, toward the end of the Mass, he will dry the chalice.
>
> On the top of the purificator, he will place the small plate called the *paten.*
>
> On the paten he places the host or bread to be consecrated in the Mass.

1. A chalice and paten. 2. This is how the chalice looks
before the veil is put over it. On the chalice are the paten, the
purificator, and the pall. 3. A corporal and burse. 4. A ciborium.
The hosts used for Communion are kept in the ciborium.

Over the host he places the *pall*, a piece of linen about six inches square. This is usually doubled and stiffened by a cardboard.

He then covers all with the *chalice veil*, a covering usually of the same color as the vestments of the priest.

On top of the chalice veil, the priest places the *burse*, a folded container, in which is the *corporal*. The corporal is a square piece of linen that is placed under the chalice and host during the Consecration.

Vestments of the Priest. After the chalice and the host have been prepared for the Mass, the priest puts on the *vestments* or garments especially used for this purpose.

The first vestment put on by the priest is the *amice*. This is a piece of linen rectangular in shape, 2½ feet long by 2 feet wide, provided

Amice.

with long strings and ornamented with a cross in the center.

The priest touches his head with the amice, then puts it around his neck, crosses it on his breast and ties the strings to keep it in position.

This was originally a cover of the head (a hood) and later a scarf.

"Put, O Lord, the helmet of salvation upon my head, that I may overcome the assaults of the devil."

The second vestment put on by the priest is the *alb*. This is a white linen garment with sleeves, and reaching to the feet. The bottom is sometimes made of lace. The alb covers the cassock completely.

"Cleanse me, O Lord, and purify my heart: that being made white in the Blood of the Lamb, I may have the fruition of everlasting joys."

The *cincture* is a girdle used for gathering in the alb at the waist. It is a cord-like band, made of linen, hemp, or silk. It may be white, or the same color as the vestments, except black. It is tied about the waist.

"Gird me about, O Lord, with the girdle of purity and extinguish in my loins the desire of lust: so that the virtue of continence and chastity may ever abide with me."

1. Alb.   2. Cincture.   3. Maniple.

The fourth vestment put on by the priest is the *maniple*. This is a band placed over the left arm so that it falls equally on both sides. It is an ornamental vestment, which formerly served the purpose of a handkerchief. It is ornamented with one cross in the center, and usually with one at each end.

"May I be worthy, O Lord, so to bear the maniple of tears and sorrow: that with joy I may receive the reward of my labor."

The fifth vestment put on by the priest is the *stole*. It is a long narrow strip of silk generally fringed at the end, and is ornamented like the maniple.

The stole is worn around the neck and crossed over the breast. (A bishop wears both ends hanging down in front.) Priests wear it in the exercise of any sacred function.

"Restore to me, O Lord, the stole [robe] of immortality which I lost by the transgression of the first parent and although unworthy I draw near to Thy sacred mystery, may I yet be found worthy of everlasting joy."

Stole.

The sixth vestment put on by the priest is the *chasuble*. This is the outside garment of the priest with which we are most familiar. The chasuble is usually made of silk and its color depends on the special character of the Mass. The chasuble was first in the form of a cloak, but now it is much simpler. It is a long, somewhat rectangular silk garment with a (circular) or V-shaped opening in the center for the head. It is over 3 feet long (40 to 46 inches) in front and rear. It is a little over 2 feet wide (26 to 30 inches). A Cross is usually embroidered on the back of the chasuble.

"O Lord, who hast said: My yoke is easy, and My burden is light: make me so to be able to bear it, that I may obtain Thy favor. Amen."

Another vestment of the priest which is seen most often in the Benediction of the Blessed Sacrament is the *cope*. This is a long cape or cloak.

Chasuble.

Sanctuary. The place of the Holy Sacrifice of the Mass is the altar within the *sanctuary*, or more particularly the altar stone in the center of the altar table. Let us clearly identify the various places where the ceremonies in connection with the Holy Sacrifice of the Mass take place.

The *Sanctuary* (meaning the Holy Place) is all the space included within the altar rail. The central place is the altar. This place is reserved for priests and their immediate assistants, including altar boys or acolytes.

The *Sacristy* is the room just off the sanctuary, in which the priest prepares the vessels for the Mass and puts on his vestments. It is here that the liturgical linen, vestments, vessels, books, etc., are kept when not in use.

The *altar rail* is a railing separating the sanctuary from the remainder of the church, particularly where the laity are. It is a low railing at which we ordinarily receive Holy Communion.

The *altar* is the central structure. The altar steps, of which there must be at least one, lead up to it. It is the table on which the Eucharistic Sacrifice takes place. This is the *altar table*.

The word *altar* means a high mountain or high place. It probably recalls the time when

A cope. This is the large cape worn by the priest at Benediction.

sacrifices were made to God on high places or hills and mountains, and not indoors. Later they were built indoors as in Solomon's temple. And with the early Christians, who were persecuted, they were located underground in the *catacombs*.

The *tabernacle* is the small house at the center of the altar—a Holy of Holies—in which Christ in the Most Blessed Sacrament lives. It is because Christ is here that we kneel or genuflect when we come into Church or leave it, and that we raise our hats as we pass the Church on the street. The sign that Christ is in the tabernacle is the ever-burning *sanctuary lamp* which usually hangs toward the front of the sanctuary.

The sides of the altar are given special names. The side to your right as you sit in your pew is called the *Epistle side*, because it is there that the priest reads from the Epistle in the Mass. On your left side as you sit in your pew is the *Gospel side* where the priest reads the Gospel during the Mass.

The *crucifix* is placed in a prominent position on the altar so that the priest and people can always see it to remind them of Calvary. It is, as you know, a cross with a figure of Christ nailed to it recalling His crucifixion. It is very appropriate that it should be given this prominent place above the tabernacle.

The *altar stone* is an essential part of the altar. Ordinarily every altar must be made of stone or at least must contain an altar stone large enough to hold the host and the greater part of the base of the chalice. This stone contains five crosses: one in the center, and one in each of the four corners, in memory of the five wounds of Christ's body. Because the early Masses said in the catacombs were read over the tomb of a martyr (the top of which was the altar

The priest is vesting for Mass.
What vestments does he already have on?

table) it is now required that relics of martyrs be placed below the altar table or in the altar stone.

The *credence table* is a small table or shelf on the Epistle side of the altar where the cruets (or bottles) of wine and of water, and the finger bowl and towel are placed. In solemn High Masses, the chalice, paten and host covered by the humeral veil is kept there until the Offertory and returned after the ablutions.

Three altar cloths made of linen or hemp must cover the altar. These must be blessed by the bishop or his delegate. Three cloths are used so that if the Precious Blood should be spilt, it would be absorbed by the cloths before it reached the stone. The three cloths also symbolize the Trinity. They symbolize, too, the winding sheets in which the Body of Jesus was wrapped for burial.

Altar candles remind us that Christ called Himself Light, and the Light of the world. The candles must be made of beeswax. There is a beautiful symbolism attached to this. The pure wax which the bees take from the flowers is a symbol of the pure flesh of Christ, whose source was Mary the Immaculate—the purest flower of creation. The wick is a symbol of the soul of Christ, and the flame a symbol of His Divinity.

Symbolism of Vestments*

There is included here for reference only the special meanings (symbolism) which have been given to the vestments of the priest. For each vestment there is a special meaning too, with reference to the Passion of our Lord. These meanings are indicated by the word *Passion* after the meaning.

Amice:
- the helmet of salvation (formerly covered the head)
- mortification of the tongue.
- cloth with which jailers cover Jesus' face in the court of the high priest (Passion)

Alb:
- purity of soul (whiteness)
- white garment Herod ordered that Jesus be clothed in (Passion)

---

* For the explanation of this symbolism, see especially MacMahon's (M.S.) *Liturgical Catechism*, Gill, Dublin, pp. 49-57.

Cincture:	• chastity
	• bonds with which Jesus was held captive in Garden of Olives (Passion)
Maniple:	• fetters with which Jesus was bound and led forth as a criminal (Passion)
Stole:	• sanctifying grace and immortality
	• the yoke of the Lord
	• fetters which bound Jesus to the pillar and the cross on His shoulders (Passion)
Chasuble:	• charity which covers a multitude of sins
	• sweet yoke of our Lord
	• the cross which Jesus bore (Passion)

What Did I Learn from This Chapter?

1. Who is the High Priest at every Mass?
2. Who is included in the Mystical Body of Christ? Who is the Head?
3. How does the priest get the power to say Mass?
4. Identify each vessel used in the Mass from a picture. (This child will have identified each vessel itself during the study.) Use these pictures.
5. Tell what each of the vessels used in the Mass is:
   a) chalice
   b) purificator
   c) paten
   d) pall
   e) chalice veil
   f) burse
   g) corporal
6. Have students identify each of the garments of the priest used in the Mass (if available).

7. Have students identify a picture of each of the garments used by the priest in the Mass.

8. Tell what each of the following garments is:
   - a) amice
   - b) alb
   - c) cincture
   - d) maniple
   - e) stole
   - f) chasuble

9. On the altar identify each of the parts of the sanctuary and sacristy.

10. Make a drawing of a sanctuary and sacristy naming each part.

11. Tell what each of the following is:
   - a) sanctuary
   - b) altar rail
   - c) altar
   - d) tabernacle
   - e) crucifix
   - f) altar stone
   - g) credence table
   - h) altar cloths
   - i) altar candles

My Part

1. I shall tip my hat (if a boy) every time I pass a Catholic Church because the Blessed Sacrament is on the altar.

2. I shall always:
   - (a) be quiet in church and particularly at Mass, keeping from talking; and
   - (b) pay attention to what the priest is doing; and
   - (c) follow the prayers he is saying by using my Missal as my prayer book.

3. I shall prepare my Missal for the Mass of next Sunday.

Prayers

Learn the prayer the priest says when he puts on the chasuble, and train yourself to say it each time you enter the Church for Mass. (If you prefer one of the other prayers the priest uses in vesting himself, learn that one.)

Problems and Activities

1. In what way has the fact that early Christians had to say Mass in the Catacombs influenced the altar today or the vessels and things used in the Mass today?

2. Prepare a booklet on the "Altar and the Vestments." Use photographs, pictures from catalogues, or make drawings from books. Include any prayers or poems you may find. Include a picture of the Pope, any bishops or archbishops, as well as priests.

3. If possible, construct an altar on a small scale that follows the laws of the Church. Secure the co-operation of your pastor or assistant who may be teaching your class. Perhaps the girls in the school (if there are any) can make the vestments, or the Altar Society of the Church might co-operate with you.

4. If you do not know the following poems, learn at least one of them:

The Sanctuary Lamp — Yvonne Dolphin
God's Home — Edward F. Garesché, S.J.
The Blessed Candle — James Kinney Collins

Vocabulary

The meaning of the following words is taught by association with the thing itself. These object lessons are supplemented by pictures and drawings.

Chalice	Amice	Sanctuary
Purificator	Alb	Sacristy
Paten	Cincture	Tabernacle
Pall	Maniple	Crucifix
Chalice veil	Stole	Cruets
Burse	Chasuble	Credence table
Corporal	Cope	

Representative: a person who acts for another. The priest acting for Christ in the Mass.

Mystical: having a secret meaning. Cannot be seen; such as the mystical presence of Christ on the altar in the Mass.

Extinguish: to put out, such as a fire.

Immortality: that which cannot die. Life forever, everlasting life.

Transgressor: a sinner, a person who violates a law.

Catechism (Christian Doctrine)

- What is the Sacrament of Holy Orders? (278)
- What is necessary to receive Holy Orders worthily? (279)
- How should Christians look upon the priests of the Church? (280)
- Who can confer the Sacrament of Holy Orders? (281)
- When did Christ give His priests the power to change bread and wine into His body and blood? (249)
- How do the priests exercise this power of changing bread and wine into the body and blood of Christ? (250)

The humeral veil. The word *humeral* means "shoulder."
This is the veil which the priest wears over his shoulders when
he gives Benediction. It is white or gold in color.

Chapter VIII

THE PSALMS AND THE MASS

I. The Book of Psalms

The great source of the prayers of the Mass is the Holy Bible, both the Old and the New Testaments. The prayers of the Mass are not taken generally from all the books of the Holy Bible. Most of the 46 books of the Old Testament and the 27 books of the New Testament are used, but not all to the same degree. The Gospels are always taken from one of the four Holy Gospels of Jesus Christ according to St. Matthew, St. Mark, St. Luke, and St. John. The Epistles are usually taken from the Epistles (letters) of St. Paul, although the Epistles of the other Apostles are also used, and in some cases, other books of the New or Old Testaments.

Psalms, a Source of Prayers for Mass. From the Old Testament there are especial favorites. Isaias, for example, the great Prophet who foretold the coming of Christ, is used many times. But the source most often used—in fact in every Mass—is the "Psalms," of which there are one hundred and fifty. Occasionally a whole Psalm is quoted but usually only a verse or two is quoted.

The Authors and Division of the Psalms. The principal inspired writer of the Psalms is King David. Others are thought to be written by Moses, Solomon, and others whose names are given in the titles. In all collections there are one hundred and fifty Psalms, though the individual

Psalms do not always contain the same verses. For example, what in the Catholic Douay version is called the 22nd Psalm is referred to in other versions as Psalm 23. This is a Psalm you should know:

PSALM 22
A Psalm for David

The Lord ruleth me: and I shall want nothing. 2. He hath set me in a place of pasture.

He hath brought me up, on the water of refreshment: 3. He hath converted my soul.

He hath led me on the paths of justice, for His own name's sake.

4. For though I should walk in the midst of the shadow of death, I will fear no evils, for Thou art with me.

Thy rod and Thy staff, they have comforted me.

5. Thou hast prepared a table before me, against them that afflict me.

Thou hast anointed my head with oil; and my chalice which inebriateth me, how goodly is it!

6. And Thy mercy will follow me all the days of my life.

And that I may dwell in the house of the Lord unto length of days.

Messianic Character of the Psalms. The Hebrew word for the Book of Psalms is *Tehillim* which means "Hymns of Praise." Sometimes in the book they are called canticles. Sometimes they were sung with instrumental accompaniment and sometimes not. The Book of Psalms was the national hymn book of the Hebrews. In it, in a general way, they expressed their longing for the King that was to come, the Messias. They express the longing for their Saviour who, as we know, is Christ. This was true not only of the book as a whole, but it is true in a special way of certain Psalms which are Psalms 2, 8, 15, 21, 44, 87,

109, and 131. Some of these Psalms tell us of the coming of the Messias. For that reason we call them Messianic. This is the way St. Paul understood them, and uses them in his Epistles. Even more important is the fact that Christ Himself uses them to show that they tell of His coming. This makes certain this Messianic character of the Psalms. One of these Messianic psalms you might learn by heart is the 8th Psalm.

> 2. O Lord, our Lord, how admirable is Thy name in the whole earth!
>
> For Thy magnificence is elevated above the heavens.
>
> 3. Out of the mouth of infants and of sucklings Thou hast perfected praise, because of Thy enemies, that Thou mayest destroy the enemy and the avenger.
>
> 4. For I will behold Thy heavens, the works of Thy fingers: the moon and the stars which Thou hast founded.
>
> 5. What is man that Thou art mindful of him? or the son of man that Thou visitest him?
>
> 6. Thou hast made him a little less than the angels, Thou hast crowned him with glory and honor: 7. and hast set him over the works of Thy hands.
>
> 8. Thou hast subjected all things under his feet, all sheep and oxen: moreover the beasts also of the fields.
>
> 9. The birds of the air, and the fishes of the sea.
>
> 10. O Lord, our Lord, how admirable is Thy name in all the earth!

Penitential Psalms. There is a famous series of Psalms expressing sorrow called the *Seven Penitential Psalms.* There are others besides these seven, but these are given the name. One of these is the very famous 129th Psalm:

> Out of the depths I have cried to Thee, O Lord: 2. Lord, hear my voice.
>
> Let Thy ears be attentive to the voice of my supplication.
>
> 3. If Thou, O Lord, wilt mark iniquities: Lord, who shall stand it.

4. For with Thee there is merciful forgiveness: and by reason of Thy law, I have waited for Thee, O Lord.

My soul hath relied on His words: 5. My soul hath hoped in the Lord.

6. From the morning watch even until night, let Israel hope in the Lord.

7. Because with the Lord there is mercy: and with Him plentiful redemption.

8. And He shall redeem Israel from all his iniquities.

Brief Verses from Psalms. One could turn to almost any of the Psalms to find a verse expressing what is in your heart. If your feeling is a desire to express praise and thanksgiving to God, you open to Psalm 137:

I will praise Thee, O Lord, with my whole heart: for Thou hast heard the words of my mouth.

I will sing praise to Thee in the sight of the angels: 2. I will worship toward Thy holy temple, and I will give glory to Thy name.

For Thy mercy or Thy truth: for Thou hast magnified Thy holy name above all.

3. In what day soever I shall call upon Thee, hear me: Thou shalt multiply strength in my soul.

4. May all the kings of the earth give glory to Thee: for they have heard all the words of Thy mouth.

5. And let them sing in the ways of the Lord: for great is the glory of the Lord.

If you feel sorrow or contrition for your sins, you will find Psalm 139 helpful:

2. Deliver me, O Lord, from the evil man: rescue me from the unjust man.

3. Who have devised iniquities in their hearts: all the day long they designed battles.

4. They have sharpened their tongues like a serpent: the venom of asps is under their lips.

5. Keep me, O Lord, from the hand of the wicked: and from unjust men deliver me.

If you want to express to God how happy you are for all His benefits, Psalm 33 puts it in words for you:

> 2. I will bless the Lord at all times, His praise shall be always in my mouth.
> 3. In the Lord shall my soul be praised: let the meek hear and rejoice.
> 4. O magnify the Lord with me; and let us extol His name together.
> 5. I sought the Lord, and He heard me; and He delivered me from all my troubles.

Or if you want to tell God how much you really depend on Him, Psalm 72 would be helpful:

> 25. For what have I in heaven? and besides Thee what do I desire upon earth?
> 26. Thou art the God of my heart, and the God that is my portion forever.

In the prayers of the Church for morning and evening especially, the Psalms are also used very much indeed. Some of the most beautiful prayers in the daily prayer book of priests, called the "Breviary" are made up from these Psalms.

Our Lord Himself used the Psalms as His own prayers. It seems good to know that we can pray to God in the very same words which Jesus Himself used. These verses are the prayers, too, of the Chosen People before the Messias came. These prayers from the Psalms are also, as we shall see, the prayers of the Mass.

2. The Psalms and the Ordinary of the Mass

Judica Me—Psalm 42. In the Ordinary of the Mass there are two long quotations from the Psalms—the prayer at the foot of the altar at the beginning of the Mass, and the prayers at the time of the washing of hands. The

David sings a psalm to God. The Psalms were used as prayers
by Christ Himself.

prayer at the foot of the altar is Psalm 42. This is one of the few times a Psalm is quoted completely in the Mass. We give it here:

> 1. Judge me, O God, and distinguish my cause from the nation that is not holy: deliver me from the unjust and deceitful man.
> 2. For Thou art God my strength: why hast Thou cast me off? and why do I go sorrowful whilst the enemy afflicteth me?
> 3. Send forth Thy light and Thy truth: they have conducted me, and brought me unto Thy holy hill, and into Thy tabernacles.
> 4. And I will go in to the altar of God: to God who giveth joy to my youth.
> 5. To Thee, O God my God, I will give praise upon the harp: why art thou sad, O my soul? and why dost thou disquiet me?
> 6. Hope in God, for I will still give praise to Him: the salvation of my countenance, and my God.

The prayer of the Mass is made by quoting first the fourth verse:

> I will go in to the altar of God: to God who giveth joy to my youth.

Then the whole Psalm is given, expressing David's longing for the temple and altar of God, and his desire to give praise to Him who is David's hope and strength and salvation. One would think the Psalm was written expressly for the Mass. It tells exactly how the priest and the people should feel in approaching the altar of God.

Verses from the Psalms in the Ordinary

This prayer at the foot of the altar is ended by a quotation of one verse from Psalm 122. It is:

> Our help is in the name of the Lord, who made heaven and earth.

It is in this form of a verse or a few verses that the Psalms are used in the Mass, particularly, as we shall see later, in

the Proper of the Mass. Just before the priest ascends to
the altar, for example, two verses of Psalm 84 are quoted:

> Thou wilt turn, O God, and bring us to life: and Thy people
> shall rejoice in Thee.
> Show us, O Lord, Thy mercy: and grant us Thy salvation.

And immediately after is a verse from Psalm 101:

> Hear, O Lord, my prayer and let my cry come unto Thee.

Again as the priest is incensing the altar in a solemn
high Mass, his prayer is a quotation of three verses from
the Psalms:

> Let my prayer, O Lord, be directed as incense in Thy sight:
> the lifting up of my hands as the evening sacrifice. Set a door
> round about my lips; that my heart incline not to evil words, to
> make excuses in sins.

How perfectly these short prayers fit the action of the
priest! If we would become acquainted with the Psalms
we would remember such brief quotations to say in time of
temptation or depression, and to give praise or thanksgiving
to God.

Let us see if there are other uses of just a verse or two
of the Psalms in the Ordinary of the Mass. In the *Sanctus*
is a line from a verse (26) of Psalm 117:

> Blessed is He that cometh in the Name of the Lord.

After the priest receives the Body of Christ, he expresses in
the words of Psalm 115 his desire to give praise to the Lord.

> What shall I render to the Lord for all the things that He
> hath rendered to me? I will take the chalice of salvation and I
> will call upon the Name of the Lord.

And this is followed by a verse (4) from Psalm 17:

> Praising I will call upon the Lord and I shall be saved from
> my enemies.

PSALMS AND THE MASS

Lavabo—Psalm 25. So much for the use of one or two verses from the Psalms in the Ordinary of the Mass. It was noted that there are two longer quotations from the Psalms in the Ordinary of the Mass. The first was the prayer, *Judge me, O Lord,* at the foot of the altar at the beginning of Mass. This is the whole of Psalm 42. The other longer use of a Psalm is found immediately after the priest makes the offering, and washes his fingers. As he does so he prays in the words of Psalm 25 (verses 6-12) that he may be cleansed and redeemed spiritually:

> I will wash my hands among the innocent; and will compass Thy altar, O Lord:
> That I may hear the voice of Thy praise: and tell of all Thy wondrous works.
> I have loved, O Lord, the beauty of Thy house; and the place where Thy glory dwelleth.
> Take not away my soul, O God, with the wicked: nor my life with bloody men:
> In whose hands are iniquities: their right hand is filled with gifts.
> But as for me, I have walked in my innocence: redeem me, and have mercy on me.
> My foot hath stood in the direct way: in the churches I will bless Thee, O Lord.

3. Psalms in the Proper of the Mass

The Psalms are very often used in the Proper of the Mass. The prayers of the Proper of the Mass are rather short, and often they are made up of a verse from one of the Psalms. This is true especially of the Introit, the Gradual, the Alleluia, the Tract, the Offertory, and the Communion.

In the Mass of the Catechumens. The *Introit* was originally a long Psalm sung as the priests came in in solemn procession. When these solemn processions no longer took place, the quotation from the Psalm was very much reduced. Ordinarily it is but one verse. This is illustrated in the Introit for the first Mass on Christmas Day, which is taken from the 2nd Psalm. It is as follows:

> The Lord hath said to me: Thou art My Son, this day have I begotten Thee. Why have the Gentiles raged, and the people devised vain things?

The Glory be to the Father, and to the Son, and to the Holy Ghost, etc., is said and the first part of the Introit is repeated.

The Lessons of the Mass, including the Gospel and the Epistle, were separated by short prayers. Usually there are only two of these. The first is the *Gradual*.

The *Gradual*, in the early Church, was sung from a step (Latin word, *gradus*) called an *ambo* (a kind of pulpit), and has the most elaborate music of any of these parts. The music required much repetition of the words. This made impossible the quotation of a full Psalm and, consequently, a single verse is often used and repeated in the singing. For example, the Gradual for the Second Mass on Christmas Day at dawn is taken from Psalm 117 as follows:

> Blessed be He that cometh in the Name of the Lord; the Lord is God, and He hath shone upon us. This is the Lord's doing; and it is wonderful in our eyes.

The *Alleluia* has much the same character as the Gradual, consisting on Holy Saturday, for example, of a verse from Psalm 117:

> Give praise to the Lord, for He is good: for His mercy endureth forever.

The *Tract*, for example, on this same day is a verse from Psalm 116, as follows:

> O praise the Lord, all ye nations: and praise Him, all ye people. For His mercy is confirmed upon us: and the truth of the Lord remaineth forever.

Originally this was a full Psalm, but is now, ordinarily, only a brief part of a Psalm. On some special Sundays, it is longer, particularly on Palm Sunday when it contains sixteen verses.

In the Mass of the Faithful. As we come to the Mass of the Faithful, the *Offertory Verse*, which begins this part of the Mass, is often a quotation from a Psalm. For example, the Offertory for the second Sunday after Epiphany is a verse from Psalm 65, as follows:

> Shout with joy to God, all the earth: sing ye a psalm to His Name; come and hear, all ye that fear God, and I will tell you what great things the Lord hath done for my soul, alleluia.

At the end of the Mass the *Communion Antiphon* often is made up of a verse from the Psalms. The Communion, for example, for Ascension Day is from Psalm 67, as follows:

> Sing ye to the Lord, who mounteth above the heaven of heavens to the east, alleluia.

Just as the Church finds in the Psalms appropriate prayers and thoughts for its life throughout the year, so the individual may likewise find in the Psalms thoughts of thanksgiving, of praise, of sorrow, and of love and adoration of God, and for guidance in his daily life.

What Did I Learn from This Chapter?
1. Is the Book of Psalms part of the Bible?
2. Is it a part of the Old or the New Testament?
3. Who is the principal author of the Psalms?
4. Who else wrote psalms, included in the Book of Psalms?
5. How many psalms are there in the Book of Psalms?
6. Are they always given the same number?
7. What is another word meaning psalm?
8. What is a penitential psalm?
9. How many of the penitential psalms are usually grouped together?

10. Find in the Book of Psalms a line or verse which expresses:
    a) praise of God.
    b) sorrow for our sins.
    c) thanksgiving to God.
    d) dependence on God.
11. Quote from memory one complete psalm.
12. Tell about the psalm that the priest quotes at the beginning of the Mass at the foot of the altar. Why is this fitting?
13. Tell about the psalm that the priest uses after he makes the offering in the Mass of the Faithful. Why is this fitting or appropriate?
14. Find out from what psalms the following parts of the Proper of the Mass of next Sunday are taken:
    a) Introit
    b) Gradual
    c) Alleluia
    d) Tract
15. Are the psalms ever used in the Mass of the Faithful? When?
16. Find in the Book of Psalms verses that speak of the Messias (Christ).
17. Review the questions in Chapter II.

My Part

1. I shall learn a verse from a psalm
    a) to say whenever I am tempted.
    b) to show God I am thankful.
2. I will (do) tip my hat every time I pass a Catholic church.
3. I am (will be) in my pew in church five minutes before the Mass begins.
4. I do not leave the Church until the priest has left the altar and is in the sacristy.
5. I am receiving Communion
    a) weekly
    b) monthly

6. I use my Missal every time I attend Mass following the priest in his prayers and joining mine with his.

7. I listen attentively to the Gospel and the Sermon so as to be ready for our talk about it on Monday morning.

8. I am saying as I enter the Church for Mass the prayer the priest says when putting on his chasuble:

"O Lord, who hast said: My yoke is easy, and My burden is light: make me so to be able to bear it, that I may obtain Thy favor. Amen."

Prayers

I will learn the following brief prayers (or ejaculations) from the Psalms:

"I will praise Thee, O Lord, with my whole heart.

I will bless the Lord at all times, His praise shall always be in my mouth.

I will go to the altar of God: to God who giveth joy to my youth.

Our help is in the name of the Lord, who made heaven and earth," etc.

Problems and Activities

1. Tell when you might use the brief prayers given under *Prayers* (above);

e.g.: when you are grateful for your health,

when you are grateful for the goodness of your parents,

when you wish to give thanks to God.

2. Find out the facts about King David, the psalmist (if you have your book *Before Christ Came*). Secure additional information if you can, and also some pictures of King David.

3. Find out how many of the Communion prayers given in *Life of the Soul*, the third grade book, are from the Psalms, or if you have a Daily Missal, turn to the Communion of the Masses for this month and find out how many are from the Psalms.

4. Make a small booklet in which you print some brief prayers from the Psalms which you like very much. Give the

booklet the title *Brief Prayers from the Psalms for Me.*

5. Watch next Sunday for the word *Lavabo* as you did for the word *Credo. Lavabo* is the Latin word for "I will wash." It is the first word of that part of Psalm 25 which the priest uses as he washes his fingers after he receives the offering.

6. I shall listen closely next Sunday while the priest is at the foot of the altar to see if I can hear and recognize the *Judica Me,* which are the first Latin words of Psalm 42, Judge me.

7. Begin a list "Latin Words from the Mass that I Know." Give the meaning and tell when the words are used in the Mass. Begin with:

   a) *Credo.*
   b) *Judica Me.*
   c) *Lavabo.*

8. Tell when you would use each of the following verses:

> Psalm 22, Verse 1.
> Psalm 22, Verse 4.
> Psalm 8, Verse 4.
> Psalm 8, Verse 5.
> Psalm 129, Verses 1 and 2.
> Psalm 137, Verse 1.
> Psalm 33, Verse 5.
> Psalm 72, Verse 26.

9. Have you a Catholic Bible in your home? If not, on Mother's or Father's birthday or at Christmas time give her or him a New Testament (joining with your brothers and sisters if necessary). Be sure you are getting a Catholic Bible. How can you tell?

10. Ask the teacher to read Psalm 21 in class. Remember that this was written a thousand years before the Crucifixion. To what incidents of the Crucifixion does it refer?

11. For the following brief prayers from the Psalms used in the fourth grade, tell which of the purposes given in the following definition of prayer from the Catechism are fulfilled:

> (Prayer is the lifting up of the mind and heart to God, to adore Him, to thank Him for His benefits, to ask His forgiveness, to beg of Him all the graces we need whether for body or soul.)

a) Have mercy on me and hear my prayer (Ps. 4).

b) O Lord, my God, in Thee have I put my trust: save me from all them that persecute me and deliver me (Ps. 7).

c) I will give praise to Thee, O Lord, with my whole heart (Ps. 9).

d) Preserve me, O Lord, for I have put my trust in Thee (Ps. 15).

e) My God is my helper, and in Him will I put my trust (Ps. 17).

f) To Thee, O Lord, have I lifted up my soul. In Thee, O my God, I put my trust, let me not be ashamed (Ps. 24).

g) I will bless the Lord at all times. His praise shall be always in my mouth (Ps. 33).

h) Forsake me not, O Lord my God: do not Thou depart from me. Attend unto my help, O Lord, the God of my salvation (Ps. 37).

i) Have mercy on me, O God, according to Thy great mercy (Ps. 50).

Using the Missal

1. Review Exercise:

a) Find in your Missal where the Ordinary of the Mass begins.

b) Find where the Proper of the Mass next Sunday begins.

c) What is the Gospel for next Sunday?

d) Read the Collect for next Sunday.

e) Read the Communion for next Sunday.

2. Find in the Missal:

a) *Judica me*—Judge me.

b) *Lavabo*—I will wash.

c) *Credo*—I believe.

3. Tell for each:

a) Is it part of the Mass of the Catechumens or Mass of the Faithful?

b) Is it part of the Ordinary of the Mass or of the Proper of the Mass?

c) Do any of these prayers belong in the Canon of the Mass?

4. I am using my Missal in praying the Mass with the priest every Sunday. I try to be exactly where he is. (The Latin words, *Credo* and *Lavabo*, help me to follow the Mass.)

Bible Passages

For the following passages:

1. Tell whether they are from the Old or New Testament.
2. Name the Book from which they are taken.
3. Tell where in the Mass they are used.

"Our help is in the name of the Lord who made heaven and earth."

"I will go in to the altar of God, to God who giveth joy to my youth."

"I will wash my hands among the innocent."

"Blessed is He that cometh in the Name of the Lord."

"I will take the chalice of salvation and I will call upon the Name of the Lord."

"This is My Blood."

Vocabulary

Anoint: to make sacred. The meaning comes from the fact that in religious ceremonies persons were made sacred by pouring oil on them.

Penitential: sad, sorrowful.

Iniquities: sins, evils, bad acts, such as a violation of God's law.

Salvation: the act of gaining heaven, on saving of one's soul.

Catechism (Christian Doctrine)

•Did God abandon man after he fell into sin? (60)
•Who is the Redeemer? (61)
•Did the Son of God become man immediately after the sin of our first parents? (72)
•What is prayer? (304)
•Is prayer necessary to salvation? (305)
•At what particular times should we pray? (306)

Chapter IX

THE MASS AND REDEMPTION AND THE COMMANDMENTS OF THE CHURCH

Men have always, as we have seen, offered sacrifices to God in order to honor Him, to atone for their own sins, to give thanks to God, or to ask for His blessings. The Holy Sacrifice of the Mass is the greatest sacrifice of all religion. It is the supreme, perfect sacrifice. But why is it necessary? In order to understand why the Sacrifice of the Cross and the Sacrifice of the Mass are necessary we must go back to the story of our first parents, Adam and Eve.

The Fall of Man. Man's disobedience in the Garden of Eden separated him from God. The glories of Paradise were denied him further. He was expelled, or sent out, from the Garden. Death, sickness, and all the ills of human nature came to man. He lost grace. He lost everything supernatural. He still had hope that God would not forsake him, though he had to suffer for his disobedience.

Promise of a Redeemer. What could man himself do to satisfy fully the justice of God? The sinner himself could offer nothing to atone for his great sin of disobedience. He could offer the sacrifice of animals. He could offer the fruits of the earth or the fruits of the flock. He could offer the bloody and unbloody sacrifices of the old law. But this was not enough. A Redeemer had been promised. The promise of a Redeemer was made to Adam in the Garden of Eden by God Himself. The promise or prophecy of a clean oblation—a pure and holy sacrifice—was made by the prophet Malachias. The Jews never realized how closely related these two promises or prophecies were. Until, in the fullness of time, Christ came to earth, no man really knew. Christ is the Redeemer. His Body and Blood is the clean oblation.

God's Love of Man in the Redemption. It was only God who could have thought of and brought about what did happen. It was only by the power of God it could be brought about. Only God's love of sinful man could do as much for man as He did. The Redeemer who was to come was God Himself made man. It was Jesus Christ, the God-man. He was conceived by the Holy Ghost, born of the Virgin Mary, suffered under Pontius Pilate, was crucified, died and was buried. The third day He arose again from the dead. He ascended into heaven, where He sits at the right hand of God the Father Almighty, and from whence He shall come to judge the living and the dead. We can see now what St. John the Evangelist meant when he said: "God so loved the world as to give His only-begotten Son that whoever believeth in Him may not perish but may have life everlasting."

Redemption and the Clean Oblation. The plan of Redemption that God had in mind to save men became clear in the life of Christ—particularly at the end of His life. Christ, the Son of God, dying on the cross satisfied the justice of God. It was a great satisfaction. The offering of the bread and wine at the Eucharistic Banquet on the first Holy Thursday was to be the Sacrifice of the New Law, the clean oblation. This, as is said in the Mass, is

> a pure Host
> a holy Host
> a spotless Host
> the holy Bread of eternal life, and
> the chalice of everlasting salvation.

With the ascension of Christ into heaven at the right hand of the Father and the sending of the Holy Ghost upon the Apostles, the plan of Redemption became even clearer. The Church was organized to carry on this sacrifice—"Do this in commemoration of Me." A priesthood was provided after the order of Melchisedech. And so this sacrifice would be offered from the rising of the sun to the setting thereof and forever.

Meaning of the Sacrifice on the Cross. We know that the sacrifice of God made Man on Calvary was a bloody sacrifice. "He was wounded for our iniquities, He was bruised for our sins." The Priest and Victim in this great Sacrifice was Christ Himself, and the altar was the cross. Christ wished to make this sacrifice—He wished to die for us, and gave up His life of His own free will. The death of Christ on the cross was the greatest victory ever won in this world. It was a full victory over sin, and it satisfied all the claims of divine justice. By it heaven was opened again, supernatural life was won for our souls, and the Heavenly Father once more looked down with pleasure on men. They could again be His children, heirs of His kingdom, partakers of His nature. The enemy of mankind—the evil spirit—was overcome. The Creator's justice satisfied, heaven opened, grace purchased, hell conquered—these are the fruits of that great sacrifice of the God-man on Mount Calvary.

Grace of God for Man. The justice of God was satisfied by Christ's sacrifice on the cross. Wonderful graces were won for man. Man would need this grace in his struggle against sin. This grace comes to man through the sacraments and through the daily renewal of the Sacrifice of Calvary in the Holy Sacrifice of the Mass. From this we can see how necessary the organized Church is in God's plan for the Redemption of man, and how important are the priest, bishop, and pope. They bring us, in God's plan, the means of salvation.

Mass as a Source of Grace. Even if there were no commandment to attend Mass, we should want to go to Mass. It is man's greatest privilege after baptism to hear Mass and to receive Holy Communion. Many of us would attend Mass without the commandment because of God's love of us. We should want, too, with all our heart to receive Holy Communion often. To go once a year would seem to be stingy with God. As we understand more clearly that the Mass is a real sacrifice, we shall feel as many do that to hear Mass without going to Communion is not to fulfill the intention Christ had when He instituted the Mass.

Third Commandment of God. What the Church commands us is really the very least we should do. We could hardly do less. In the third commandment of God He commands us:

To Keep Holy the Sabbath Day

We know that the day set aside in a special way for the service of God is Sunday, and not Saturday, as it was among the Jews. The reason for this is, as you know, to commemorate the fact that "on Sunday Christ arose from the dead, and on Sunday He sent the Holy Ghost upon the Apostles."

First Commandment or Precept of the Church. It was the most natural thing in all the world, therefore, that the Church should require us to celebrate the day set aside in a special manner for the worship of God by attending Mass. What more fitting way is there? The great mysteries of religion which the Church wishes us especially to recall

Jesus gives Communion to His Apostles.

are celebrated on days on which the faithful are required to hear Mass. That, too, is very fitting, as you will see, when you study the Masses for the Holydays of Obligation. The first commandment of the Church follows from the third commandment of God, and its desire to emphasize the great mysteries of religion and the virtues of the saints. The first commandment of the Church is, as you will recall:

To Hear Mass on Sundays and Holydays of Obligation

Holydays of Obligation. The Holydays of Obligation in the United States are:

1. All the Sundays of the year.
2. January 1, the Feast of the Circumcision.
3. Ascension Day.
4. August 15, the Assumption of the Blessed Virgin Mary into heaven.
5. November 1, All Saints Day.
6. December 8, the Feast of the Immaculate Conception.
7. December 25, Christmas Day.

Fourth Commandment of the Church. In connection with this commandment or precept to hear Mass on Sundays and other Holydays of Obligation, one thinks also of the fourth commandment of the Church:

To Receive the Holy Eucharist During the Easter Time.

Easter time in the United States extends from the first Sunday in Lent to Trinity Sunday.

As has been said, this is the least we can do. Communion ought ordinarily be a part of our participation in the Mass. We should receive the Holy Eucharist at least during the period of the year when it was instituted, and when we live again each year with Christ, His Crucifixion, Resurrection, and Ascension. Weekly or at least monthly Communion is the very least we should do. Many people go to Communion every day.

Practical Rules for Attending at Mass. You will understand the following simple rules without long explanations:

1. You should hear the whole of the Mass.
2. You should plan to be in your seat five minutes before the beginning of the Mass.
3. You should not leave your seat until the priest has left the altar when the Mass is finished.
4. You must be bodily present at a Mass. You cannot satisfy your obligation by "joining" in a Mass over the radio.
5. You must keep your mind and heart on the celebration of the Mass. Do not let yourself be distracted.
6. You should participate in the prayers of the priest by praying with the priest, using your Missal.
7. You should make an offering, or contribution, according to your means. If you will deny yourself some little thing during the week (candy, for example), and save the penny, or nickel, or dime, to give to the collection on Sunday, it will be a real offering of the money and of yourself.
8. You should, whenever possible, go to Holy Communion.

What Did I Learn from This Chapter?

1. State the relation to the Christian plan of redemption of each of the following:
    a) The Fall of Adam
    b) The Promise of a Redeemer
    c) The prophecy of a clean oblation
    d) The Last Supper
    e) The Sacrifice on Calvary and the Resurrection
    f) The Church
    g) The Catholic priesthood
    h) The Mass
    i) Holy Communion
2. Show the meaning in the Christian plan of redemption of:
    a) Christmas
    b) Easter
    c) Pentecost
3. What is grace? In terms of grace what was the purpose of the Redemption?
4. What do we mean by the supernatural part of man's life? (grace)
5. What does the word *Redeemer* mean? *Saviour?* Apply these meanings to Christ.
6. What was the prophecy of Malachias? Was it fulfilled? Tell how.
7. Tell how the clean oblation is described in the Mass itself.
8. What is the meaning of the Sacrifice of the Cross?
9. What is the need now for the continuation or repetition (in the Mass) of the Sacrifice of the Cross?
10. How was God's justice satisfied for Adam's disobedience?
11. What is the third commandment of God?
12. What is the first commandment or precept of the Church?
13. What is the fourth commandment or precept of the Church?
14. What are the holydays of obligation in the United States?

15. For the purpose of the fourth precept of the Church, when does Easter time begin in the United States? When does it end?

16. Tell the priest's place in God's plan of redemption.

My Part

1. I shall recite the prayer that the priest uses in putting on the chasuble as I enter the Church for Mass.

2. I shall be in my seat five minutes before the Mass begins.

3. I shall prepare my Missal on Saturday evening for the Mass of the next day.

4. I shall use my Missal in praying the Mass with the priest.

5. I shall make an offering of money at every Mass I attend which will represent some little sacrifice or self-denial on my part.

6. I shall go to Holy Communion as often as possible.

7. I shall remain in my seat after the Mass is over until the priest has left the altar and is in the sacristy.

8. I shall tip my hat every time I pass a Catholic church (boy).

9. I shall tip my hat every time I meet a priest.

10. How do you show your love of God?

Problems and Activities

1. Write in your own words God's plans of Redemption from the disobedience of Adam to the first Pentecost.

2. Find in the New Testament the quotation: "God so loved the world, as to give His only-begotten Son; that whosoever believeth in Him, may not perish, but may have life everlasting." (............) Tell how it came to be said.

3. Prepare a booklet of poems, pictures, and other material on the Redemption of Man by Jesus Christ. Give your booklet a title of your own such as:

    a) Adam and Christ

    b) God's Love of Man

    c) Sin and Love

    d) Eden and Calvary

Tell why these might be good titles.

4. Prepare a booklet on the holydays of obligation in the United States.

5. Review the facts about the Christmas cycle under the headings:

    a) Preparation

    b) Celebration

    c) Continuation of the Celebration

6. At the Last Supper:

    a) Who was the Priest?

    b) Who was the Victim Offered?

    c) To whom was the Victim offered?

    d) What for?

7. At the Crucifixion:

    a) Who was the Priest?

    b) Who was the Victim offered?

    c) To whom was the Victim offered?

    d) What for?

8. In the Mass last Sunday:

    a) Who was the Priest? the High Priest?

    b) Who was the Victim offered?

    c) To whom was the Victim offered?

    d) What for?

9. Find out what you can about the ceremonies when a person is made a priest—that is, when a priest is *ordained*. This is, as you know, the reception of the sacrament of holy orders.

10. What is the Holy Sacrifice of the Mass? Show:

    a) That it is a sacrifice.

    b) That it is holy.

11. Review especially the chapter on the First Mass.

Memorize

"Do this in commemoration of Me."

"God so loved the world, as to give His only-begotten Son; that whosoever believeth in Him, may not perish, but may have life everlasting."

"He was wounded for our iniquities; He was bruised for our sins."

Bible Passages

For each of the passages given above:

    1. Tell whether it is from the Old Testament or the New Testament.

    2. Name the book from which it is taken.

    3. Tell how it came to be made.

Vocabulary

Supernatural: more than natural, above nature.

Redemption: buying back, paying for, saving, rescue, salvation.

Crucifixion: the punishment formerly given criminals of nailing them to a cross.

Infinite: without an end; lasting forever.

Precept: rule or law, or requirement, such as the law of the Church to attend Mass on Sunday.

Communion: the receiving of the Body and Blood of Christ under the form of the Bread by the people, or under the form of the bread and wine, by the priest.

Mysteries: things impossible or difficult to understand fully; such as the doctrine of the Trinity.

Immaculate: pure, without spot.

Assumption: means, when applied to the Blessed Virgin, that she was taken up into heaven after death.

Obligation: something required; a duty. It is an obligation or duty to receive Holy Communion during the Easter season.

Catechism (Christian Doctrine)

   • Who were the first man and woman? (39)

   • Were Adam and Eve innocent and holy when they came from the hand of God? (40)

   • Did God give any command to Adam and Eve? (41)

   • Which were the chief blessings intended for Adam and Eve had they remained faithful to God? (42)

   • Did Adam and Eve remain faithful to God? (43)

   • What befell Adam and Eve on account of their sin? (44)

• What evil befell us on account of the disobedience of our first parents? (45)
• What other effects followed from the sin of our first parents? (46)
• Who is the Redeemer? (61)
• Which are the means instituted by our Lord to enable men at all times to share in the fruits of the Redemption? (114)
• What is the Church? (115)
• Why did Christ found the Church? (120)
• What is the Holy Eucharist? (238)
• When did Christ institute the Holy Eucharist? (239)
• Who were present when our Lord instituted the Holy Eucharist? (240)
• What is the Mass? (263)
• What is a sacrifice? (264)
• Is the Mass the same sacrifice as that of the cross? (265)
• How is the Mass the same sacrifice as that of the cross? (266)
• What were the ends for which the sacrifice of the cross was offered? (267)
• What is the sacrament of holy orders? (278)
• What are we commanded by the third commandment? (354)
• How are we to worship God on Sundays and holydays of obligation? (355)
• Is it a mortal sin not to hear Mass on a Sunday or a holyday of obligation? (390)
• Why were holydays instituted by the Church? (391)
• How should we keep the holydays of obligation? (392)
• What sin does he commit who neglects to receive Communion during the Easter time? (400)
• What is the Easter time? (401)

PART II
Study of the Ordinary of the Mass

Chapter X

THE MASS OF THE CATECHUMENS PREPARES US

Priest Prepares for Mass. We have noted, as the priest put on his vestments, the prayers he offered as a part of his preparation for the Mass. He prays that every stain of sin may be wiped away from his soul, that he may overcome temptation, that he may be cleansed and purified, and that he may have everlasting joys. He prays for purity and that all bad desires may be blotted out and, as he draws near to the sacred mystery of the Eucharistic sacrifice, he prays for everlasting joy, and that he may be worthy, and that he may be able to bear the yoke of Christ and win His favor. This is the priest's spirit in preparing for the Mass.

Mass—A Real Sacrifice. We must prepare ourselves for the Mass as if we were to be present at the first Sacrifice of the Cross. We must prepare for our part with the same spirit as the priest. The sacrifice in which we are now to take part is not a mere representation of what happened on the first Holy Thursday and Good Friday. It is a continuation of the great sacrifice of Calvary. We are to take part in a great mystery of religion. God becomes actually present on the altar! There is the *real presence of Christ*. There is Christ, Priest and Victim of the Holy Sacrifice of the Mass.

Proper Respect at Mass. Our feeling should be one of great reverence and respect. We will be in our pew before Mass begins. We will be silent during the Mass except for our prayers. We shall not talk to our neighbor. We shall follow the priest intently. We shall find out what is the special feast of the day and enter into the spirit of it with the Church by using our Missals. We shall realize that we are part of what is happening. We must prepare to confess that we have sinned. We must be sorry. We must be ready to offer ourselves with Christ. We are not merely to listen to the Mass. We are not even merely to read the prayers along with the priest. We, ourselves, mind, body, and soul must take part in the Sacrifice. In the Mass of the Faithful the priest will address us as follows:

> Brethren, pray that my sacrifice and yours may be acceptable to God the Father almighty.

This shows us that we are expected to take part in the Sacrifice of the Mass. It is our Sacrifice. It is the Priest's. It is Christ's.

Be Early for Mass. Our thoughts have turned to the Mass while we are preparing to leave our house. We leave home in plenty of time so that we arrive at the Church before Mass begins. We should plan to be there at least five minutes before Mass begins. We should know what Sunday it is and arrange our Missal so that the prayers of the Mass that change can be easily found.

How Can We Enter Fully Into the Mass? How can we enter fully into the Mass and not merely listen? you may ask. Perhaps together we can answer that question. We shall take each prayer that is used in the Mass, as given in our Missal, try to understand what it means, and then try to express these thoughts in our attitude every time we read them in the Mass.

We should always be in Church at least five minutes before Mass
begins. The children in this picture are going to nine o'clock Mass.
How early are they?

Asperges. Before the beginning of the Mass on Sunday the priest, if it is to be a High Mass, proceeds down the center of the aisle sprinkling the people with holy water, and then returns to the foot of the altar. While he goes down the aisle he says:

Thou shalt sprinkle me, O Lord, with hyssop, and I shall be cleansed; Thou shalt wash me, and I shall be made whiter than snow.

Ps. Have mercy on me, O God, according to Thy great mercy.

V. Glory be to the Father, the Son and the Holy Ghost, etc. Amen.

Ant. Thou shalt sprinkle me. . . .

V. Show us O Lord, Thy mercy.

R. And grant us Thy salvation.

V. O Lord, hear my prayer.

R. And let my cry come unto Thee.

V. The Lord be with you.

R. And with thy spirit.

Let Us Pray:

Hear us, O holy Lord, Father Almighty, everlasting God, and vouchsafe to send Thy holy Angel from heaven, to guard, cherish, protect, visit, and defend, all that dwell in this house; through Christ, our Lord. Amen.

This ceremony is called the *Asperges.* The name is taken from the first word of the prayer in Latin. It means "thou shalt sprinkle."

Vidi Aquam. During Eastertide the *Asperges* is not said but in its place is said the *Vidi Aquam* (I saw the water). The psalm is also changed. During the Eastertide the words that are said are:

Ant. I saw water flowing from the right side of the temple, alleluia; and all to whom that water came were saved, and they shall say: Alleluia, alleluia.

Praise the Lord for He is good; for His mercy endureth forever. Glory be to the Father.

Ant. I saw water. . . .

Prayers at the Foot of the Altar. The Mass of the Catechumens opens with the prayers at the foot of the altar. These are prayers which help to prepare us for the great sacrifice. They show the spirit with which the priest and the people should begin the Mass. The prayers at the foot of the altar include:

1. The Sign of the Cross.
2. The Psalm, "Judge me" (*Judica Me*).
3. The Public Confession (*Confiteor*).

Let us learn the meaning and use of these prayers.

The Sign of the Cross. It is quite fitting that this great Sacrifice should begin with the simple reminder of the original Sacrifice—the Sign of the Cross. Christ dying on the cross on Calvary comes to mind. It directs our attention from the very beginning to the central thought of the Mass, the Sacrifice of Christ. We shall always make this Sign of the Cross in the same reverent spirit with which we make it at the beginning of the Mass. As we use our Missal at Mass we shall notice how many times the cross is referred to and this simple sacramental used in the Sacrifice of the Mass. Perhaps we can think more about the Sign of the Cross every time we make it.

42nd Psalm. The priest then announces simply his intention: "I will go unto the altar of God." And the server answers: "To God who giveth joy to my youth." So likewise we, too, must go unto the altar of God with the priest. How shall we show that? What shall we think of? The Psalm (42) which we now recite with the priest helps us to answer these questions. The Psalm is:

Judge me, O God, and distinguish my cause from the nation that is not holy ; deliver me from the unjust and deceitful man.

The Mass begins with the prayers at the foot of the altar.

For Thou, O God, art my strength; why hast Thou cast me off? And why go I sorrowful whilst the enemy afflicteth me?

Send forth Thy light and Thy truth; they have led me and brought me unto Thy holy hill and into Thy tabernacles.

And I will go in unto the altar of God; unto God who giveth joy to my youth.

To Thee, O God, my God, I will give praise upon the harp; why art thou sad, O my soul, and why dost thou disquiet me?

Hope in God, for I will still praise Him; who is the salvation of my countenance and my God.

Glory be to the Father, and to the Son, and to the Holy Ghost.

As it was in the beginning, is now, and ever shall be, world without end. Amen.

The priest is full of the great joy that is his in offering the Sacrifice. So likewise we should be joyful indeed for the privilege of taking part. But although the privilege for the priest and people is very great, there are naturally other feelings too. We fear the Lord because of our sins, and have a childlike faith in God as our strength, we hope in Him who is our salvation, and trust in His help because we are His creatures. These are the feelings with which we must begin the Mass. Then we ask God:

"Send forth Thy light and Thy truth; they have led me and brought me unto Thy holy hill and into Thy tabernacles."

This Psalm, *Judica me*, is omitted during the Passion time.

Read through these words from Psalm 42 silently. Then under the direction of the teacher a student will read it aloud. Then talk over these questions in class:

1. What is the first feeling on going to the altar?
2. Is this feeling continued?
3. What feeling is expressed in the verse beginning "Judge me"?
4. What is the importance for you in the words, "not holy," "unjust," "deceitful."
5. How is your dependence on God expressed?

6. What do we pray for in the third verse?
7. What, for us, is the "holy hill" and "Thy tabernacles"?
8. What verses express:
   a) praise of God?
   b) hope in God?
   c) joy in God's service?

There follows after the psalm the praise of God (called the lesser doxology—that is, Glory be to the Father, and to the Son, and to the Holy Ghost, etc.) which will appear frequently in the Mass. In this prayer, or doxology:

1. We give praise and glory to God (Holy Trinity).
2. We name each person of the Blessed Trinity.
3. We state the idea that God is eternal and never changes, in the beginning, now, and forever.

We repeat the idea of joy in going to the altar of God, and acknowledge that it is from God that we are to receive help. Now we bow to acknowledge God as Creator.

Notice how fitting or appropriate this beginning of the Mass is. How happy we are to go to the altar of God, and then comes the fear that we may not be pure or holy or just enough. But God is our strength and we shall depend on Him. We welcome, too, the chance or opportunity to give glory to Him and praise. We have hope in Him and our help is in His Name.

The Confiteor. Throughout this opening of the Mass there runs the feeling of priest and people of its greatness. This is shown in the priest's public confession that he is a sinner. Here in the very presence of God Himself, man might very well be ready to confess his sins and be fearful.

Though every Catholic child knows the *Confiteor*, we print it here as it is said in the Mass by the server to bring out some points:

I confess
    to Almighty God,
    to blessed Mary, ever Virgin,
    to blessed Michael the Archangel,
    to blessed John the Baptist,
    to the holy Apostles Peter and Paul,
    to all the saints, and
    to you, Father,
that I have sinned exceedingly
    in thought, word, and deed,
    (*strike breast three times as sign of sorrow for our sins*)
    through my fault,
    through my fault,
    through my most grievous fault.

Therefore
I beseech
    blessed Mary, ever Virgin,
    blessed Michael, the Archangel,
    blessed John the Baptist,
    the holy Apostles Peter and Paul, and
    all the saints, and
    you, Father,
to pray
    to the Lord our God
    for me.

Notice that it has two parts:

    1. A confession of sins,
    2. Petition to all the Saints to pray for us.

The *Confiteor* is made to almighty God and to all the saints, especially the ones named. The petition is to these saints to pray to God for us. The confession is made to all the saints as well as to God, in order to have the saints pray for us.

The priest says the *Confiteor* first, and the server and we with him ask for mercy and forgiveness and everlasting life for him in the words:

"May Almighty God have mercy upon thee, and forgive thee thy sins, and bring thee to everlasting life."

In saying the *Confiteor*, the priest bows low and prays with his hands joined together. Like the humble publican in the parable he will not so much as lift up his eyes to heaven. Immediately afterwards the server and all of us repeat the *Confiteor*, confessing that we, too, are sinners. The priest then repeats the prayer "May Almighty God," etc.

The *Confiteor* gets its name from its first word in Latin. *Confiteor* means "I confess." It is a confession of sins, and a request for prayers for ourselves, and forgiveness. Notice the custom of referring to the prayers of the Mass by the first words of the Latin form. It will help us if we learn to refer to the prayers of the Mass by the Latin word.

Then making the Sign of the Cross, the priest prays for the "pardon, absolution and remission of our sins"—his and ours.

This same spirit is continued in the verses that are recited before the priest ascends the altar. They are as follows:

V. O God, turn and give us life.
R. And Thy people will rejoice in Thee.
V. Show us, O Lord, Thy mercy.
R. And give us Thy salvation.
V. O Lord, hear my prayer.
R And let my cry come unto Thee.
V. The Lord be with you.
R. And with thy spirit.

Through the *Confiteor* we say that as sinners we come to the altar of God to serve Him, and pray for the pardon of our sins. Perhaps we do not realize that we are making this public confession of our sins and desire for pardon, absolution, and remission of our sins. You see, every time you go to Mass you admit that you have sinned and pray for pardon of your sins.

Priest and People Together Offer Mass. It is significant that here at the beginning of the Mass and, as we shall note, at several places during the Mass, the priest prays that the Lord will be with the people; and the server, for and with the people, prays for the priest. Then the priest says *Oremus*: Let *us* pray.

It must be quite clear from this that priest and people must join together and pray the Mass together. Now notice how in the following prayers the priest uses the word we. In other words, he joins the people with himself in the prayers of the Mass.

As the priest ascends the altar he repeats the desire of himself and of the persons attending the Mass that may be forgiven their sins and begin the Mass in a right spirit.

The priest says:

> Take away from us
> our iniquities,
> we beseech Thee, O Lord:
> that we may be worthy to enter with pure minds
> into the Holy of Holies.
> Through Christ our Lord. Amen.

Again we (priest and people) beseech the Lord, that is, we ask Him earnestly through the saints, particularly those whose relics are here (in the altar stone), that our Lord forgive the priest his sins. The priest says this prayer, having reached the top of the steps, while kissing the altar:

> We beseech Thee, O Lord,
> by the merits of Thy saints whose relics are here,
> and of all the saints,
> that Thou wouldst vouchsafe
> to forgive me all my sins. Amen.

At Solemn High Mass the priest blesses incense, and incenses the altar.

Introit. The Mass of the Catechumens continues with the *Introit.* This is ordinarily a verse from the Psalms with the *Gloria Patri* and part of the verse repeated. When processions were more frequent, the Psalms used were longer.

The word *introit* means entrance. This was the beginning of the Mass—the public service of the Church. It is chanted in the High Mass by the choir upon the entrance of the priest. The Introit is a changeable part of the Mass. It varies from day to day. The special character of each Mass is ordinarily indicated by the Introit. It indicates the main idea of the Mass or the season in which the Mass occurs—e.g., Advent.

The Masses are ordinarily named from the first word of the Introit. The first word of the Introit for the fourth Sunday of Lent is *Laetare,* and so the Sunday is called *Laetare Sunday.* If you look in a rather complete Missal (e.g., St. Andrew's Daily Missal), you will notice that this title is printed at the heading of the Mass. The Introit is not a part of the Ordinary of the Mass. It is a part of what is called the *Proper of the Season.* It varies or changes from Sunday to Sunday. Later we shall study the special Masses as we are now studying the Ordinary of the Mass, and at that time we shall study the different Introits.

We print the Introit for the first Sunday of Advent, which shows the character of the Season in the phrase "none of them that *wait* on Thee, O Lord, shall be confounded." We print this Introit to show its form: ordinarily a verse from a psalm as introduction, then one or more verses from the same psalm, then the "Glory be to the Father," and a final repetition of the introductory verse.

In the *Kyrie Eleison* we ask for God's Mercy.

1. "To Thee, O Lord, have I lifted up my soul: in Thee, O my God, I put my trust; let me not be ashamed: neither let my enemies laugh at me: for none of them that wait on Thee shall be confounded. (Ps.) Show me, O Lord, Thy ways, and teach me Thy paths."

2. Glory be to the Father, and to the Son, and to the Holy Ghost. As it was in the beginning, is now, and ever shall be, world without end. Amen.

3. "To Thee, O Lord, have I lifted up my soul: in Thee, O my God, I put my trust; let me not be ashamed: neither let my enemies laugh at me: for none of them that wait on Thee shall be confounded."

Kyrie Eleison. The next part of the Mass of the Catechumens, which is always the same, is the appeal to the Persons of the Blessed Trinity for mercy. It continues the spirit of the opening of the Mass. Its form is simple. The language is Greek, the language in which the Mass was said in the first two centuries.

Kyrie,	eleison	Lord,	have	mercy
Kyrie,	eleison	Lord,	have	mercy
Kyrie,	eleison	Lord,	have	mercy
Christe,	eleison	Christ,	have	mercy
Christe,	eleison	Christ,	have	mercy
Christe,	eleison	Christ,	have	mercy
Kyrie,	eleison	Lord,	have	mercy
Kyrie,	eleison	Lord,	have	mercy
Kyrie,	eleison	Lord,	have	mercy

This prayer is addressed to the Father, to the Son, and to the Holy Ghost. It is a prayer for mercy, or the love of God. It must be devoutly repeated, as indeed it will be if we have entered into the spirit of the prayers at the beginning. It leads us naturally into the next part of the Mass.

Gloria in Excelsis Deo. In the next prayer we turn more completely to God. We desire His glory. In the Mass particularly we praise Him, we bless Him, we adore Him, we glorify Him. We give thanks—for His great glory. Then we address the Trinity again in prayer.

In the opening words we hear again the words sung by the angels on the first Christmas night. After the praise of God there is the special prayer to each of the persons of the Blessed Trinity: to God, the Father Almighty; to Jesus Christ, the only-begotten Son; and to the Holy Ghost.

Now, in these prayers our hearts are fully turned toward God. It is His glory we seek. It was for His glory that Christ died on Calvary. It is for His glory that this Mass and all Masses are said. And here in one of the world's most glorious prayers we are telling of this glory. The teacher will read this aloud in class. You will read it aloud often by yourself. You will memorize it.

The very language of the *Gloria* should arouse in us deep feelings of affection and love for the Holy Trinity. The Mass has carried us along to a very high point. Let us give glory to God with our whole heart, and mind and soul. Let us say the *Gloria* with joy and with love.

Glory be to God on high, and on earth peace to men of good will.
> We praise Thee.
> We bless Thee.
> We adore Thee.
> We glorify Thee.
> We give Thee thanks for Thy great glory.
O Lord God, heavenly King, God the Father Almighty.
O Lord Jesus Christ, the only-begotten Son.
O Lord God, Lamb of God, Son of the Father.
Who takest away the sins of the world, have mercy on us.
Who takest away the sins of the world, receive our prayer.
Who sittest at the right hand of the Father, have mercy on us.

For Thou only art holy.
Thou only art the Lord.
Thou only art most high, O Jesus Christ,
Together with the Holy Ghost
  in the glory of God the Father.
Amen.

This prayer is omitted during the penitential seasons of Advent, of Septuagesima, and in Lent.

The Gloria is sometimes called the *Greater Doxology*. The *Lesser Doxology* is the *Gloria Patri*, etc. (Glory be to the Father). *Doxology* means a hymn or statement praising God.

Reviewing This Chapter

1. What is the purpose of the first part of the Mass of the Catechumens? Show this by referring to the prayers of this part of the Mass.

2. What phrases show the priest's and our sorrow for our sins and our desire for mercy in the following prayer of the first part of the Mass of the Catechumens:
   a) Psalm 42.
   b) The *Confiteor*.
   c) The prayer as the priest ascends the altar.
   d) The prayer as the priest kisses the altar.
   e) The *Kyrie, Eleison*.
   f) The *Gloria*.

3. From your answer, what is your attitude as you begin the Mass? Do you feel in your heart this sorrow? Do you desire and ask for mercy in your heart as you repeat the words of the Mass?

4. Show in this part of the Mass how the priest speaks for you. Make a list of all the places where he includes you.

5. Do you join with the priest in saying the Mass? Do you offer up your sins? Do you follow the prayers with the priest?

6. Is the *Kyrie, Eleison* for you a ninefold cry for mercy and forgiveness to the Father, the Son, and the Holy Ghost? Try next Sunday to realize the meaning of this cry for mercy.

7. Can you repeat the *Gloria in Excelsis Deo?* If not, read it now. Do you realize the appeal to the Father, the Son, and the Holy Ghost? Where is there here a desire for mercy and forgiveness?

8. Tell in your own words why this part of the Mass of the Catechumens is a fitting introduction to the whole Mass.

9. What is meant in the Mass by the following words:
   a) *Introit.*
   b) *Confiteor.*
   c) *Kyrie, Eleison.*
   d) *Christe, Eleison.*
   e) *Gloria in Excelsis Deo.*
   f) *Oremus.*

10. Tell what you can about the *Introit.*

11. About the *Confiteor*, tell:
    a) What are the two parts?
    b) Confession of sins is made to whom?
    c) The request to pray for us is made to whom?
    d) Who in the first list is omitted in the second?
    e) Where and how is forgiveness asked?

12. About the *Gloria in Excelsis Deo,* tell:
    a) What is said about the Trinity in the first part?
    b) What is said about God, the Father?
    c) What is said about Jesus Christ?
    d) What is said about the Holy Ghost?

Using the Missal

1. Find in your Missal:
   a) *Confiteor.*
   b) Prayers at the foot of the altar.

      c) Judge me, O Lord.

      d) *Kyrie, Eleison.*

      e) *Introit.*

      f) *Gloria.*

2. Tell for each after you have found it:

      a) Is it part of the Mass of the Catechumens or of the Mass of the Faithful?

      b) Is it part of the Ordinary of the Mass or Proper of the Season?

      c) Is it fixed or changeable?

3. Find in your Missal the *Introit* for the following days:

      a) Midnight Mass at Christmas.

      b) Ascension Day.

      c) Third Sunday of Advent.

      d) Third Sunday after Pentecost.

      e) Next Sunday.

      f) One you especially like.

4. Find in your Missal:

      a) What prayer comes before the Introit.

      b) What prayer follows the Introit.

5. Take your Missal and follow the first part of the Mass of the Catechumens for next Sunday. (You do not have to read each prayer.)

My Part

1. I am using my Missal at every Mass I attend.

2. I prepare my Missal the evening before the Mass.

3. I know how to find the Introit and its place in the Mass.

4. I make an examination of conscience before attending Mass in order to enter into the spirit of the first part of the Mass of the Catechumens.

5. I shall join with the priest more heartily in the Confiteor.

Prayers

    1. Say the *Confiteor* hereafter in two parts with a slight pause after the confession of sin, then pray for the help of Mary and the saints.

    2. In time of temptation you might use the *Kyrie, eleison.*

    3. Repeat from memory the *Gloria in excelsis Deo.*

Bible Passages

For each of the following passages from the Bible tell:

    1. Who said it.

    2. To whom it was said.

    3. When and where.

    4. Where is it used in the Mass?

"Glory to God in the Highest, and on earth peace to men of good will."

"Lamb of God who takest away the sins of the world."

"I will go unto the altar of God."

Vocabulary

ENGLISH WORDS

Tabernacle: a place to worship God (a tent among the Hebrews).

Life everlasting: life forever, life in heaven, life with God.

Grievous: very great (fault for our sins).

Beseech: to ask earnestly (of God).

Salvation: saving the soul, freeing from sin, gaining heaven.

Iniquities: sins.

Relics: something belonging to a saint. (Every altar has some relics of a saint.)

Only-begotten: only-born. "Only-begotten Son" means "only Son."

Absolution: forgiveness or pardon of sins.

LATIN WORDS

Gloria Patri: Glory be to the Father.

Judica me: judge me.

Confiteor: I confess.

Dominus vobiscum: the Lord be with you.

Et cum spiritu tuo: and with thy spirit.

Gloria in excelsis Deo: Glory to God in the Highest.

GREEK WORDS

Kyrie, eleison: Lord, have mercy.

Problems

1. Arrange the following parts of the Mass of the Catechumens in the order in which they occur, indicating the order by numbering:

> Confession (*Confiteor*)
> *Gloria in excelsis Deo*
> *Introit*
> The Psalm, *Judica Me*
> *Kyrie, Eleison*

2. Tell what the congregation should do at each part of the Mass of the Catechumens as given above :

    a) Sit

    b) Stand

    c) Kneel

3. Tell where the priest says each of the prayers listed above:

    a) At the foot of the altar.

    b) On the Gospel side of the altar.

    c) At the center of the altar.

    d) On the Epistle side of the altar.

Catechism (Christian Doctrine)

  •Why did God make you? (6)

  •Is there but one God? (21)

- Why can there be but one God? (22)
- How many persons are there in God? (23)
- Is the Father God? (24)
- Is the Son God? (25)
- Is the Holy Ghost God? (26)
- What do you mean by the Blessed Trinity? (27)
- Are the three Divine Persons equal in all things? (28)
- Are the three Divine Persons one and the same God? (29)
- Can we fully understand how the three Divine Persons are one and the same God? (30)
- What is a mystery? (31)
- What is the Mass? (263)
- What is a sacrifice? (264)
- Is the Mass the same sacrifice as that of the cross? (265)
- How do we make the sign of the cross? (295)
- Why do we make the sign of the cross? (296)
- How is the sign of the cross a profession of faith in the chief mysteries of our religion? (297)
- How does the sign of the cross express the mystery of the Unity and Trinity of God? (298)
- How does the sign of the cross express the mystery of the Incarnation and death of our Lord? (299)

Chapter XI

THE MASS OF THE CATECHUMENS
INSTRUCTS US

The first part of the Mass of the Catechumens was a preparation for the main part of the Mass. It showed our love for God and our desire to be worthy of the great sacrifice of the Mass by acknowledging our sins and desiring forgiveness. We prayed also to the Trinity and showed our desire to glorify the Trinity in the lovely and moving words of the *Gloria in Excelsis Deo*. We are ready now to receive the instruction of the second part of the Mass of the Catechumens.

Teaching Great Truths of Religion. This second part of the Mass of the Catechumens is mostly instruction. In this part of the Mass, the Apostles, or a prophet of the Old Testament, instructs us in the Epistle. Christ is the teacher in the Gospel. Then, when we have been enlightened by these teachings, we rise and declare again our faith in the principal doctrines of the Catholic Church. This is the Creed.

Three Main Points. In the Ordinary of the Mass these three things are the most important parts of this second part of the Mass of the Catechumens:

The Epistles, or Sayings of the Apostles or Prophets.

The Gospels, or Sayings of our Lord.

The Creed.

Let us follow these different parts so that we shall understand them still better.

Having finished the *Gloria*, the priest turns to us
and greets us with "*Dominus Vobiscum.*"

Greeting the People. With the great words of the *Gloria in Excelsis Deo* still echoing in our ears and in our hearts, the priest turns from the center of the altar to greet the people:

> Priest: *Dominus Vobiscum*
> Server: *Et cum spiritu tuo*

We should learn to recognize these Latin words and memorize them. They mean:

> Priest: The Lord be with you.
> Server: And with thy spirit.

Collect. The *Collect* is a general prayer, which changes with the feast or Sunday. It is said before the reading of the Epistle, or Lesson. It contains ordinarily an address to God, a request and a reason that would move God to grant our petition. It is made through the intercession of Christ. The Collect ends with praise of the Trinity. The petition in the Collect quoted is expressed in the word *grant.* The word *beseech* is often used. Find some other. You can see from the Collect for the Midnight Mass what kind of prayer it is:

> O God, who hast made this most holy night to shine forth with the splendor of the True Light; grant, we ask Thee, that we, who have known the Mysteries of that Light on earth, may rejoice also in its happiness in heaven. Who with Thee. . . .

This prayer is said on the left, or Epistle side of the altar (your right).

Epistles, Writings of the Apostles or Prophets. Then follows a reading from a letter of one of the Apostles or of that great Apostle who came after the twelve, St. Paul, or from some Prophet of the Old Testament. The words of these saints and prophets are meant for our instruction. They are selected because of the character of the Mass of the day. This reading is in keeping with the Introit and the Collect. This is one of the changeable parts of the Mass. It is read at the left (your right) side of the altar. This gives the left side of the altar the name of the "Epistle side" of the altar.

We should listen attentively to these great words of the Epistle or Lesson inspired by God, as we read them the first time while the priest reads them at the altar in Latin, and more particularly when he reads them (ordinarily) in English to the people in the church.

In a high Mass the people sit during the reading of the Epistle. At the end of the Epistle the server and the people say "thanks be to God" (*Deo gratias*). They are thanking Him for the instruction of the Epistle.

In the earlier days, the Mass of the Catechumens continued with the further instruction of the people in three lessons: one taken from the Old Testament, a second from the New Testament (not part of the Gospels), and a third from the Gospels themselves. These lessons or instructions were separated by chants or songs. The Epistles and the Gospels are all that remain of these lessons. The chants, however, have remained, though in somewhat shorter form.

The first of these, the *Gradual,* gets its name from the fact that it was originally sung or chanted from a step (*gradus*). It is usually a text from a Psalm, though sometimes it is taken from other books of the Bible or from other religious works. It has at times the same lesson as the Epistle, or it emphasizes the same idea as the other changeable parts of the Mass.

The Gradual for the Mass at dawn on Christmas Day is:

> Blessed be He that cometh in the name of the Lord: The Lord is God, and He hath shone upon us. This is the Lord's doing; and it is wonderful in our eyes.

The priest reads the Epistle—a part of a letter of one of the Apostles.

The *Alleluia* verse was added to the Gradual and is very much like the Gradual. It is made up of a verse and a response. It is ordinarily taken, as the Gradual is, from the Psalms, or other books of the Bible or other religious works.

When the Alleluia (which means: "Praise ye the Lord") is omitted from Septuagesima to Easter and on some special feasts, a penitential psalm is put in its place. This is called a *Tract*, which is from the Latin word meaning to go "straight on"—that is, without a response.

A Hymn was added to the Gradual, Alleluia, or Tract, which is called the *Sequence*. Five Sequences still remain in the Missal. They will be studied when we study special Masses. The *Veni Sancte Spiritus* (Come, Holy Spirit) of Pentecost is one of them.

Gospel and Preparation for It. We are now to hear the very words of Christ. Surely we would be eager to hear what Christ would say if we had lived when He was walking the earth, telling men about the Kingdom of God. We are to hear His very words now. Let us be waiting reverently for them.

Prayers to be Worthy. The priest, before he reads the words of Christ, prays that he may be worthy, that he may be cleansed. He prays that his lips may be cleansed with a live coal as happened to the Prophet Isaias:

> Cleanse my heart and my lips, O Almighty God, who didst cleanse the lips of the Prophet Isaias with a burning coal; and vouchsafe through Thy gracious mercy, so to purify me, that I may worthily proclaim Thy holy Gospel. Through Christ our Lord. Amen.

In the Low Mass the priest prays again:

> The Lord be in my heart and on my lips, that I may worthily and in a becoming manner proclaim His holy Gospel. Amen.

The priest greets the people again with the familiar: *Dominus vobiscum.* The reply is: *Et cum spiritu tuo.*

The priest announces where the Gospel reading is taken from: "Continuation of the holy Gospel according to St. Matthew" or "St. Mark," etc. The server answers: "Glory be to Thee, O Lord."

Then the words of the Holy Gospel are read to the people, who stand out of respect for the words of Christ. How attentively we should listen to those words that tell the incidents of the life of Christ, His parables and His miracles.

At the end of the Gospel reading, the server says:

> Praise be to Thee, O Christ!

and the priest says the very simple prayer:

> By the words of the Gospel may our sins be blotted out.

Sermon.   At this point in the Sunday Mass comes usually the instruction of the people.   This we call the "Sermon," preached in English after the reading of the Epistle and the Gospel in English.

The Gospel changes from Sunday to Sunday and from day to day.   It keeps very much the spirit of the Introit, Collect, Gradual, and other changeable parts of the Mass.

Special Reverence for the Gospel.   The ceremonies centering around the Gospel show the special reverence which the Church has for the words of Christ.   This is indicated in several ways:

> 1. The Missal is moved from the left to the right (our "right to left") side of the altar, which is the side of honor.
>
> 2. The priest says a special prayer at the center of the altar that he may be worthy (*Cleanse my heart and my lips, O Almighty God*).
>
> 3. When he stands before the Missal he makes the sign of the cross upon it and himself.
>
> 4. When he finishes reading, he kisses the Missal.

The priest reads the Gospel. All stand in reverence for the words of Christ.

And so, likewise, do the people (laity) show special reverence:

> 1. By standing erect during the reading.
>
> 2. By making three signs of the cross on the forehead, lips, and breast, that Christ may be in their minds, on their lips, and in their hearts.

This is shown also in solemn high Mass by the lights and the incensing of the book.

Nicene Creed. And then to end the Mass of the Catechumens and to prepare us for the Mass of the Faithful, we repeat again our faith in the teachings of Christ, His Apostles, and His Church. This we do by reciting with the priest the *Nicene Creed*. It is very much like the Apostles' creed, which we know. It repeats the same doctrines.

The Mass of the Catechumens has instructed us, so that we can better understand the creed which we are now to say. This wonderful creed was put together, or formulated, more than sixteen hundred years ago. It was first composed by the First Council of Nicea (A.D. 325) and revised by the Council of Constantinople (A.D. 381). In it:

> • We repeat our faith in the one God.
> • We repeat our faith in God, the Father, the Creator.
> • We repeat our faith in God, the Son, with a statement of the principal facts of His life, which we lovingly recall.
> • We repeat our faith in God, the Holy Ghost, the Life Giver, and
> • We repeat our faith in the Church, itself, and the great doctrines of baptism and of the resurrection of the dead.

Read aloud this wonderful creed (*Credo*) and meditate, or think over, each of its great parts.

> I believe in one God, the Father Almighty, Maker of heaven and earth, and of all things, visible and invisible.
>
> And in one Lord, Jesus Christ, the only-begotten Son of God.

Born of the Father before all ages.

God of God; Light of Light; true God of true God.

Begotten, not made, consubstantial with the Father, by whom all things were made.

Who for us men, and for our salvation, came down from heaven.

And was incarnate by the Holy Ghost of the Virgin Mary: and was made Man.

He was crucified also for us, suffered under Pontius Pilate, and was buried.

And the third day He rose again according to the Scriptures.

And ascended into heaven, and sitteth at the right hand of the Father.

And He shall come again with glory to judge both the living and the dead, and His kingdom shall have no end.

And in the Holy Ghost, the Lord and Giver of Life,

Who proceedeth from the Father and the Son.

Who, together with the Father and the Son, is adored and glorified; Who spoke by the Prophets.

And one holy, Catholic and Apostolic Church.

I confess one baptism for the remission of sins.

And I look for the resurrection of the dead,

And the life of the world to come. Amen.

The Mass of the Catechumens ends with the Creed. As was said before, the catechumens—that is, those who were not as yet baptized—were dismissed, and only those who were baptized were permitted to remain for the Mass of the Faithful. Now all remain (even visitors) for the Mass of the Faithful, hoping that to all the grace of God may come.

Summary. The latter half of the Mass of the Catechumens is given over to instruction, as the earlier half is given over largely to prayers for forgiveness of our sins and of adoration of the Most Blessed Trinity. This instruction changes from Sunday to Sunday and from day to day. It is given to us through the Epistle and the Gospel and sermon. As we study special Masses, we shall study the Epistles and Gospels. These often give the Mass its special character. The Mass of the Catechumens closes in the resounding phrases of the Creed. This is the Nicene Creed. It is practically the same as the Apostles' Creed.

Now we understand better that the Creed is not merely a summary of the things we must believe, but it is a great prayer.

1. Arrange the following parts of the Mass of the Catechumens in the order in which they occur, indicating the order by numbering:
   - Credo
   - Introit
   - Gospel
   - Collect
   - Kyrie, eleison
   - Gloria in excelsis Deo
   - Gradual
   - Public confession (Confiteor)
   - Epistle
2. Tell what the congregation should do at each part of the Mass of the Catechumens as given above:
   - a) Sit
   - b) Stand
   - c) Kneel
3. Tell where the priest says each of the prayers listed above:
   - a) At the foot of the altar
   - b) On the Gospel side of the altar
   - c) At the center of the altar
   - d) On the Epistle side of the altar

Reviewing This Chapter

1. What does the earlier half of the Mass of the Catechumens do?
2. What is the purpose of the latter half of the Mass of the Catechumens?
3. What words are used in the Collects to show it is a prayer of petition?
4. For the Mass for next Sunday see if you can find a relation between the Collect, the Epistle, and the Gospel. (Ask pastor

to explain for the next Sunday or for any feast day.)

5. What should your attitude be when you are being instructed? Does this apply to this part of the Mass?

6. Who are the instructors in this part of the Mass? What respect do you owe them?

7. What actions of the Mass show special reverence and respect for the words of the Gospel?

8. What attitude, if you are properly prepared, does the first part of the Mass of the Catechumens give you toward the instruction of the second part?

9. Repeat slowly and articulately the words of the Nicene Creed or the words of the Apostles' Creed.

10. Is there any real difference between the two creeds? Write them in parallel columns.

11. Mark off the parts of the Nicene Creed addressed to:
    a) God
    b) The Son
    c) The Father
    d) The Holy Ghost
    e) The Holy Catholic Church

12. What is:
    a) The Gradual
    b) The Alleluia
    c) Sequence
    d) Tract

13. Tell about the life of St. Paul.

14. Find out more about the Epistles than is given in this book.

Examen

1. Do you enter heartily into the marks of respect for the words of the Gospel?

2. Do you try to understand the application of the Epistles and Gospels to your own life?

3. Do you give close attention when you stand while the priest reads the Gospel of the day?

4. Do you kneel reverently when the priest says the words "and

was incarnate by the Holy Ghost, of the Virgin Mary; and was made Man"?

My Part

1. I am using my Missal at every Mass I attend.

2. I prepare my Missal the evening before the Mass.

3. I make an examination of conscience before attending Mass in order to enter into the spirit of the first part of the Mass of the Catechumens.

4. I join with the priest most heartily in saying the Confiteor.

5. I join heartily, too, in the petition to God in the Collect.

6. I shall pay close attention to the priest as he reads the Epistles and the Gospels and preaches his sermon.

7. I shall kneel reverently when the priest says in the Creed: "and was incarnate by the Holy Ghost, of the Virgin Mary; and was made Man."

Using the Missal

1. I am using my Missal in praying every Mass I attend.

2. In your Missal find the Collects for the following days:
    a) Second Sunday of Advent.
    b) Second Sunday after Epiphany.
    c) Second Sunday after Pentecost.
    d) Second Sunday of Lent.
    e) Next Sunday.
    f) One you like very much.

3. In what does the end of the Collect for the Second Sunday of Advent differ from the others mentioned in Question 2?

4. In each of these Collects list the verbs which tell the petition.

5. Find the Epistles for the following days:
    a) Feast of the Immaculate Conception.
    b) Second Mass on Christmas Day.
    c) Sixth Sunday after Pentecost.
    d) Next Sunday.

6. Find the Gospels for the Sundays listed in Question 5.

Prayers

Memorize three Collects that you especially like. You will know on what day they are said.

Vocabulary

ENGLISH WORDS

Cleanse: to make clean or pure (our souls).

Incarnate: to become human (as Christ), to take a form or shape.

Apostolic: going back to the Apostles (the Church), like the Apostles.

LATIN WORDS

Deo Gratias: Thanks be to God.

Credo: I believe.

Catechism (Christian Doctrine)

- What must we do to save our souls? (9)
- How shall we know the things which we are to believe? (10)
- Where shall we find the chief truths which the Catholic Church teaches? (11)
- Say the Apostles' Creed. (12)
- Is there but one God? (21)
- Why can there be but one God? (22)
- How many persons are there in God? (23)
- Is the Father God? (24)
- Is the Son God? (25)
- Is the Holy Ghost God? (26)
- What do you mean by the Blessed Trinity? (27)
- Are the three Divine Persons equal in all things? (28)
- Are the three Divine Persons one and the same God? (29)
- Can we fully understand how the three Divine Persons are one and the same God? (30)
- What is a mystery? (31)

Chapter XII

THE MASS OF THE FAITHFUL

1. The Offertory

It is to the Mass of the Faithful that the phrase, "the holy sacrifice of the Mass," really belongs. It is the fulfillment of the sacrifice of Melchisedech. It is the clean oblation of which Malachias prophesied. In it God Himself comes down to our very altars, not as a symbol but really. This mystery of our Catholic faith we call the Real Presence.

The change of the bread and wine into Christ's Body and Blood, we call transubstantiation. The bread and wine become the Body and Blood of Christ. We should approach this wonderful miracle which comes to pass in our churches every day with a sense of the greatness of what is about to happen.

Offering in the Early History of the Church. In old days people brought bread and wine and other gifts, including money, to the Church. The priest set apart those *offerings* which were to be used in the Mass, the bread and the wine. The others he blessed and laid aside. These offerings are our acknowledgment that all things, including ourselves, belong to God. We no longer bring offerings of bread and wine but instead we make an offering of money. But it would be a mistake to think that this would be the important offering. Just as Christ as High Priest is going to *offer* Himself as the sacrifice or oblation, so we *must offer ourselves,* mind and heart and soul. We must join ourselves with Christ, the High Priest, with the priest we see on the altar, and with other Catholics in the Sacrifice of the Mass.

Main Parts of the Mass of the Faithful. The central act of the Mass, and indeed the central act of all Catholic worship, is the Consecration. The other parts of the Mass are grouped around it. Some lead up to it. Some follow it. In the Mass of the Faithful there is a prayer, blessing (and in solemn high Mass, incensing) which leads up to the Consecration. This part is known as the Offertory. Then after the Consecration there is the Eucharistic Banquet which is the Communion of the priest and of the people. This is followed naturally by some acts of thanksgiving. So in the Mass of the Faithful we shall look for:

1. The Offertory, including offering of ourselves.
2. The Consecration.
3. The Communion.
4. Thanksgiving.

Beginning of the Mass of the Faithful. After the Credo, which ends the Mass of the Catechumens, the priest opens the Mass of the Faithful by greeting the people:

Dominus vobiscum (The Lord be with you),

and the server and the people answer:

Et cum spiritu tuo (and with thy spirit).

Then the priest says simply:

Oremus (Let us pray).

Though this is now a general invitation to pray, in earlier days it was followed by specific prayers.

Offertory Verse. The Offertory is introduced by a verse, or verses, from some part of Holy Scripture that strikes the spirit of the day or the season. This is shown in the Offertory verse of the First Mass on Christmas Day, at midnight:

"Let the heavens rejoice, and let the earth be glad before the face of the Lord, because He cometh."

These are verses 11 and 13 of Psalm 95.

The verses for Easter Sunday are numbers 9 and 10 from Psalm 75:

"The earth trembled and was still when God arose in judgment. Alleluia."

Offertory. As has been said, in earlier days the people brought the bread and wine which was used in the sacrifice. These were the offerings. The bread and wine is now provided by the Church. People now make an offering of money at the "collection" taken up at this part of the Mass. To enter truly into the Mass they must offer up themselves. This must be for them, the real offering—not their money, but themselves.

Offering of the Bread. The priest now takes the veil from the chalice and places it to the right. He also places the chalice on the right. He removes the pall and then takes the paten and Host in both hands. He is ready for the first part of the Offertory which is the offering of the bread. The priest offers up to the Father the bread or Host. After making the sign of the cross with it, he places it on the corporal.

The spotless Host is offered up to God. The priest feels himself unworthy to offer it to his "living and true God." And so again he prays for forgiveness of his own sins, and also for the people's sins.

The offering is made:

1. For his own countless sins, offenses, and negligences.
2. For all present in the Church.
3. For all faithful Christians living and dead.

The offering is made that all these people may have salvation unto everlasting life.

The Host is offered for the salvation of all faithful Christians.

Accept,
O Holy Father, Almighty and Eternal God,
this unspotted Host,
which I, Thine unworthy servant,
offer unto Thee,
my living and true God,
for my innumerable sins, offenses, and negligences, and for all
here present;
as also for all faithful Christians, both living and dead; that it may
avail both me and them for salvation unto life everlasting.
Amen.

Offering for All Christians. It should be noticed that the offering is made not only for the priest and the particular congregation, but for *all Christians.* The whole Mystical Body of Christ—all Christians—are joined together in all Masses. We should try to remember at every Mass, that we, too, are joined in this great body of Christians making a sacrifice to God.

Mixture of Water and Wine. The priest now blesses the water (which represents the faithful) and mixes it with wine. He prays to God, first recalling the fact how marvelous and noble was human nature when He created man (Adam) and how He more marvelously renewed the life of grace in man after the Fall. He then makes the wonderful request (which, however, Christ made possible) that by the mystical union of water and wine we may become divine (sons of God) as Christ became human (a man). We become, in the language of the Last Gospel, "Sons of God." The prayer which the priest says while mixing the water and the wine, is:

O God,
Who, in creating human nature, didst wonderfully honor it,
and still more wonderfully restore it,
grant that,

by the Mystery of this water and wine,
we may be sharers in His divinity,
Who did stoop to share our humanity,
Jesus Christ Thy Son, our Lord,
Who liveth and reigneth with Thee,
in the unity of the Holy Ghost,
world without end.
Amen.

Meaning of Ceremonies. This idea is carried out, too, in the ceremony that goes with this prayer. The water is blessed but the wine is not blessed. This is done because the wine as symbol of divinity needs no blessing, but for water as the symbol of humanity (and the faithful) a blessing is proper.

The mixture of the water and wine has two meanings. In the first place it symbolizes the union in Christ of God (His divine nature) and man (His human nature). It also symbolizes the union of Christ (wine) and the people (water). When the wine and water is offered in the chalice it means that the faithful, or the people, are offered up with Christ.

Offering of the Chalice. The chalice is then offered up by the priest for our salvation and *for that of the whole world,* through the clemency, or mercy, of God.

We offer unto Thee,
O Lord,
the chalice of salvation,
beseeching Thy mercy,
that it may ascend before Thy divine Majesty as a sweet odor, for
    our salvation, and for that of the whole world.
Amen.

This is followed by two verses of the prayer of the three young men in the fiery furnace (called the Canticle of the Three Children) (Dan. iii. 39-40). It is a prayer that we may be received by God and that our sacrifice may be pleasing to Him. Perhaps we do not have the heroic spirit of the three young men, but their example should inspire us to join with Christ in the sacrifice of the Holy Mass:

> May we be received by Thee, O Lord,
> in the spirit of humility and contrition of heart,
> and grant that the sacrifice we offer this day
> in Thy sight, may be pleasing to Thee, O Lord God.

The offering is concluded in the beautiful short prayer asking the blessing of the Holy Ghost:

> Come, O Sanctifier, Almighty and Eternal God, and bless this Sacrifice, prepared for Thy Holy Name.

Incensing of Offerings and Faithful. The next part of the Offertory at a solemn high Mass (but not at a high Mass or low Mass) is the incensing of the offerings and of the faithful. The priest asks God to bless the incense, through the prayers of the Archangel Michael and of all the saints. He incenses the water and wine, the Crucifix and altar, and then says the prayer:

> May the Lord enkindle within us the fire of His love, and the flame of everlasting charity. Amen.

After this the priest is incensed and finally the people are incensed.

Washing of the Hands—Lavabo. The priest, after incensing the altar (and even when there is no incensing), washes his hands, or the tips of the first fingers of the hands. This is a mark of respect for the Body of Christ, which he will touch after the Consecration. As he does so, he recites six verses (6 to 12) of the 25th Psalm.

> I will wash my hands among the innocent: and will walk in procession around Thine altar, O Lord.
> That I may hear the sound of Thy praise; and tell of all Thy wondrous works.

I have loved, O Lord, the beauty of Thy house: and the place where Thy glory dwelleth.

Take not away my soul, O God, with the wicked; nor my life with men of blood.

In whose hands are iniquities; their right hand is filled with gifts.

But I have walked in my innocence; redeem me, and have mercy on me.

My foot hath stood in the direct way: in the churches I will bless Thee, O Lord.

Glory be to the Father, etc.

He expresses again the love, praise, and glory of God in the first three verses. Then with the Psalmist he thinks again of his sins and his fear of sinful men. He then expresses his desire for redemption and his good will toward God. As we come nearer to the Consecration we are lifted up in spirit, but are never quite able to forget our sins.

Prayer to the Blessed Trinity. We now ask the Most Blessed Trinity to accept the offering in memory of the Passion, Resurrection, and Ascension of our Lord, Jesus Christ, and also for the honor of Mary, St. John the Baptist, Peter and Paul, and all the saints. We ask for their prayers. The prayer is made to the Trinity through the same Christ, our Lord:

Receive, O Holy Trinity, this offering which we make to Thee,
in memory of the
Passion,
Resurrection, and
Ascension of our Lord Jesus Christ,
and in honor of Blessed Mary, ever Virgin,
of blessed John the Baptist,
of the holy Apostles, Peter and Paul,
and of all the saints,
that it may avail to their honor and our salvation;
and may they, whose memory we celebrate on earth,
be pleased to pray for us in heaven,
Through the same Christ our Lord.

Orate Fratres. The priest now turns to the people and says in a low voice: "Brethren pray," and then turns toward the altar and says the rest of the prayer in a quiet voice.

The prayer is answered in a way that clearly shows the threefold purpose of the Sacrifice. Let us look at the words:

> Brethren, pray that my sacrifice and yours may be acceptable to God the Father Almighty.

And the answer is:

> May the Lord receive the sacrifice from thy hands, to the praise and glory of His name, to our benefit, and to that of all His holy Church.

We have pointed out here the true spirit that should be in our hearts and minds and on our lips in this Sacrifice; that is, the praise and glory of God. This is most important. All the other things will surely be added onto you. This is the spirit that must guide our thoughts and feelings here and in all parts of the Mass.

Notice also that the priest speaks of the Sacrifice as "*my* sacrifice and *yours*." The Eucharistic Sacrifice is the Sacrifice of Christ and the whole Church—the Head and members of the Mystical Body. With the bread and wine both priest and people offer up themselves. After the Consecration, as we shall see, both priest and people offer up the Body of Christ and themselves in union with Christ. Of course, the important part in the sacrifice is the power of the priest, given him by Christ, to change the bread and wine into the Body and Blood of Christ. That is, of course, *the* sacrificial act of the Mass.

Secret. The Offertory, or first part of the Mass of the Faithful, is ended with the prayer called the *Secret*. In the early days of the Church, this was the prayer said over the offerings of the people that were to be actually used in

The priest asks us to pray that his sacrifice and ours
may be pleasing to the Lord.

sacrifice. This and the Offertory Verse are the only parts of the Offertory that change. The Secret is very much like the Collects and other changeable parts of the Mass. It is usually a prayer asking God to accept the gifts offered up and to bless those who offer them. The kind of prayer the Secret is, is shown in the Secret for Pentecost:

> Sanctify, O Lord, we beseech Thee, the gifts offered: and cleanse our hearts by the enlightening of the Holy Spirit. Through our Lord…in the unity…

This prayer is called the Secret, because the priest says it in a very low voice; that is, secretly. That is one explanation. It is also explained by the fact that it is the prayer which was said in olden times over the bread and wine which had been separated from the other offerings and set aside. The Latin word expressing this idea is *Secreta*.

The Parts of the Mass

1. Indicate which of the following parts of the Mass belong to the Mass of the Catechumens, and which to the Mass of the Faithful:

    Secret
    Gloria in excelsis Deo
    Credo
    Kyrie, eleison
    Lavabo
    Gospel
    Offering of Bread and Wine (Offertory)
    Confiteor
    Orate fratres
    Epistle

Copy the parts which belong to the Mass of the Faithful in the order in which they occur.

2. Tell what the people should do at each part of the Mass as given above:

    a) Sit

    b) Stand

    c) Kneel

3. Tell where the priest says each of the prayers, or performs the acts, listed above:

    a) At the foot of the altar.

    b) On the Gospel side of the altar.

    c) At the center of the altar.

    d) On the Epistle side of the altar.

Reviewing This Chapter

1. Into what two major parts is the Mass divided?

2. Into what divisions may the Mass of the Faithful be divided?

3. How has the Mass of the Catechumens prepared for the Mass of the Faithful?

4. In what way can you offer yourself up with the priest?

    a) By being sorry for your sins?

    b) By resolving not to sin again?

    c) By resolving to be charitable and practice the other virtues?

5. Do you feel that this part of the Mass is solemn?

6. Do you think, as the bread and the wine are offered, about the great thing that is to happen?

7. Do you notice how the prayers express our unworthiness for such a great event as is about to happen?

8. Do you want to wash your hands and cleanse your heart in preparation for it?

9. Do you study the prayer to the Most Holy Trinity with great devotion?

10. Do you gladly join with the priest when he asks the people to pray—*Orate fratres?*

11. What is the effect of praying for all men?

12. Show in what ways the Mass now takes on the character of a sacrifice.

13. What is being offered up? to whom? Quote the prayer.

14. Is the offering you make in money the most important offering you should make?

15. Show why offerings apart from the sacrifice itself are necessary if the Church is to do its work in the world.

16. What does *Orate fratres* mean in English?

17. How can we take on Christ's divinity? What is grace?

18. Show where in the prayers of the Offertory the whole Church or others besides those present are prayed for.

19. Why is water used with the wine in the offerings?

20. For the prayer when the priest mixes the water and the wine ("O God, who in creating human nature") answer these questions:

    a) To whom is the prayer addressed?

    b) What word shows it is a petition?

    c) What is the great petition of this prayer?

    d) How does God renew our human nature?

    e) When did Christ take on our humanity?

    f) How can we take part in His divinity?

21. For the Prayer to the Most Holy Trinity answer these questions:

    a) To whom is the prayer made?

    b) What word expresses the request or petition?

    c) What is the Most Holy Trinity asked to receive?

    d) In memory of what? (Notice here and elsewhere that the Ascension is joined with the Passion and Resurrection.)

    e) In honor of whom?

    f) What two purposes are stated here of the offerings?

    g) What do we desire of the saints (including Mary)?

    h) Who is the mediator for us to the Most Blessed Trinity?

My Part

1. I am using my Missal in praying every Mass I attend.

2. I shall do my part in the Mass of the Catechumens as stated on page 131.

3. I will try always to make my offering to the collection mean at least a little sacrifice on my part.

4. I shall recall at this point the examination of conscience and offer up myself for my sins.

5. I shall try to lessen my "sins, offenses, and negligences."

6. I shall keep in mind my privilege in joining with the priest in offering the unspotted Host: Christ.

7. I shall want to wash my hands and cleanse my heart at the Lavabo.

8. I shall keep in mind the meaning of the water in the offerings.

9. I shall gladly join with the priest at the *Orate Fratres*.

Using the Missal

1. Find in your Missal:
   a) *Orate Fratres*.
   b) Creed.
   c) *Lavabo*.
   d) The Secret.
   e) Asking the Offering to be received by the Most Holy Trinity.
   f) Collect.
   g) Offering the Bread and Wine.
   h) *Confiteor*.
2. Tell for each of the parts after you have found it:
   a) Whether it is a part of the Mass of the Catechumens or of the Mass of the Faithful.
   b) Whether it is part of the Ordinary of the Mass or of the Proper of the Mass.
   c) Whether it is fixed or changeable.

3. Find the Secret for the following days:
   a) Next Sunday.
   b) The Third Mass of Christmas.

Prayers

Memorize the following three prayers after you have studied them:

1. O God, who in creating human nature.
2. Prayer to the Most Holy Trinity.
3. *Orate Fratres.*

Vocabulary

ENGLISH WORDS

Eternal: having no beginning or end (true only of God).

Divinity: God or like God.

Clemency: mercy.

Intercede: to ask or plead (for us).

Intercession: the act of asking or pleading for another.

Vouchsafe: give (to us); make sure we get; guarantee.

Redeem: to save, to buy back, to pay off.

Brethren: the members of the congregation, brothers, fellow members.

Acceptable: satisfactory, all right, agreeable.

LATIN WORDS

Oremus: Let us pray.

Lavabo: I wash.

Orate fratres: Pray, brethren.

Catechism (Christian Doctrine)

• Who is the Holy Ghost? (94)
• Is the Holy Ghost equal to the Father and the Son? (96)
• Why did Christ send the Holy Ghost? (100)

- When and where are the bread and wine changed into the body and blood of Christ? (262)
- What is the Mass? (263)
- What is a sacrifice? (264)
- Is the Mass the same sacrifice as that of the Cross? (265)
- How is the Mass the same Sacrifice as that of the Cross? (266)
- What were the ends for which the Sacrifice of the Cross was offered? (267)
- Is there any difference between the Sacrifice of the Cross and the Sacrifice of the Mass? (268)
- How should we assist at Mass? (269)
- Which is the best manner of hearing Mass? (270)

Chapter XIII

THE MASS OF THE FAITHFUL

2. The Consecration

We come now to the actual sacrifice of the Mass. The very heart of the Mass is the consecration of the host and of the wine. This is when the Transubstantiation takes place. By the power of Christ acting through the priest, the bread and wine is actually changed into the Body and Blood of Christ. Christ becomes really present on the altar. This should stir—us to pray, make us want to praise God, give glory to His Name, and offer thanksgiving as His creatures. However, before we come to the Canon of the Mass, which is fixed and does not change, there is a special preparation called the Preface.

Introduction to the Preface. Before the Preface itself is read there is an introduction. This part of the Mass opens with the usual greeting of the priest:

> The Lord be with you. (*Dominus vobiscum.*)

and the response for the people:

> And with thy spirit. (*Et cum spiritu tuo.*)

Then with fine appropriateness the prayer begins:

> Lift up your hearts. (*Sursum corda.*)

and the response comes :

> We have them lifted up to the Lord.

And then the priest continues:

> Let us give thanks to the Lord our God.

and the response comes again:

> It is fitting and just.

Which leads us into the first words of the Preface.

Preface.   The Preface echoes the invitation of its introduction or beginning to give praise, glory, and thanksgiving to God. We give glory and thanks to God through Christ, and we join with the angel choirs and other heavenly hosts to give glory to God. The Preface for Trinity Sunday, which is used on all Sundays that have not Prefaces of their own, expresses this well:

> It is truly fitting and just, right and for our salvation,
> that we should at all times and in all places,
> give thanks
> unto Thee
> O holy Lord, Father almighty, everlasting God,
> Who together with Thine only-begotten Son,
> and the Holy Ghost,
> art one God, one Lord;
> not in the singleness of one Person, but in the Trinity of one
>   Substance.
> For what we believe, by Thy revelation, concerning Thy glory,
> the same do we believe of Thy Son,
> the same of the Holy Ghost
> without difference or distinction.
> So that, in confessing the true and everlasting Godhead,
> distinction in persons,
> unity in essence,
> and equality in Majesty
> may be adored.
> Which the Angels and Archangels,
> the Cherubim also and Seraphim
> do praise who cease not to cry out,
> with one voice saying:

There are fifteen Prefaces. There is a Common Preface for Feasts when there are no special Prefaces. If you will

In the Preface we join with the angel choirs to give glory to God.

look in your Missal, you will find all the Prefaces are very much alike except for one part which belongs to the special Feast Day or Season. These are the different prefaces:

> Common Preface
> Preface of the Blessed Trinity
> Preface of the Nativity
> Preface of the Epiphany
> Preface for Lent
> Preface of the Cross
> Preface for Easter
> Preface for Ascension
> Preface for Pentecost
> Preface for the Feast of the Sacred Heart
> Preface for the Feast of the Kingship of Christ
> Preface of the Blessed Virgin Mary
> Preface of St. Joseph
> Preface of the Apostles
> Preface for the Dead

Sanctus. The prayer which ends the Preface is a prayer of praise offered to the Holy Trinity:

> Holy, Holy, Holy, Lord God of Hosts, Heaven and earth are full of Thy glory. Hosanna in the highest. Blessed is He that cometh in the Name of the Lord. Hosanna in the highest.

In its opening is the prayer of the Prophet Isaias (vi. 3), and in its conclusion are the words with which the Jewish people greeted Christ in His triumphant entry into Jerusalem on Palm Sunday. How well these words of the great Prophet, Isaias, the Psalmist, David, and of the Evangelist, St. Matthew, help us to forget ourselves as we give praise and glory to God for the redemption of men, through Christ our Lord.

The bell is rung at the Sanctus as a special signal that we are coming to the most solemn part of the Mass: the Consecration.

Three Parts of the Preface. The Preface begins with the request to lift up our hearts to God and ends in the *Sanctus, Sanctus, Sanctus (Holy, Holy, Holy)*. We can be helped in praying this part of the Mass if we remember the three parts:

1. The Introduction—the invitation to lift up our hearts to God and to give Him thanks.
2. The Preface proper.
3. The Sanctus.

Canon. The Canon of the Mass begins with a series of five prayers: a prayer that the offerings be accepted by God, a prayer for the Church Militant, a Memorial of the Living, a memorial of the Church Triumphant, and then a prayer in preparation for Consecration, when the priest spreads his hands over the host and chalice and asks God to accept the offering and give us eternal salvation, and then asks God to bless the offering and make it worthy, that it may become the Body and Blood of Christ.

The priest bows low, kisses the altar, and quietly asks God to accept the offerings. All parts of the Canon are said with great quietness—with a hush. All parts are said at the center of the altar. The priest prays with outstretched hands that this sacrifice is offered for "Thy holy Catholic Church," and "all true believers and professors of the Catholic and Apostolic Faith," and more particularly for those present, "who offer the sacrifice of praise for themselves and theirs." The first prayer is addressed to God the Father. It is a prayer and petition through Christ to accept the gifts, the offerings, the sacrifice.

It is as follows:

> Wherefore, O Most merciful Father, we humbly pray and beseech Thee, through Jesus Christ Thy Son, our Lord, that

Thou would vouchsafe to receive and bless these gifts, these offerings, this holy and unblemished sacrifice.

These offerings are made in the next prayer (1) for the Catholic Church throughout the world; (2) for the Pope; (3) for your own bishop or archbishop, and (4) for all Catholics.

These in the first place we offer up to Thee for Thy holy Catholic Church,
that it may please Thee to grant her peace,
to protect, unite and govern her throughout the world,
together with thy servant N. our Pope, N. our Bishop,
and all true believers and professors of the Catholic and Apostolic Faith.

The next prayer is the Memento for the Living, who should be named where the *N.* and *N.* are placed. These are persons we wish especially to pray for. Included in the prayer, are also all present and their relatives or friends. What is desired for them here, as throughout the Mass, is their eternal salvation.

Be mindful, O Lord, of Thy servants and handmaids N. and N. and of all here present, whose faith and devotion are known to Thee: for whom we offer, or who offer up to Thee this sacrifice of praise for themselves and theirs, for the redemption of their souls, for the hope of their safety and salvation, and who now pay their vows to Thee, the eternal, living, and true God.

And again the priest prays, this time to honor the Church Triumphant, and to honor the memory first of Mary, then of the Apostles, of certain early popes, and of other martyrs venerated in Rome, and of all the saints. This prayer is as follows:

In union with...and venerating the memory first of the glorious Mary ever Virgin, Mother of our God and Lord Jesus Christ; likewise of Thy blessed Apostles and Martyrs, [*Apostles*] Peter and Paul, Andrew, James, John, Thomas, James, Philip,

The Priest prays the Memento for the Living,
desiring their eternal salvation.

Bartholomew, Matthew, Simon and Thaddeus, [*Popes*] Linus, Cletus, Clement, Xystus, Cornelius, [*other Martyrs venerated in Rome*] Cyprian, Lawrence, Chrysogonus, John and Paul, Cosmas and Damian, and of all Thy saints; by whose merits and prayers grant that in all things we may be defended by the help of Thy protection. Through the same Christ, our Lord. Amen.

This prayer is usually named from the first word as the priest says it in Latin: *Communicantes.* This is sometimes translated by "communicating with," but we have used a simpler form: "in union with." All the persons named are from the very early years of the Church. We join ourselves especially with these members of the Church Triumphant and all the saints in making the petition for God's protection through Christ, our Lord.

After the opening words of this prayer we have placed a mark (...) indicating an omission. Words are added here on certain days: on Christmas, Epiphany, Easter, Ascension, Pentecost, Holy Thursday, and Holy Saturday.

The words inserted for Easter, for example, are:

And keeping Thy most holy day of the resurrection of our Lord Jesus Christ according to the flesh.

Find the words added on the other feast days in your Missal.

Hanc Igitur. Then follows the prayer in immediate preparation for the Consecration. The first part of this prayer (called the *Hanc Igitur*, from the first words in Latin) is a petition "mercifully to accept this offering of our service, as also of Thy whole family." These phrases need a further word of explanation. Here clearly we are to offer up ourselves—the offering of our service—the whole Church, in fact, with Christ in the Eucharistic Sacrifice. We join with ourselves the whole family of Christ—His Mystical Body in the Mass. We are all joined together.

We therefore beseech Thee,
O Lord,
mercifully to accept
this offering of our service,
as also of Thy whole family:
and to dispose our days in Thy peace:
and bid us to be delivered from eternal damnation,
and to be numbered among the flock of Thy elect.
Through Christ our Lord.
Amen.

Prayers for the Transubstantiation. Then the prayer goes on to ask that this offering be blessed and that it become the Body and Blood of Christ for us:

Which offering do Thou, O God, be pleased in all things to bless, approve, confirm, make worthy and acceptable; that it may become for us the Body and Blood of Thy most beloved Son our Lord Jesus Christ.

Transubstantiation. Now we come to the main part of the Mass. The same events that happened on the first Holy Thursday are re-enacted. This is done as Christ had commanded on that memorable night: "Do this in commemoration of Me." The bread is turned into His Body and the wine into His Blood. This is done to recall the death on Calvary where the Blood of Christ was separated from His Body. This is a mystery of our religion which we do simply because Christ commanded. It indicates clearly that the Sacrifice of the Mass is the same as the Sacrifice of the Cross.

Consecration of the Host. The priest consecrates the host, first recalling the events of the first Holy Thursday night. The priest genuflects, raises the Host on high and genuflects again. With each action the server rings the bell. The words of Consecration, which you learned in earlier grades are, as you know:

The priest elevates the Host which has now become the Body of Christ. Now and at the elevation of the Chalice we should say: "My Lord and My God."

Who the day before He suffered
took bread into His holy and venerable hands,
and with His eyes lifted up toward heaven,
unto Thee, God, His almighty Father,
giving thanks to Thee,
blessed,
broke
and gave to His disciples,
saying: Take and eat ye all of this,
FOR THIS IS MY BODY.

And now on the altar in place of the Bread is the Body of Christ.

Consecration of the Wine. Then follows immediately the consecration of the wine. The priest genuflects first, then raises the chalice containing the Precious Blood on high, and then genuflects again—the server ringing the bell with each act of the priest, as in the consecration of the host. The words of Consecration are:

In like manner,
after He had supped,
taking also this excellent chalice
into His holy and venerable hands,
and giving thanks
to Thee,
He blessed and gave to His disciples,
saying:
Take and drink ye all of this,
FOR THIS IS THE CHALICE OF MY BLOOD,
OF THE NEW AND ETERNAL TESTAMENT:
THE MYSTERY OF FAITH:
WHICH SHALL BE SHED FOR YOU AND FOR MANY
UNTO THE REMISSION OF SINS.
As often as ye shall do these things,
ye shall do them in remembrance of Me.

In that quietness Christ, through the priest, performs a great miracle—a mystery of our religion. No longer does the chalice contain wine—the wine has become the Blood of our Saviour. Christ has come down to that altar. He is really present. It is no wonder it is so quiet. It is no wonder there is a great hush. It is no wonder we seem to hold our breath.

The Victim is Offered to God. The Victim, Christ, having been sacrificed, the priest proceeds with arms outstretched to offer Him up to God, calling to mind His life on earth, His Passion and His Ascension. Especial attention is called to the pure and holy character of the Victim. The offering of the Victim to God is made in the following prayer:

> Wherefore, O Lord,
> we Thy servants,
> as also Thy holy people,
> calling to mind the blessed Passion of the same Christ Thy
>   Son our Lord,
> and also His glorious ascension into heaven,
> offer
> unto Thy most excellent Majesty,
> of Thy gifts and presents,
> a pure Host,
> a holy Host,
> a spotless Host,
> the holy Bread of eternal life,
> and the Chalice of everlasting salvation.

Prayer that God Will Accept the Sacrifice. In the next prayer the priest prays that the sacrifice which has just been made shall be acceptable to God as were the sacrifices of Abel, of Abraham, and of Melchisedech. Continuing, as it were, the prayer of offering the Victim to God, the priest says:

> Upon which
> vouchsafe to look with a propitious and serene countenance,
> and to accept them,

as Thou wert graciously pleased to accept
the gifts of Thy just servant Abel,
and the sacrifice of our Patriarch Abraham,
and that which Thy high priest Melchisedech offered to
　Thee,
a holy sacrifice,
a spotless Host.

Preparing for the Eucharistic Banquet. The prayer of offering with the petition of acceptance is now followed by a prayer that the Angel may carry up to heaven ("Thy altar on high") the Sacred Body and Blood, that there may flow down to those who receive Holy Communion, "every heavenly blessing and grace." As always, this petition is made "through the same Christ our Lord." The words of this third prayer after the Consecration are:

> We most humbly beseech Thee, almighty God, command these things to be carried up by the hands of Thy holy Angel to Thine altar on high, in the sight of Thy divine majesty, that as many of us, as, by participation at this altar, shall receive the most sacred Body and Blood of Thy Son may be filled with every heavenly blessing and grace. Through the same Christ, our Lord. Amen.

Reading of the Diptychs. In the early Church, a folded tablet containing the names of those for whom the priest was to pray, was kept on the altar. This was a *diptych*. Hence it applies to the lists of names to be commemorated in the Mass.

The priest now mentions the Church—the Church Suffering, the Church Militant, the Church Triumphant. He prays first for the dead. This commemoration—or memory—of the dead has two parts: the first part asks God to be mindful of these persons, and the second, to grant them a place of refreshment, light, and peace. And this is asked of God through Christ our Lord. The prayer is:

Be mindful, O Lord, of Thy servants and handmaids N. and N., who are gone before us with the sign of faith, and slumber in the sleep of peace.

To these, O Lord, and to all that rest in Christ, grant, we beseech Thee, a place of refreshment, light and peace. Through the same Christ, our Lord. Amen.

The following prayer is for "us sinners," that we may have some part and fellowship with the saints in heaven, and particularly with those named in the prayer—all martyrs. They represent many walks of life: a prophet, a deacon, an apostle, a disciple, a bishop, a pope, a priest, and a cleric, married women, virgins, and widows. The prayer is:

> And to us sinners, Thy servants,
> hoping in the multitude of Thy mercies,
> vouchsafe to grant some part and fellowship with
> Thy holy Apostles and Martyrs: with John, Stephen,
>   Matthias, Barnabas, Ignatius, Alexander, Marcellinus,
>   Peter, Felicitas, Perpetua, Agatha, Lucy, Agnes, Cecilia,
>   Anastasia, and with all Thy saints,
> into whose company, we beseech Thee, admit us,
> not considering our merit,
> but granting Thine own free pardon.
> Through Christ, our Lord.

Final Prayers of the Canon. The final prayers of the Canon remind us that all good things come through Christ—and through Him all honor and glory is given to God. These very brief prayers are, first:

> Through whom, O Lord, Thou dost always create, sanctify, quicken, bless, and give us these good things.

Now lifting up the Host and Chalice to heaven, in what is called the minor elevation, the Victim of the Sacrifice is finally offered up to God:

By Him, and with Him, and in Him, is to Thee, God the Father almighty, in the unity of the Holy Ghost, all honor and glory. Forever and ever.

This is called the *minor elevation.*

And the priest, raising his voice with the last words, calls from the people the word of approval—"Amen." So is it!

The Parts of the Mass

1. Mark the following parts of the Mass of the Faithful to indicate:
     a) which belong to the Offertory
     b) which belong to the Consecration
          Lavabo
          Offering of the Bread and Wine
          Preface
          Memento of the Living
          Consecration of the Host
          Communicantes
          Prayer to the Most Holy Trinity
          Sanctus
          Consecration of the Wine
          Memento of the Dead
          Minor Elevation

   Arrange the parts of the Consecration in the order in which they occur.

2. Tell what the congregation should do at each part of the Mass as given above:
     a) Sit
     b) Stand
     c) Kneel

3. Tell where the priest says each of the prayers, or performs the acts, listed above:
     a) At the foot of the altar

    b) On the Gospel side of the altar

    c) At the center of the altar

    d) On the Epistle side of the altar

Reviewing This Chapter

1. What is meant by Consecration?
2. What is meant by the Doctrine of the Real Presence?
3. What is meant by Transubstantiation?
4. Show that the Holy Sacrifice of the Mass is a genuine sacrifice.
5. Show from the language used in this part of the Mass that we all form one body—priest, congregation, and all Christians—with Christ in the sacrifice.
6. What relation has this to the doctrine of the Mystical Body of Christ? The Communion of Saints?
7. What is the Canon of the Mass? What is the Preface a preface to? What Preface is used on the Sundays of the Year? What is the *Sanctus?*
8. What was the sacrifice of Abel? of Abraham? of Melchisedech?
9. What references are there in this part of the Mass to the:
    a) Church Triumphant
    b) Church Militant
    c) Church Suffering
10. Find the sentences or phrases in the Preface for Trinity Sunday which gives the same ideas as the Catechism answers:

    Q. What do you mean by the Holy Trinity?

    A. By the Blessed Trinity I mean one God in three Divine Persons.

    Q. Are the three Divine Persons equal in all things?

    A. The three Divine Persons are equal in all things.

    Q. Are the three Divine Persons one and the same God?

    A. The three Divine Persons are one and the same God, having one and the same Divine nature and substance.

11. Who is the present or reigning pope?
12. Who is your bishop or archbishop?

13. How does the list of saints given before the Consecration differ from the list given after?

14. For whom are prayers said in this part of the Mass?

Examen

1. At the beginning of this part of the Mass do you really "lift up your heart"? (*Sursum Corda*)

2. Do you realize in the Consecration that you are participating in a great action—the coming of God in our midst?

3. Which of the prayers besides the words of Consecration do you like? Do you ever linger over them? Do you ever think of them outside of Mass?

4. Repeat quietly the words of the Consecration of the Host.

5. Repeat quietly the words of the Consecration of the Wine.

6. As you pray do you keep in mind all Christians and join them?

7. Do you name persons who have died for whom you wish to pray?

8. Do you pray for your parents?

9. Do you say for yourself at the Consecration those words of St. Thomas: "My Lord and my God"?

10. Do you pray for the pope and for your bishop?

My Part

1. I am using my Missal in every Mass I attend.

2. I shall do my part in the Mass of the Catechumens.

3. I shall try always to make my offering to the collection mean at least a little sacrifice on my part.

4. I shall recall at this point the examination of conscience with which I began the Mass and offer up myself for my sins.

5. I shall try to lessen my "sins, offenses, and negligences."

6. I shall keep in mind my privilege in joining with the priest in offering the unspotted Host, Christ.

7. I shall want to wash my hands and cleanse my heart at the *Lavabo*.

8. I shall keep in mind the meaning of the water in the offerings.

9. I shall gladly join with the priest at the *Orate Fratres*.

10. I shall try to lift up my heart in prayer in the Preface.

11. I shall pray to the Father through Christ that the offerings of the Mass may be pleasing to Him.

12. I shall pray for my parents and relatives, living and dead, and for the whole Church.

13. I shall try to repeat with the priests the words of the consecration of the bread and of the wine and realize what is happening on the altar.

Using the Missal

Find in your Missal in the Canon the following prayers:

    a) For the dead.

    b) For the living.

    c) To the Father to accept the gifts and offerings.

    d) Consecrating the wine.

    e) Consecrating the Host.

    f) Referring to the Sacrifices of the Old Testament.

    g) The end of the Canon.

Is there any part of the Canon that is part of the Proper of the Mass? Why?

Prayers

Be sure your knowledge of the Consecration of the Host, Consecration of the Wine is exact. Memorize the Memento of the Dead.

Vocabulary

ENGLISH WORDS

Hosanna: loud shout of praise to God.

Seraphim: angels.

Redemption: salvation, buying back, rescue.

Oblation: what is offered in a Sacrifice, the victim.

Venerable: sacred, worthy of respect (Christ's hands).

Testament: that which is left to children or relatives (what Christ left to all the world).

Host: the bread used in the Mass and in Communion.

Propitious: favorably or with approval.

Diptychs: a folded tablet containing lists of names.

Multitude: a great or very large number.

LATIN WORDS

Vere dignum et justum est: It is truly fitting and just.

Hanc igitur: this, therefore.

Memento: Be mindful (remember).

Catechism (Christian Doctrine)

- Which are the means instituted by our Lord to enable men at all times to share in the fruits of the Redemption? (114)
- What is the Church? (115)
- Who is the invisible Head of the Church? (116)
- Who is the visible Head of the Church? (117)
- Why is the pope, the bishop of Rome, the visible head of the Church? (118)
- Who are the successors of the other Apostles? (119)
- Why did Christ found the Church? (120)
- Are all bound to belong to the Church? (121)
- What is the Holy Eucharist? (238)
- When did Christ institute the Holy Eucharist? (239)
- Who were present when our Lord instituted the Holy Eucharist? (240)
- How did our Lord institute the Holy Eucharist? (241)
- What happened when our Lord said, "This is My body; this is My blood"? (242)
- Is Jesus Christ whole and entire both under the form of bread and under the form of wine? (243)
- Did anything remain of the bread and wine after their substance had been changed into the substance of the body and blood of our Lord? (244)

- What do you mean by the appearances of bread and wine? (245)
- What is this change of the bread and wine into the body and blood of our Lord called? (246)
- How was the substance of the bread and wine changed into the substance of the body and blood of Christ? (247)
- Does this change of bread and wine into the body and blood of Christ continue to be made in the Church? (248)
- When did Christ give His priests the power to change bread and wine into His body and blood? (249)
- How do the priests exercise this power of changing bread and wine into the body and blood of Christ? (250)
- Has the Church any marks by which it may be known? (128)
- How is the Church one? (129)
- How is the Church holy? (130)
- How is the Church catholic or universal? (131)
- How is the Church Apostolic? (132)
- In which Church are these attributes and marks found? (133)
- From whom does the Church derive its undying life and infallible authority? (134)
- By whom is the Church made and kept one, holy, and catholic? (135)

Chapter XIV

THE MASS OF THE FAITHFUL

3. The Communion and Thanksgiving

The Communion, or Eucharistic Banquet, is the third part of the Mass of the Faithful. The first part is the Offertory in which the bread and wine are offered up to God. The second part is the Consecration of the bread and wine, so that through the power of Christ it becomes the Body and Blood of Christ, and the sacrifice of Calvary actually takes place again on our altars. In this third part of the Mass of the Faithful, the priest and the people partake of the Sacrifice in the Eucharistic Banquet and which we call Holy Communion.

The Sacrifice has been made. There is now in the Church a more relaxed feeling. The tension of the Consecration is over. The intense quietness is over.

Our Father. The Communion part of the Mass begins with a familiar prayer taught by Christ Himself. It is the "Our Father." We give it here so as to bring out its seven petitions. Think of each petition as you say again this great familiar prayer:

Our Father, Who art in heaven,
1. hallowed be Thy name;
2. Thy kingdom come;
3. Thy will be done on earth as it is in heaven.
4. Give us this day our daily bread;
5. and forgive us our trespasses, as we forgive those who trespass against us.
6. And lead us not into temptation.

Then the server continues:

> 7. But deliver us from evil.

And the priest concludes:

> Amen.

Deliver Us from All Evils. Then the priest, taking up the last words of the Our Father, repeats in a quiet voice its request to deliver us from evil, past, present, and to come. He then prays for the intercession of Mary, the Apostles, Peter, Paul, and Andrew, and of all the saints to grant us peace in our days. At this point the priest makes the sign of the cross with the paten, kisses it, and places it under the Host, which since the Consecration lay on the corporal. The prayer concludes with the petition to the Trinity through Christ our Lord, that we may be free from sins and secure from all disturbances.

This is another prayer in which the priest's raising his voice on the final words is a cue to the people to join in the prayer by saying *Amen*. When, earlier in the Mass, besides the *Secret*, was this the case? This prayer is really an enlargement of the last petition of the Our Father. It is:

> Deliver us, we beseech Thee, O Lord, from all evils, past, present, and to come: and by the intercession of the blessed and glorious Mary ever Virgin, Mother of God, together with Thy blessed Apostles Peter and Paul and Andrew, and all the saints, mercifully grant peace in our days; that by the assistance of Thy mercy we may be always free from sin, and safe from all disturbances.
>
> Through the same Jesus Christ Thy Son, our Lord,
>
> Who with Thee in the unity of the Holy Ghost, liveth and reigneth, God.
>
> World without end.

And the server and people respond:

> Amen.

Peace of the Lord. The prayer which has just been made for peace—that is, grace—is continued in the next prayer. It is a very brief prayer. After breaking the Host in three parts, the priest makes the sign of the cross three times over the Chalice, with one of the pieces of the Host, praying:

The peace of the Lord be always with you.

and the server and people respond:

And with thy spirit.

This simple prayer means much. The peace desired is the peace of the Lord. Peace here does not mean what it means ordinarily—quiet, absence of noise, or of wars or quarrels. It means fullness of grace. It means the blessings of salvation. It means union with God. It means spiritual peace and it means everlasting happiness. That is a real delivery from all evils. It gives more meaning to this prayer of the priest. How heartily we should enter into it, for the priest here prays that we may have the peace of the Lord, which is the precious fruit of the Sacrifice of the Mass. What a preparation for Communion that is—the peace of God!

The priest, after making the three signs of the cross, drops the particle of the Host into the chalice and continues to pray:

May this mixture and Consecration of the body and Blood of our Lord Jesus Christ be effectual unto eternal life for us that receive it. Amen.

Meaning of the Acts. In the Consecration, the bread and the wine are separately consecrated, indicating the separation of the Body and Blood of Christ, and therefore His death. Here in this simple act, the mixture or joining together of the bread and wine is, to the eye of faith, a uniting of Body and Blood. And so the Victim on the altar is "not a dead Victim but a Victim glorious and immortal." He is a risen Lord. This simple act represents also the joining of all Christians as the Mystical Body of Christ with the Head, Christ Himself. What feelings should be ours as we follow the priest and realize the wonderful things that happen on our altars. Deep love and reverence should be in our hearts as we are moving to the Communion rail. It was the intention of the Lord, as St. Chrysostom said, that all should receive Communion. Not to receive Communion is not to fulfill the intention of our Lord. If for any reason we cannot receive Communion sacramentally, let us desire to do so in our hearts—a spiritual Communion.

Agnus Dei. The priest now strikes his breast three times, repeating the words of St. John the Baptist, announcing, as a voice in the wilderness, the Messias who is to save them. Notice how the desire for peace or salvation is expressed again:

Lamb of God, Who takest away the sins of the world, have mercy upon us.

Lamb of God, Who takest away the sins of the world, have mercy upon us.

Lamb of God, Who takest away the sins of the world, grant us peace.

After the *Agnus Dei* (Lamb of God), there follows another prayer for peace. This prayer recalls Christ's words, "My peace I give unto you." The priest, desiring the peace of Christ but fearful of his sins, asks Christ to look not upon his sins but upon the faith of the Church and grant her peace and unity. This prayer is in preparation for the "kiss of peace" which is given in solemn high Mass by the celebrant to the deacon, and then to the others in

Knowing his own unworthiness, the priest strikes
his breast three times before receiving Communion,
reciting the words of the centurion.

the sanctuary. It is not given in a simple high Mass or low Mass. This prayer for peace is as follows:

> Lord Jesus Christ, who said to Thine Apostles, peace I leave with you, My peace I give unto you, look not upon my sins, but the faith of Thy Church; and grant to it that peace and unity which is agreeable to Thy will. Who livest and reignest, God, forever and ever. Amen.

Priest's Preparation for His Communion. The two following prayers are spoken in the first person. They are the priest's personal preparation for Holy Communion. The ideas which the priest expresses for himself, each member of the congregation might use for his personal preparation for Communion. In the first prayer, the priest asks Christ who, in fulfilling the Father's will, and by cooperation of the Holy Ghost, has given His life for the world, to deliver him from sin and from all evils, and to make him always keep God's Commandments. He asks Christ to do this through His most holy Body and Blood. This is an excellent prayer for us for our own preparation for Communion. It is as follows:

> Lord Jesus Christ, Son of the living God, who, according to the will of the Father, through the co-operation of the Holy Ghost, hast by Thy death given life to the world; deliver me by this Thy most sacred Body and Blood from all mine iniquities and from all evils; and make me always adhere to Thy commandments, and never suffer me to be separated from Thee; Who with the same God the Father and Holy Ghost, livest and reignest, God, forever and ever. Amen.

The priest then says another prayer that is suitable for us in our preparation for Communion. He prays that he may not receive the Body and Blood of Christ unworthily.

> Let not the participation of Thy body, O Lord Jesus Christ, that I, unworthy, presume to receive, turn to my judgment and

condemnation: but through Thy goodness may it avail me for a safeguard and a remedy of body and soul: Who livest and reignest with God the Father in the unity of the Holy Ghost, God, forever and ever. Amen.

The three prayers which the priest says before receiving the Body and Blood of Christ should also be our preparation for Holy Communion.

The Priest Receives the Body and Blood of Our Lord. Then the priest kneels (genuflects), takes the Host and says:

> I will take the bread of heaven, and call upon the name of the Lord.

Then, knowing his own unworthiness, he strikes his breast three times and says a short prayer taken from the words of the centurion who asked Christ to heal his servant. The server rings the bell three times. The priest's prayer is:

> Lord, I am not worthy that Thou shouldst enter under my roof; say but the word, and my soul shall be healed.

He then makes the sign of the cross with the Host in his right hand, and says:

> May the Body of our Lord Jesus Christ preserve my soul to life everlasting. Amen.

He receives the Body of our Lord Jesus Christ. Then repeating the Psalm which Christ used at the Last Supper, he says as a thanksgiving:

> What shall I render to the Lord for all He hath rendered unto me? I will take the chalice of salvation, and call upon the name of the Lord. Praising, I will call upon the Lord, and I shall be saved from mine enemies.

The priest, filled with gratitude and confidence, gathers up the small pieces which may have broken from the Host and drops them into the chalice. Again expressing his faith and confidence, he makes the sign of the cross and says:

When the priest receives Communion,
we are reminded of Christ's burial.

> May the Blood of our Lord Jesus Christ preserve my soul to everlasting life. Amen.

Preparation for Communion of the People.   To prepare for the Communion of the people, the server, in the name of the people themselves, says the *Confiteor*. We should be sure to make this act of contrition, also, especially if we go to Holy Communion. The priest gives the absolution which takes away venial sins, in the following words:

> May almighty God have mercy upon you, forgive you your sins, and bring you to life everlasting.

To which the server responds:

> Amen.

Behold the Lamb of God.   The priest then takes one of the Sacred Hosts in his right hand, and with the Ciborium (which contain the Hosts for the people), in his left hand, turns to the people. He holds the Sacred Host above the Ciborium, while he says:

> Behold the Lamb of God, behold Him who taketh away the sins of the world.
>
> Lord, I am not worthy that Thou shouldst enter under my roof: say but the word and my soul shall be healed, (three times)

Holy Communion for the People.   The people, especially those who are going to receive Holy Communion, say, with the priest the words:

> Lord, I am not worthy that Thou shouldst enter under my roof: say but the word and my soul shall be healed.

The priest then goes to the altar rail, to give Communion to the faithful there. As he gives to each the Sacred Host, he says in Latin:

> May the Body of our Lord Jesus Christ preserve thy soul to life everlasting. Amen.

We should plan to go to Communion as often as we can. To hear Mass without receiving Communion, said a great saint, John Chrysostom, is not to carry out the intention of our Lord. We will prepare ourselves for Communion by making a good confession the previous evening (if we are not already in the state of grace) and we must fast from midnight. If we have sinned, we are in greater need for the food of the soul. We must not get the idea that Communion is only for those who are perfect or at least very good. It is for all men. It is a source of grace. It is part of Christ's plan for bringing to men the grace of the Redemption. There is a very simple poem that expresses this idea. It is:

THE VERY TIME

I used to think, if I'd been bad,
    I'd better stay away
From You, dear God; I used to think
    I might as well not pray.
I used to think, if I'd been bad
    You wouldn't want me to—
And so I didn't pray, but now
    Of course I always do.
Now when I have been bad, dear God,
    I always quickly fall
Down on my knees, for then—Oh, then
    I need You most of all!

Mary Dixon Thayer

It is but natural that in taking an active part in the Sacrifice of the Mass, we should receive Holy Communion. It is intended for us sinners. For that is the reason that Christ came—that *all* men might have salvation. Why not make use of this wonderful Gift when it is so easily done, so natural, and so helpful to our souls!

Thanksgiving. The fourth and last part of the Mass of the Faithful is the Thanksgiving. It is very short, but the person who has received Communion should spend some time in making his own thanksgiving, besides saying these public or liturgical prayers of the Church in the Mass.

The first prayer of this part of the Mass is the request that we who have received the Body and Blood of our Lord may have a pure mind, and that this divine Food may be an eternal remedy for our sick souls. The prayer uses the form "*we.*" It is a prayer for all communicants. It shows the need for right attitudes and right dispositions—"a pure mind." We must co-operate with God's grace. The prayer is:

> Grant, O Lord, that what we have taken with our mouth, we may receive with a pure mind: and that from a temporal gift it may become for us an eternal remedy.

The second prayer is said by the priest in the first person. It is said while the server pours water and wine into the chalice to cleanse his fingers. In this prayer the priest prays that the Communion of the Body and Blood—the two species—may have its full effect in him. The people should use the same prayer to express the same wish, even though they received the Body and Blood of Christ under one species only. The prayer is:

> May Thy Body, O Lord, which I have received, and Thy Blood which I have drunk, cling to my inmost heart: and grant that no stain of sin may remain in me, to whom these pure and holy sacraments have given new strength: Who livest and reignest world without end. Amen.

Communion and Postcommunion. Then are read the prayers known as the Communion and Postcommunion, which change in their form from day to day. They are prayers that may be used often in many

The priest reads the Communion and Postcommunion
from the Epistle side of the altar.

ways. The Communion for the Third Mass on Christmas Day shows what this prayer is like:

> All the ends of the earth have seen the salvation of our God.

The Postcommunion for this day is as follows:

> Grant, we beseech Thee, Almighty God, that as the Saviour of the world born on this day is the author of our divine generation, so He may Himself also be to us the giver of immortality. Who with Thee...(*etc.*)

The priest then goes to the middle of the altar, kisses it, and says:

> *Dominus vobiscum.*
>
> *Et cum spiritu tuo.*

Dismissal. And then the priest uses a form of dismissal, facing the people, and all give thanks simply:

> *Ite Missa est.* (Go, the Mass is ended)
>
> *Deo gratias.* (Thanks be to God)

Or, in some Masses this is done facing the altar, in this form:

> *Benedicamus Domino.* (Let us bless the Lord)
>
> *Deo gratias.* (Thanks be to God)

The first form of dismissal is used on days which are more or less joyful and the second form on days of penance and of fasting.

The *Ite Missa est* is not actually the end of the Mass. The priest, as it were, summarizes all the prayers of the entire Mass in the prayer which follows:

> May the performance of my homage be pleasing
> to Thee, O holy Trinity;
> and grant that the sacrifice
> which I, unworthy, have offered up
> in the sight of Thy Majesty

> may be acceptable to Thee,
> and through Thy mercy
> be a propitiation for me
> and for all those for whom I have offered it.
> Through Christ our Lord.
> Amen.

Here the priest, realizing keenly the greatness of the Mass, and his own sense of unworthiness, makes this prayer. He desires above all that it shall be a "propitiation"—that is, a satisfaction to the Trinity for him and for all for whom it is offered. In this last prayer to the Holy Trinity, he wants to recall the purposes for which Christ died and for which the Mass is said.

Last Blessing. Then, in a most fitting way, there follows at once the blessing. The priest faces the altar, raises his eyes to heaven, stretches out his hands, raises them and joins them, bowing before the crucifix. He then turns toward the people, and makes the sign of the cross over them, saying:

> May almighty God bless you: the Father, the Son, and the Holy Ghost.

And the server and the people receiving the blessing, say:

> Amen.

No one should leave the church before this blessing of Holy Mother Church. It is a part of the Mass. Its value comes from the tremendously great value of the Mass. It would be well if there was no movement, even the slightest, to leave the church until the priest has actually left the altar and is in the sacristy. This, of course, is not until the prayers after Mass (low Mass) are said. Those who have received Holy Communion should remain for a personal thanksgiving in a form recommended by the Church.

The priest sends the people away from Mass with a blessing.

Last Gospel. Then the priest goes to the Gospel side of the altar, and while he reads the first fourteen verses of the first chapter of the Gospel of St. John, the people stand. It reminds us of our opportunity as "Sons of God, born not of blood, nor of the will of flesh, nor of the will of man, but of God." How appropriate is this Gospel to end the Mass. It speaks of the Incarnation. It acknowledges God as Creator. It tells the story of Christ and the redemption of man. And it ends most gloriously:

> We saw His glory, as it were the glory of the only-begotten of the Father, full of grace and truth.

And again the server and the people express their thanksgiving:

> *Deo gratias.* (Thanks be to God.)

The words of the Last Gospel are:

> In the beginning was the Word,
> and the Word was with God,
> and the Word was God.
> The same was in the beginning with God.
> All things were made by Him,
> and without Him was made nothing that was made.
> In Him was life,
> and the life was the light of men:
> and the light shineth in darkness,
> and the darkness did not comprehend it.
>
> There was a man sent from God,
> whose name was John.
> This man came for a witness, to give testimony of the light,
> that all men might believe through him.
> He was not the light,
> but was to give testimony of the light.
>
> That was the true light,
> which enlighteneth every man that cometh into this world.
> He was in the world,

and the world was made by Him,
and the world knew Him not.
He came unto His own,
and His own received Him not.
But as many as received Him,
He gave them power to be made the sons of God:
to them that believe in His name:
who are born,
not of blood,
nor of the will of the flesh,
nor of the will of man,
but of God,
AND THE WORD WAS MADE FLESH (*all genuflect*),
and dwelt among us:
and we saw His glory,
as it were the glory of the only-begotten of the Father,
full of grace and truth.
Thanks be to God.

The Parts of the Mass

1. Tell (or write) which parts of the Mass of the Faithful listed
   belong:
       a) to the Offertory,
       b) to the Consecration,
       c) to the Communion and Thanksgiving.
           Lavabo
           Consecration of the Host
           Postcommunion
           Agnus Dei
           Preface
           Pater Noster
           Communicantes
           Lord, I am not worthy
           Confiteor by the Server
Arrange those parts of the Mass that come after the Consecration
    (the Communion and the Thanksgiving) in the order in
    which they occur in the Mass.

2. Tell what the congregation should do at each part of the Mass as given above:

    a) Sit

    b) Stand

    c) Kneel

3. Tell where the priest says each of the prayers, or performs the acts, listed above:

    a) At the foot of the altar.

    b) On the Gospel side of the altar.

    c) At the center of the altar.

    d) On the Epistle side of the altar.

Reviewing This Chapter

1. Explain what each of the seven petitions of the Our Father means.

2. After having finished the study of this chapter, tell why the Our Father is such an appropriate beginning for this chapter.

3. With what part of the Sacrifice is this chapter identified?

4. What is meant by the peace of the Lord?

5. What is sanctifying grace?

6. Why should we plan to go to Communion whenever we attend Mass?

7. Is the Commandment of the Church about Easter Communion all we should do? Explain your answer.

8. Repeat the words in Latin which the priest uses in giving you Communion. What is the meaning in English?

9. Is Christ received fully by the people under the species of bread alone? Explain.

    Why was the method adopted?

10. Under what forms does the priest receive Holy Communion?

Examen

1. Repeat the prayers you would use at Communion if you did not have your Missal with you.

2. What prayers do you like in this part of the Mass? Do you know them by heart?

3. Say the *Our Father*, emphasizing each of its seven petitions.

4. How do you make a Spiritual Communion?

5. How is the idea of the peace of the Lord carried forward in the prayers? (You may look in your Missal.)

6. Read aloud the prayer asking to be "delivered from evil" beginning with the *Our Father*.

7. At times pause (do not read) to think of the great event that is happening before you.

8. Find out why the priest says: "Behold the Lamb of God." Let this enliven your faith.

9. What is the best way for you to express your Thanksgiving? Recall Christ's phrases: "Go and sin no more"; "Keep my commandments"; or use other phrases.

My Part

1. I am using my Missal in praying every Mass I attend. (I am doing my part as outlined on page 131.)

2. I shall try to receive Communion as often as possible.

3. I shall say the *Our Father* with emphasis on each of the seven petitions.

4. I shall say the *Confiteor* toward the end of the Mass in a real spirit of contrition.

5. I shall say, too, in the same spirit the "Lord, I am not worthy."

6. I shall remain in my seat until the priest has left the altar at the end of the Mass and is in the sacristy.

Using the Missal

1. Find in your Missal:

   a) The *Agnus Dei* (Lamb of God).

   b) Lord, I am not worthy.

   c) *Lavabo*.

   d) *Pater Noster* (Our Father).

    e) Priest's Communion.

    f) Preface.

    g) Postcommunion.

    h) Dismissal.

    i) Creed.

    j) Communion.

    k) *Kyrie Eleison*.

    l) Collect.

2. For each of the parts of the Mass listed above tell:

    a) Whether it is part of the Mass of the Catechumens or Mass of the Faithful.

    b) To which part of these two main subdivisions does it belong.

    c) Whether it is part of the Ordinary of the Mass or of the Proper of the Season.

3. Find the prayer that is said after the *Our Father*. Answer the following questions regarding it.

    a) What is its relation to the "Our Father"?

    b) What is the petition of the opening clauses?

    c) What is asked for through the intercession of the Blessed Virgin Mary and all the saints?

    d) What does "peace" mean here?

    e) What is asked through the mercy of God?

    f) Who is the mediator?

4. Find the two prayers which the priest says just before he takes the Host in preparation for Communion.

For the first one (beginning "Lord Jesus Christ, Son of the living God") answer these questions:

    a) To whom is the prayer addressed?

    b) What is the petition?

    c) How is this to be done?

    d) What two additional petitions are made?

    e) What references are there to the Most Holy Trinity in this prayer?

5. Find the Communion for:
   a) Easter Sunday.
   b) Fifth Sunday after Pentecost.
   c) Fifth Sunday after Epiphany.
   d) All Saints Day.
   e) Next Sunday.

Prayers

1. Be sure the words of the "Our Father" you know are exactly correct. Write it out first, and then compare your copy with the printed copy.

2. Memorize the prayer beginning "Deliver us, we beseech Thee."

3. Memorize the prayer beginning "Lord Jesus Christ, Son of the Living God."

4. Memorize the Agnus Dei.

Bible Passages

1. For the following passages from the Bible tell:
   a) Whether it is from the Old or New Testament.
   b) From which book? What chapter and verse? Who said it?
   c) To whom was it said?
   d) When and where was it said?

   "Our Father, Who art in Heaven."
   "Lamb of God, Who takest away the sins of the world."
   "Lord, I am not worthy that Thou shouldst enter."
   "I will take the chalice of salvation."

2. For a few "Communions" tell where they are taken from.

Vocabulary

ENGLISH WORDS

Precepts: rule or direction.

Redeemer: Saviour, Jesus Christ.

Trespasses: sins.

Bounteous: giving freely, generous.

Deliver: to save us from (sins), to give up.

Adhere to: to keep (the Commandments).

Preserve: to save (our souls), to keep.

Temporal: for a while, in time, opposite of eternity.

Propitiation: in satisfaction for (Christ's death for our sins).

Comprehend: to understand.

LATIN WORDS

Pater noster: Our Father.

Pax domini: The peace of the Lord.

Agnus Dei: Lamb of God.

Domine, non sum dignus: Lord, I am not worthy.

Ite Missa est: Go, the Mass is ended.

Corpus Domini nostri Jesu Christi custodiat animam tuam in vitam aeternam. Amen: May the Body of Our Lord Jesus Christ preserve thy soul to life everlasting. Amen.

Catechism (Christian Doctrine)

- Which are the chief effects of the Redemption? (102)
- What do you mean by grace? (103)
- How many kinds of grace are there (104)
- What is sanctifying grace? (105)
- What do you call those graces or gifts of God by which we believe in Him, hope in Him, and love Him? (106)
- What is Faith? (107)
- What is Hope? (108)
- What is Charity? (109)
- What is actual grace? (110)
- Is grace necessary to salvation? (111)
- Can we resist the grace of God? (112)
- What is the grace of perseverance? (113)
- Is Jesus Christ whole and entire both under the form of bread and under the form of wine? (243)

- Why did Christ institute the Holy Eucharist? (251)
- How are we united to Jesus Christ in the Holy Eucharist? (252)
- What is Holy Communion? (253)
- What is necessary to make a good Communion? (254)
- Does he who received Communion in mortal sin receive the body and blood of Christ? (255)
- Is it enough to be free from mortal sin to receive plentifully the graces of Holy Communion? (256)
- What is the fast necessary for Holy Communion? (257)
- Is anyone ever allowed to receive Holy Communion when not fasting? (258)
- When are we bound to receive Holy Communion? (259)
- What is the Easter time? (401)
- What sin does he commit who neglects to receive Communion during Easter time? (400)

The sacrifice of the Cross is always kept before the people
during Mass. Notice the large painting of the crucifixion
over the altar in this picture.

Chapter XV

REVIEW OF THE MASS:
FOUR SPECIAL STUDIES

Introductory

The Mass can be studied from many points of view. We have been studying each part of the Ordinary of the Mass. At the end of the study of each part we have reviewed what we have learned. We have now completed this study of each part of the Ordinary of the Mass. We might now go back and look at the Mass as a whole. As we do this, we will study some of the very important ideas in the parts of the Mass. We might list these great ideas as follows:

1. The Sacrifice of the Cross is kept before the mind of the priest and the faithful, not only by the presence of the crucifix in the most prominent place on the altar, but by the number of times we make the sign of the cross recalling the sacrifice on Calvary.

2. The sacrifice of the Mass is offered to the Most Holy Trinity and there are many ways which, if we study closely, we can see how the Mass keeps before us the idea of the Holy Trinity. The sign of the cross also does this.

3. While the Mass is *primarily* addressed to the Holy Trinity, it is through Christ's mediatorship (i.e., through the fact that Christ by His death brought together man and God who had been separated by man's disobedience in the Garden of Eden) that it secured for us grace and salvation. It is this "going between" by Christ that saved man. This idea also is brought out in many ways throughout the Mass, as we shall see.

4. What is really expected of the faithful in their attendance at Mass? They must take active part, not merely be mute spectators. The mere reciting of the prayers is not enough.

What occurs is a great sacrifice. As we study the prayers of the Mass closely, we shall find out how often the priest speaks not only for us, but with us, and how in many ways we must show our co-operation.

In studying the Mass again from these four points of view, we shall find that our knowledge and understanding become clearer and deeper. We shall study each one of these points.

I

Special Study: The Sign of the Cross

Objective:
- To bring out the importance and meaning of the sign of the cross.
- To review the entire Mass from this special point of view.

As in the Mass, it would be a very good practice to begin all our actions with the sign of the cross. Let us do that now.

Let us start by reading the story of the Crucifixion from St. Matthew as given on pages 36 and 38 of this book.

Let us review now the five questions and answers in the Catechism regarding the sign of the cross. (#295-299)

Now let us look through the Ordinary of the Mass in our Missal to see how often the sign of the cross is made. Let us, too, try to understand in each case why it is used. In some Missals a little cross marks each place where the sign of the cross is to be made.

The purpose of this study is not to find out merely the number of times the sign of the cross is made. The purpose is to review the whole Mass with special reference to the importance and the meaning of the places where the sign of the cross is made.

For your guidance in this study the following information is given regarding the total number of times the priest makes the sign of the cross:

- Thirty-three times over the offering.
- Sixteen times on himself.
- Twice, when he turns and blesses the people.
- Each time when he gives Holy Communion to each communicant.

The priest makes the sign of the cross, therefore, fifty-two times.

Have members check over each place where the sign of the cross is made and the reason for it.

II

Special Study: The Most Blessed Trinity

Objective:
- To show the dominant place of the Most Holy Trinity in the Mass.
- To review the entire Mass from this special point of view.

In a special study we have seen that the sign of the cross, with its continual reminder of the Most Holy Trinity, is used over fifty times in the Mass. It is natural that it should be used so often when we understand that the Mass is offered to the Most Holy Trinity through Christ our Lord.

We can understand the importance of the Most Holy Trinity in the Mass by reading the Missal with this single object in mind. Apart from the number of times the sign of the cross is made, how and in what ways is the Most Holy Trinity mentioned? or referred to?

You will naturally not miss the longer references in:

1. Kyrie eleison.
2. Gloria in excelsis Deo.
3. The Credo.
4. Preface for the Feast of the Most Holy Trinity.

Notice what is said in "2," "3," and "4" about each Person of the Most Blessed Trinity, and what is said about the Trinity as a whole (e.g., unity of essence, equality of majesty, and distinction of the persons).

For further study take, for example, a prayer in the beginning of the Mass of the Faithful.

It opens:

> O God, who in a marvelous manner did create . . .

It ends:

> Jesus Christ, Thy Son, our Lord, who liveth and reigneth with Thee in the unity of the Holy Ghost one God, world without end. Amen.

Notice how just before the Communion of the priest, this prayer is addressed to Christ:

> Lord Jesus Christ, Son of the living God, who, according to the will of the Father, through the co-operation of the Holy Ghost, . . .

And it ends:

> Who with the same God the Father and Holy Ghost livest and reignest God forever and ever. Amen.

Find as many examples in the Mass as you can in which the Most Holy Trinity is mentioned. Note in each case to whom the prayer is addressed, and then note how the other persons are mentioned at the end of the prayer as given above. You will therefore notice the beginning and end of the prayers of the Mass to see how the Trinity is included.

III

Special Study: Jesus Christ, the Mediator

Objective:
- To emphasize the mediatorship of our Lord, Jesus Christ.
- To review the entire Mass from this point of view.

We have seen how in God's plan for redemption Christ becomes the mediator between God and man. He satisfies God by His sacrifice on Calvary for man's disobedience. He became the High Priest at the Last Supper and continues so in the Mass.

Christ is the mediator between God and man. He restored fully the friendship of God and Man. By His sacrifice, the rift between God and man was healed. Man could again have the supernatural character—grace— which he lost in the Garden of Eden by his disobedience.

This idea of Christ as mediator is brought out in another way in the Mass besides the offering of the bread and wine. It is in the prayers in the Mass which are offered "through Christ our Lord," or simply "through our Lord." Many prayers in the Mass end in this way.

Now read through the Ordinary of the Mass and make a list of the number of times the phrase "through Christ our Lord" or one like it appears at the end of the prayers of the Ordinary of the Mass.

Check your list against this one:

1. Prayers at the foot of the altar.
2. Prayer before the Gospel is read.
3. Prayer over incense.
4. Prayer to the Most Holy Trinity.
5. Commemoration of the Saints.
6. The Oblation Prayers.
7. Prayer over Body and Blood.
8. Commemoration of the Dead.
9. Prayer to the Most Holy Trinity at the end.

Give a reason for the use of this ending of the Prayer in each case.

In the Proper of the Mass, we might also study for certain Sundays in this same way.

1. The Collects
2. The Secret
3. The Postcommunion

IV

Special Study: "I" and "We" in the Mass

Objective:

- To emphasize the participation of the faithful in the Mass with the priest.
- To review the entire Mass from this point of view.

You shall learn also something very important about the Mass as a whole if you will go through the prayers of the Mass and notice a very simple fact:

1. When the priest speaks for himself, i.e., in the first person singular using "I" or "my" or "mine," and

2. When the priest speaks for the congregation, or for himself and the congregation together, or for the congregation, i.e., the first person plural, using "we" or "our," or the second person plural using "you" or "your."

We shall see in this way the prayers of the Mass are not the personal prayers of the priest, but are the prayers of priest and people; in fact, the prayers of the Church. It is truly the official divine service of the Church for the glory of God and the sanctification (or making holy) of our souls.

Let us take a few examples:

In the *Orate Fratres,* the priest turns to the people and asks them to pray

that my sacrifice and yours may be acceptable to God.

Immediately after the Consecration the priest prays:

Wherefore, O Lord,
we Thy servants,
as also Thy holy people.

Here notice how the priest and the people are joined together at this important place in the Mass.

You will be interested in finding out how in many ways the very words of the Mass show that you are expected to take part in the Mass. The Holy Father, Pope Pius X, says in one of his great letters (or *encyclicals*) that he does not want you to be a "mute spectator." *You must take part in the Mass.*

Does the use of "*Amen*" in the Mass help us to understand this better? What does "*Amen*" mean?

Does the "*Dominus vobiscum*" or the "*Oremus*" show that we are to join in or take part in the Mass?

DIVISION OF THE ECCLESIASTICAL YEAR

(A) CHRISTMAS CYCLE—MYSTERY OF THE INCARNATION

PREPARATION . . . . I. Advent (4 Sundays) . 4
(Purple vestments)   (From 1st Sunday of Advent to Dec. 24.)

CELEBRATION . . . {CHRISTMAS EPIPHANY} . II. Christmastide (2 to 3 Sundays) . 2
(White vestments)   (Dec. 24 to Jan. 14.)

PROLONGATION . . . . . . III. Time after the Epiphany (6 Sundays) . 6
(Green vestments)   (Jan. 14 to Septuagesima Sunday.)

(B) EASTER CYCLE—MYSTERY OF THE REDEMPTION

PREPARATION {remote, near, immediate} . I. Septuagesima (3 Sundays) . 3
(Purple vest.)   (Septuagesima to Ash Wednesday.)

   II. Lent (4 Sundays) . 4
   (Ash Wednesday to Passion Sunday.)

   III. Passiontide (2 Sundays) . 2
   (Passion Sunday to Easter.)

CELEBRATION . {EASTER PENTECOST} . IV. Eastertide (7 Sundays) . 7
(White and red vest.)   (Easter Sunday to Trinity Sunday.)

PROLONGATION . . . . . . V. Time after Pentecost (24 Sundays) . 24
(Green vest.)   (Trinity Sunday to Advent.)

Sundays = 52

(Taken from *St. Andrew's Missal*, courtesy of E. M. Lohmann Co.)

PART III
The Proper of the Season

Chapter XVI

THE SEASONS OF THE LITURGICAL YEAR

Introduction to the Study of the Proper of the Season. Each year the Church celebrates the great doctrines or mysteries of our Catholic Faith and recalls the lives and virtues of the great heroes of Christ, the saints.

The Living Christ in the Church. In the cycles of the church year we live again with Christ from day to day. We must understand that we are not merely recalling Christ's life on earth. We are to live it again in the Mystical Body of Christ. Christ promised that He would remain with the Church forever. It is the living Christ that is made known or manifested in the liturgy of the Church. "Every truth of Christ, every miracle, every event that is celebrated in the liturgy is a manifestation of the Living Christ." Let us be as near to Christ at Christmas as were the Shepherds, and let us with Magdalen at Easter announce the great news, "He is risen." Let us live in the liturgy with the Living Christ.

This spirit of living the liturgy and praying the Mass is well expressed by a learned Irish priest, Father Mac-Mahon. He says:

> "Christmas brings with it the spirit of childlike love and gladness. Epiphany awakens in us the spirit of reverent homage to our King and the spirit of zeal for the spread of His kingdom. The spirit of steadfast courage in our struggle against Satan is awakened in the first weeks of Lent, and the spirit of patience

and of suffering and the horror of sin come to us in Passiontide. At Easter the joy of victory over the enemies of our salvation floods the soul, while on the Feast of the Ascension we lift up our thoughts to heavenly things to be, by faith, like Christ, in the bosom of the Father. The Descent of the Holy Ghost endues us with power from on high and gives the spirit of fortitude which enables us to await with eager gladness the second coming of Our Lord in judgment."

A Help for Eternal Joys. Let us review the divisions and the seasons of the church year as a whole, and then let us return to each division as we study and live the great feast days of the liturgical year. We shall then learn for all feast days what is said in the Collect for the Wednesday of Easter week:

> O God who dost gladden us with the yearly celebration of our Lord's Resurrection, mercifully grant that by these festivals which we keep in life we may become worthy to attain to eternal joys hereafter.

THE CHRISTMAS CYCLE: THE ADVENT SEASON

Three Seasons. The first part of the liturgical year centers about the birth of Christ. It is called the Christmas Cycle. It is in three parts: a period of preparation, which is called the season of Advent, the period of celebration, which is called Christmastide, and the season of continuation, which dates from the Epiphany. The entire Christmas cycle lasts from the first Sunday in Advent to the Purification (or Candlemas), on February 2.

We shall now study the first part of the Christmas cycle, the season of Advent. The season of Advent includes four Sundays and ends with December 24, the Vigil of Christmas. In this season, the Church tries to have the people look forward to the coming of Christ very much as the Jewish people looked forward to the coming of the Messias. If you will turn to your Missal now and look at the Collect of any other Sunday in the year, or Feast Day, outside of the season of Advent, you will notice that nearly all the Collects end, "Through our Lord, Jesus Christ." Find out how the Collect ends when it is addressed to Christ Himself as on the feast of Christ the King. If you will now turn to the Collects in the four Sundays of Advent, you will notice that this is not so. This is only one of the ways in which the Church tries to have us enter into the spirit of Advent, or preparation. The Church tries to make us feel that the Mediator, the Redeemer, has not yet come. We await His coming.

Coming of Christ in History and in Liturgy. As we examine the prayers of this season, we notice that they call our attention to the Fall of Man and to the results of the Fall. They contain also the hope for the coming of the Messias which will save Man. It is natural that the prayers of the Church in this season should often refer to the Prophets and other great men of the Jewish race, and particularly Isaias. We await for Christ as the Jews had waited for Him for four thousand years. It is natural, too, that there should be reference to St. John the Baptist, who came to prepare the way of the Lord: "I am the voice of one crying in the wilderness, prepare ye the way of the Lord." And there is emphasis on Mary, the Virgin, through whom the Incarnation was actually brought about. You will notice, as we study this season, the continual desire of man for the Messias who was promised. These appeals are in almost every Mass. For example, the Alleluia Verse for the fourth Sunday says: "Come, O Lord, and do not delay." The Communion for the third Sunday brings out this idea also. It is: "Say to the fainthearted, take courage and fear not; *behold our God will come,* and will save us."

Christ Coming Into Our Hearts. The season of Advent also prepares for the coming of Christ into our hearts. The Collect for the Second Sunday of Advent refers to this:

> "Stir up our hearts, O Lord, to make ready the ways of Thine only-begotten Son; that through His coming we may be worthy to serve Thee with purified minds."

Christ Comes for the Final Judgment. To bring to mind more strongly the purpose for which Christ came to earth, the Mass of the first week, the first Sunday of Advent, speaks to us in the Gospel of the second coming of Christ in the last judgment. Read the Gospel from your own Missals.

Joy in the Season of Advent. In former times the season of Advent was known as a season of joy because of the coming of the Saviour. This tone of joy still continues through the season, even though it is now chiefly a season of penance. The joyous nature of the season is shown especially by the Jewish cry of joy: *Alleluia,* which has been kept in the Masses. We have it, in the Mass of the First Sunday and we have it in the last Mass of the season. On the first Sunday of Advent the Alleluia is

> Show us, O Lord, Thy mercy; and grant us Thy salvation. Alleluia.

And on the fourth Sunday of Advent the Alleluia is

> Come, O Lord, and do not delay; forgive the sins of Thy people Israel. Alleluia.

A Penitential Season. But later the period became in greater degree a season of penance. Like Lent in the Easter Cycle, the season of Advent became largely a season of penance in preparation for the Feast. In the later Middle Ages, the season of Advent was called the "Lent of Christmas." You will notice as one sign of this spirit of penance that during the season of Advent, the *Gloria* is not said and, except for the third Sunday in Advent, when rose-colored vestments may be used, the vestments are purple.*

THE CHRISTMAS CYCLE: CHRISTMASTIDE

The second part of the Christmas Cycle is Christmastide itself. This lasts from the Vigil of the Feast of Christmas to the Feast of the Epiphany on January 6. A vigil is the day immediately before the feast day. The Vigil of Christmas is therefore December 24.

Christmas is a season of great happiness. It is, as the Gospel of the first Mass on Christmas Day says, a season of great joy to all the people. We may rejoice with the angels, with the shepherds, and with the Magi. We shall "rejoice with exceeding great joy." At this period, the priest changes the purple vestments of Advent to the white vestments of Christmastide. In the Masses we shall hear again the *"Gloria in Excelsis Deo."*

The Child Jesus. The Christmastide centers about the Infancy of Christ. We come to "visibly know God by the mystery of the Word made flesh," so that in the words of the liturgy of this season we might well say: "Christ is born for us: come, let us adore Him." And with the Magi we shall "fall down before the Child and adore Him."

---

* The teacher will call the attention of students to the Ember Days of the season as they occur. The Church from the first centuries set aside in each season three days as special days of consecration and petition. They are days of fasting and abstinence.

Spirit of the Feast. It is natural, too, in the liturgy of this season that Mary and Joseph should be mentioned often; therefore, that the Feast of the Holy Family should be celebrated at this time. In this season also are the Feasts of the Holy Innocents, whom Herod killed when seeking to kill Christ Himself, and of the Holy Name of Jesus. These are not parts of the Proper of the Season, but they are from the Sanctoral Cycle. How appropriate this is. There is a note looking forward to the Easter Cycle in the prophecy of Simeon that a sword of sorrow would pierce Mary's heart. Practically all the things we know of the first twelve years of Christ's life are told over and over again in the various parts of the liturgy of the season of Christmastide.

Christ, Son of God. During this season, the truth that Christ is the Son of God, the manifestation of God to man, is brought out. In the Feast of the Epiphany, which marks the end of Christmastide, we have the revelation of the Messias, the Son of God, to the Gentiles. The liturgy of this period repeats, as we ourselves should repeat, the words of the Creed regarding Christ:

> I believe in one Lord Jesus Christ, the only-begotten Son of God, born of the Father before all ages; God of God, light of light, true God of true God; begotten, not made; consubstantial with the Father; by whom all things were made. Who for us men, and for our salvation, came down from heaven; *and was incarnate by the Holy Ghost, of the Virgin Mary.*

Threefold Meaning of Christmas. As a special privilege on this feast of Christ, the priest is allowed to say three Masses in honor of the triple birth of Christ:

1. His generation from the Father.
2. His birth as man.
3. His birth in our souls.

Threefold Meaning of the Epiphany. During the feast of the Epiphany there is a threefold manifestation of Christ referred to in the liturgy of the day:

> 1. His manifestation to the Magi, who were guided by the star in the East to Bethlehem.
> 2. The manifestation of His Divinity (My Beloved Son) at His Baptism in the Jordan by the words of the Father.
> 3. The manifestation of His power in the miracle at Cana, the marriage feast.

Gifts of the Three Kings and Your Gift. Let us, as we see the Star of Christ, do what the Three Kings did. Go and find Him. If we do not bring Him the gifts of the Three Kings, gold, frankincense, and myrrh, we can bring Him the gifts which these symbolize: Christian love or charity, prayer, self-denial or mortification. The greatest gift you can give is yourself.

THE CHRISTMAS CYCLE:
THE SUNDAYS AFTER EPIPHANY

The third part of the Christmas Cycle is the time after the Epiphany. This lasts from January 6 to February 2. After the Christmas Cycle is finished, there may be an interval before the Easter cycle begins on Septuagesima Sunday. This season may include six Sundays, but if Easter comes early it may include only two. The Masses for the Sundays omitted at this time are said after the twenty-third Sunday after Pentecost.

Emphasis on the Incarnation. The same central idea is kept in this part as in the two preceding parts, i.e., the mystery of the Incarnation. During the first part of the Christmas Cycle, the prophecies of the coming of the Messias were emphasized. In the second part, the interest centered about the childhood of Christ, so that, as St. John

In the feast of the Epiphany we celebrate a threefold manifestation of Christ's divinity: in His visit by the Magi, in His Baptism in the Jordan, and in His first miracle at Cana.

says, we may be able "to see with our eyes and handle with our hands the Word of life which was in the bosom of the Father and hath appeared to us, so that we may be able to enter into fellowship with the Father and with His Son Jesus Christ, that our joy may be full." The third part, as we shall see, reminds us that the Divinity of Christ was not only shown by the Angels or the Magi, but in the acts and words of Christ Himself.

Public Life of Christ. On the earlier Sundays we are shown the miracles which Christ did: the wedding feast in Cana of Galilee, the cleansing of the leper, the healing of the servant of the centurion of Capharnaum, the stilling of the tempest on Lake Genesareth.

In the latter Sundays of this season, the Divinity of Christ is emphasized by His teachings as told in the parable of the sower and in the parables of the mustard seed and the leaven. These Sundays after Epiphany show Christ as God in His public life. But because four of them may be used as part of the season of Pentecost or of the season of Epiphany, they do not especially refer to the Christmas Cycle. These Masses all carry the same spirit, and have the same Introit, Gradual, Offertory, and Communion.

Presentation of the Child. The Cycle is really rounded out by the feast of the "Purification of the Blessed Virgin Mary" and of the Presentation of the Child in the Temple. This may be looked upon rather as a feast of the Child Jesus than of the Blessed Mother. It was another Epiphany—a manifestation of Jesus as He comes to His temple according to the words of the prophecy of Malachias.

Candlemas. This is also Candlemas Day—the day of the blessing of the candles. The candles are a symbol of Christ. Christ is the light of the world.

The Season After Epiphany. This period is a time for growth. The vestments worn by the priest are green, symbolic of hope. The general nature of the season is one of joy at the thought that we have with us the Son of God "mighty in work and word." We can see here again that the Liturgy of the Church does not only give us a picture of what happened when Christ lived on earth but really helps us live the life of Christ with Him each year.

THE EASTER CYCLE: SEPTUAGESIMA

Two Cycles. The second part of the church year celebrates the mystery of the Redemption and centers about Easter. It is, therefore, called the Easter Cycle. In the first part of the year, the Cycle of Christmas, we see God coming down to earth and taking on the form of man. In the second part of the year, we see Jesus Christ made man, revealing His Divinity in the Resurrection and Ascension.

Three Seasons. This cycle also has a period of preparation, a period of celebration, and a period of continuation. The period of preparation is divided into three parts which are known as:

1. The Season of Septuagesima
2. The Season of Lent, the last part of which is called
3. The Passion Time

The central part of the cycle is Eastertide, extending from Easter Sunday to Trinity Sunday, and the celebration is continued in the time after Pentecost.

Septuagesima as a Bridge. The season of Septuagesima is a bridge, or a passing, from the joyful, happy Christmas time and time after the Epiphany to the sorrows of the Lenten season and Passion Time.

Septuagesima and Penance. The season reminds man of his terrible condition because of the fall of Adam and original sin. It follows this by presenting the terrible results of actual sin and its punishment in the Deluge (Sexagesima), and finally on the third Sunday of this season it presents Abraham willing to sacrifice his own son, and Melchisedech offering the bread and wine as a type of what was to happen at the end of the Passion. We are reminded, too, by the story of the workers in the vineyard and the parable of the Sower that the Redemption is to extend to all souls in all ages. You will find in it, too, the hope that by this penance the Church will prepare itself for the fruits of the Redemption.

Time of Septuagesima. The Season of Septuagesima is, of course, fixed by the date of Easter, which, as you know, is a movable feast that may extend from March 22 to April 25. It is the ninth Sunday before Easter. The names of these three Sundays, Septuagesima (seventieth), Sexagesima (sixtieth), and Quinquagesima (fiftieth), dates back from Quadragesima (fortieth), i.e., the forty days of Lent. These words are based on the system of numbering used in olden times. Now, of course, there are not ten days between the Sundays as these names might have one think. They are now just names and do not represent numbers.

Because the date of Easter changes, the Season of Septuagesima will sometimes conflict with the Season after the Epiphany. The following chart shows two examples for how the Sundays are then arranged: the first example shows what happens when Easter comes early, and the second is an example in which Easter comes later. Each has the same number of weeks, and starts and ends the same, but the movable feasts vary in between:

Example 1	Example 2
Second Sunday after the Epiphany	Second Sunday after the Epiphany
Septuagesima	Third Sunday after the Epiphany
Ash Wednesday	Fourth Sunday after the Epiphany
EASTER	Fifth Sunday after the Epiphany
Ascension Day	Sixth Sunday after the Epiphany
Pentecost	Septuagesima
First Sunday after Pentecost	Ash Wednesday
Second Sunday after Pentecost	EASTER
(other Sundays after Pentecost)	Ascension Day
Twenty-third Sunday after Pentecost	Pentecost
Third Sunday after the Epiphany	First Sunday after Pentecost
Fourth Sunday after the Epiphany	Second Sunday after Pentecost
Fifth Sunday after the Epiphany	(other Sundays after Pentecost)
Sixth Sunday after the Epiphany	Twenty-third Sunday after Pentecost
Twenty-fourth, or last Sunday after Pentecost	Twenty-fourth, or last Sunday after Pentecost

Septuagesima, a Prelude to Lent. Septuagesima is a kind of prelude or introduction to Lent. The real fasting and penance begins with the Lenten Season, but even during Septuagesima the priest wears the purple vestments and the *Gloria* and *Alleluia* are not said in the Mass.

THE EASTER CYCLE:
THE SEASON OF LENT

Time of the Season of Lent. The preparation for Easter begun in the Season of Septuagesima is continued in the Season of Lent. Lent, as we usually think of it, begins on Ash Wednesday, "the beginning of the most holy forty days," and extends to Easter. In the liturgy of the Church it is divided into two periods: from Ash Wednesday to Passion Sunday (not included), and from Passion Sunday to Easter. These periods are:

> The Season of Lent
> Passion Time

Forty Days. In the forty days' fast in Lent we live again the forty days' fast of our Lord, and we also recall:

1. Forty days' Deluge.
2. Forty days' fasting of Moses before he received the Tables of the Law.
3. Forty days' fast of Elias.

Spirit of Lent. The spirit of penance and the need for fasting is emphasized in the first four weeks of Lent. We are reminded of the warfare against the devil in the Gospel story of the first Sunday of Lent: this tells of the three temptations of Christ in the wilderness after His forty days of prayer and fasting. We have the same temptations of the devil—pride, desire for power, the lustful desires of the flesh. In the spirit of the season we must pray devoutly, make sacrifices, do acts of penance and give alms. In this spirit we approach the Masses of the Sundays and the special devotions of the season.

Following Christ in His Public Life. We must follow Christ in His preaching and in the events of His public life which are told in the Gospels of the Sunday. We should want to know more fully His teachings from the complete accounts on the Gospels according to St. Matthew, St. Mark, St. Luke, and St. John. We must listen to His teachings as if He Himself were speaking to us, particularly to that one which says: "Do penance, for the Kingdom of Heaven is at hand."

Liturgy of the Season of Lent. In the Season of Lent the spirit of penance is carried forward and strengthened to the Passion Time. The *Gloria* and *Alleluia*—which tell of joy—are omitted from the Mass. The priest wears purple vestments and in solemn high Masses certain vestments of the assisting priest are laid aside. The organ is silenced. In the week-day Masses a "Prayer Over the People" is added after the Postcommunion; this prayer begins "Let us pray. Bow down your heads before God."

THE EASTER CYCLE: PASSION TIME

Climax of the Preparation. Passion Time is the more immediate and most serious preparation for the Feast of Easter. Begun in the Season of Septuagesima, the spirit of preparation grows stronger in the first four Sundays of Lent, and reaches its highest point in Passion Time. We keep in mind here especially the great events of the last two weeks of Christ's life before the Resurrection.

A Note of Joy. In the great triumph of Palm Sunday we see the note of joy of the final triumph in the Resurrection. This joy, as it were, lightens the gloom and sadness of the season which ends in the Crucifixion and the death on the cross.

Christ of the Passion. If we read the Lenten liturgy carefully, especially the Introit, Gradual, and Tract of Passiontide, and compare it with the time that went before, we will note a great change in its spirit. In the past season the faithful expressed sorrow for sin and hope for forgiveness because of God's loving kindness. In Passiontide it is the voice of the Christ of the Passion that is heard, and we are, in the spirit of the liturgy, to suffer and to mourn with Christ.

Spirit of the Liturgy. Prayer, sacrifice, and penance are prominent in the liturgy for this period of two weeks, Passion Week and Holy Week. The vestments are of the penitential purple. Not only is the *Gloria in Excelsis* omitted, but the *Gloria Patri* is omitted in several places. The statues and pictures in the church, and even the crucifix are covered with dark veils. In stripping her altars, silencing her bells and the organ, the Church expresses the sadness which it feels in this season.

THE EASTER CYCLE: EASTERTIDE

Solemnity of Solemnities. The Eastertide extends for fifty days, from the Saturday before Easter to the Saturday after Pentecost. This feast celebrating the "Resurrection of our Lord Jesus Christ according to the flesh is the Solemnity of Solemnities and our Passover." It is the foundation of our religion. It is the best proof of the Divinity of Christ.

Easter Season. The Easter Season corresponds with the forty days that Christ appeared on earth between His Resurrection and His Ascension, and extends beyond to the time He sent the Holy Ghost (Pentecost) to begin His Church. We list here, Christ's appearances between His

The crucifixion, resurrection, and the ascension are all parts of one great act in our redemption. They are all celebrated during the Easter Cycle.

Resurrection from the dead and His Ascension into heaven to sit at the right hand of God. They are:

1. Jesus appears to Mary Magdalen (John xx. 11-18; Mark xvi. 9-11).

2. Jesus appears to the Holy Women (Luke xxiv. 9-11; Matt, xxviii. 8-15).

3. Jesus appears to Peter and to the two disciples at Emmaus (Luke xxiv. 13-35; Mark xvi. 12-13).

4. Jesus appears to the Disciples at Jerusalem (John xx. 19-23; Luke xxiv. 36-43).

5. Jesus addresses Thomas (John xx. 24-29).

6. Jesus appears near the Lake of Galilee (John xxi. 1-14).

7. Jesus gives the primacy to Peter (John xxi. 15-24).

8. Jesus appears on a mountain in Galilee (Matt, xxviii. 16-17; 1 Cor. xv. 6).

9. Jesus appears to James (1 Cor. xv. 7).

10. Jesus appears to the Eleven at Jerusalem (Luke xxiv. 44-49; Mark xvi. 14-18; Matt, xxviii. 18-20; Acts i. 4-5).

11. Jesus ascends into heaven (Acts i, iii. 6-12 ; Luke xxiv. 50- 53; Mark xvi. 19).

"The Day of the Lord"

'This is the day the Lord hath made, let us be glad and rejoice therein." "I am risen."

He is risen echoes in the feast of feasts. This is the greatest of the feasts. Alleluias resound and re-echo in this feast. It is the most glorious and the most joyous of feasts. It is the day of the Lord. It is the feast of the Redemption and of the Resurrection. The sequence expresses the victory over sin and death:

Forth to the Paschal Victim, Christians, bring your sacrifice of praise:

The Lamb redeems the sheep; and Christ the sinless One hath sinners reconciled to the Father.

Together, death and life strove in a strange conflict: The Prince of Life, who died, now lives and reigns.

What thou sawest; Mary, say, as thou wentest on the way.

I saw the tomb wherein the living One had lain; I saw His glory as He rose again; Napkin and linen clothes, and Angels twain: Yea, Christ is risen, my hope, and He will go before you into Galilee.

We know that Christ indeed has risen from the grave: Hail, Thou King of Victory, have mercy, Lord, and save. Amen. *Alleluia.*

Liturgy of the Feast. In the joy of the Resurrection the Church lays aside the purple vestments of seasons of penance and her priests wear vestments of pure white, symbol of joy and purity. The veils are taken off the statues and pictures, the organ sounds again, the bells ring, and the sanctuary is decorated. The *Gloria* is recited or sung and a joyful refrain of *Alleluia, Alleluia, Alleluia,* is added to the Introit and to other parts of the Mass. Instead of the *Asperges*, the *Vidi Aquam* is sung, reminding us of the waters of baptism.

Feast of the Ascension. During this celebration, too, there are the two great feasts of the Ascension and of Pentecost, which ends the celebration period. We celebrate the ascent of Christ as man—body and soul—to heaven. With Him He took the just souls of the past, the heroes of the Old Testament, "the divinely inspired prophets, holy Kings, penitents, holy women, virgins, and innocent children."

"Ye men of Galilee, why wonder you, looking up to heaven? *alleluia.* He shall so come as you have seen Him going up into heaven, *alleluia, alleluia, alleluia.* O, clap your hands, all ye nations; shout unto God with the voice of joy" (*Introit*).

Feast of Pentecost or Whitsunday. The Feast of Pentecost, still a part of the Eastertide, is its crown. On it we celebrate the descent of the Holy Ghost on the Apostles in the form of fiery tongues. We celebrate the founding of the Holy Roman Catholic Church. We celebrate, too, the feast of the Third Person of the Blessed Trinity, the Holy Ghost. If Christmas is in a special sense the feast of the Father, the First Person of the Blessed Trinity, and Easter the feast of the Son, the Second Person, Pentecost is the feast of the Third Person, the Holy Ghost.

THE SEASON AFTER PENTECOST

Holy Ghost Sent by Christ. The Resurrection is continued in its effects in the long period after Pentecost— from twenty-three to twenty-eight weeks. Christ ascending to heaven is the direct preparation for Pentecost. "If I go not," said Christ, "the Paraclete will not come to you, but if I go, I will send Him to you." The Holy Ghost came in the form of tongues of fire, and the Apostles were strengthened, and men from all parts of the world hear, in their own languages of the wonderful works of God.

Church. This was the beginning of the Church, and thus, as one writer says, was the Church "baptized with the Holy Ghost." The Holy Ghost had spoken by the prophets, as the Creed tells us; He was now to speak through the popes, the saints, and all members of the Mystical Body of Christ. "He will teach you all things, and bring all things to your mind, whatsoever I shall have said to you."

Seasons and the Trinity. In the Season of Advent, the liturgy celebrates the reign of God the Father over mankind, or rather, over His chosen people. In the Christmas and Easter seasons, beginning with the birth of Christ and ending with His Ascension, the liturgy celebrates the reign of the Son. Now in the period after Pentecost, the reign of the Holy Ghost in the Church is celebrated extending from Pentecost to the end of the world.

Many Appeals of this Season. The Season after Pentecost expresses the longing of the Church. It has a diffuse, or scattered, rather than a central character. In the Gospels the emphasis is on Christ's teachings and miracles. In the Epistles the instructions of the Apostles, particularly Paul, are called to our attention. The other parts often are expressions of our need for divine assistance. All should help us in securing the fruits of the Resurrection. There are many appeals to the individual soul in this season.

Beautiful Collects of the Season. In this period, too, we are encouraged to imitate Christ. The Collects of the season are especially beautiful for their thought and language. Just examine a number now. Turn, for example, to the Collect for the ninth Sunday after Pentecost for what it says about prayer.

> Let the ears of Thy mercy, O Lord, be open to the prayers of Thy suppliants: and, that Thou mayest grant the desires of them that ask, may they ask things pleasing to Thee.

Notice what is said in the Collect of the eleventh Sunday on the same subject.

> O Almighty and everlasting God, who in the abundance of Thy goodness dost go beyond at once the deserts of Thy suppliants and their requests, pour out upon us Thy mercy, pardoning what our conscience dreads, and adding besides what we presume not to ask for.

Sanctoral Cycle and the Great Feasts. In this period especially is there a group of feast days of very great importance—which, however, are not a part of the cycle itself. Some of these great feasts are:

> The Feast of the Most Holy Trinity
> The Feast of the Blessed Sacrament, or Corpus Christi
> The Feast of the Sacred Heart
> The Feast of the Finding of the Holy Cross (May 3)

The Feast of the Most Precious Blood (July 1)
The Feast of Our Lord's Transfiguration (August 6)
The Feast of the Exaltation of the Holy Cross (Sept. 14)
The Feast of the Kingship of Christ (last Sunday of October)

It is in this part of the liturgical year—the time after Pentecost—that the Sanctoral Cycle or Cycle of Saints finds its full development. Here are the great saints born of the spirit of Christ. They, too, are the manifestation of Christ in the world. It is expected of us, under the guidance of the Holy Ghost, that we shall become too, "other Christs."

Season of Joy and Hope. The season is a season of joy and hope. The vestments worn are green. The presence of the Holy Ghost in the Church gives us our basis for hope for our own salvation if we keep the commandments and do penance.

Chapter XVII

PLAN OF STUDY

The Proper of a Mass

Introductory Information

In studying the Proper of a Mass for a particular feast day, we should locate the feast day in accordance with the outline given below: as part of the introductory information, we should learn what vestments are worn by the priest.

1. The Cycle (see Chap. VI, p. 74; Chap. XV, pp. 233 ff.).
   a) The Christmas Cycle
   b) The Easter Cycle
2. The Season of the Cycle (see Chap. VI, p. 74; Chap. XV, pp. 233 ff.).
   a) Preparation:
      Advent
      Septuagesima
      Lent
      Passiontide
   b) Celebration:
      Christmas
      Easter
   c) Continuation:
      Season after Epiphany
      Season after Pentecost
3. Vestments of the Feast (see p. 80 f.).
   a) Purple
   b) Green
   c) White
   d) Red
   e) Black

Think over, then, the place of the particular feast day in the liturgical year. What is the reason for the color of the vestment? (Cf. p. 80 f.)

General Idea of This Mass. Each student should read through silently the Proper as given in his Missal. It is not essential at this time that the student should know each word.

It would probably be well for each teacher to read aloud the Proper to the class, making such incidental comment and explaining such words as will guarantee the general impression of the Mass of the particular day.

A discussion should follow at this point on these questions:

1. What is the general character of this Mass? Joyful? Sorrowful? Penitential?
2. What part of the life of Christ is referred to?
3. What is the central thought of this Mass? Where is it expressed?
4. What are the ideas or lessons taught in this Mass?
5. What is the most important part of the Proper of this Mass?
6. How can you enter into the spirit of this Mass?

At some appropriate point in this discussion, or at its end, the teacher should consult the introduction to the Mass of each Sunday in a book such as the *St. Andrew's Daily Missal.*

Study of Each Subdivision of the Mass. This will be followed now by a careful study of the meaning—with a note on the beauty—of *each part* of the Proper. The aim here is understanding.

1. Introit
2. *Gloria* (whether included or not and why)
3. Collect
4. Epistle
5. Gradual

      6. *Alleluia*
      7. Gospel
      8. Preface
      9. Communion
      10. Postcommunion
      11. The Dismissal
      12. The Last Gospel

1. What parts of the Proper are not included in this Mass?
2. What is the reason for this?
3. What does this show about the character of the Mass?
4. Give a short explanation of each part of the Proper.
5. How does this show the spirit of the liturgical season or emphasize the idea of the day? Or purposes for which Masses are offered:
      a) Thanksgiving to God
      b) Praise of God
      c) Petition to God
      d) Atonement to God for our sins
6. What part would you like to memorize? Why?

Study of Whole and Relations of the Parts to the Whole. This stage will be followed by a study of the whole Mass and the relation of its parts. Such questions as the following will guide such study.

1. What is the main effect on you of this Mass after your studying it?
2. Does this Mass include the *Gloria?* Of what significance is this?
3. Does this Mass include an *Alleluia?* Of what significance is this?
4. Does the Introit indicate the joyful or sorrowful character of this Mass? Explain.
5. What is the central idea in this Mass?
6. Where is it most strongly expressed? Read the exact words.
7. Where else is it expressed? Read each part.
8. Tell the story of the Gospel of the day.
   Tell the facts about when it occurred.
   What relation has it to the central idea of the Mass?
9. What relation has the Epistle to the central idea of the Mass?

10. What is the main thought in the Communion and Postcommunion?
11. How does the Mass end?
12. What part of the Mass should we memorize?
13. What resolution for a better life should you make as a result of the study of this Mass?
14. Do you recall any religious poem or hymn which this Mass suggests?
15. What questions, if any, in your Catechism does this Mass help you to understand better? Recall the question and answer.
16. What parts of the Proper of this Mass emphasize:
    a) The Praise of God.
    b) The Adoration of God.
    c) Thanksgiving to God.
    d) Petition to God.

Self-Examination

17. Does this Mass suggest anything regarding your own way of life?
18. Did it give you any new appreciation of religion?
19. Did it bring out more significantly any fact of the life of Christ? or its meaning?

Written Exercise

20. Tell in your own words the spirit of this Mass, and how you can enter into it.

Chapter XVIII

FIRST SUNDAY OF ADVENT

1. Part of Christmas Cycle
2. Part of Season of Advent
3. Purple Vestments (season of penance)
4. No *Gloria*
5. Has an *Alleluia*
6. The *Benedicamus Domino* is said instead of the *Ite Missa Est*.

Study of Mass as a Whole: Threefold Coming of Christ. We shall read together the various parts of the Proper of the Mass for this first Sunday in Advent—the first Sunday of the Liturgical Year. As we learn from our summary of the Season of Advent, we shall expect the coming of Christ in three ways:

1. As the Christ Child at Christmas.
2. In our own hearts.
3. As God at the Second Coming to Judge the World.

We notice that in this Mass the threefold coming of Christ is stressed. Throughout the Mass is emphasized the coming of the Christ Child at Christmas. Along with this is the continual reference to our sins. We must be delivered from our sins, to make way for Christ in our hearts. And there is the Gospel with the Second Coming of Christ as told by St. Luke. The need to be sorry for our sins and to sin no more must be clear from this general view of this Mass. This, of course, gives the Mass its spirit of penance and is why the priest wears purple vestments. The *Alleluia* expresses the note of hope, however, which gives the season its mixed character.

The spirit of the Jews begging for the Messias should be our
spirit during Advent.

Coming of Christ at Christmas. The first Sunday of Advent is the beginning of the Church year. It is part of the Christmas Cycle, and so it has the great expectation of the Incarnation—the Advent. This is the attitude we should have in our own participation in the Mass. This idea can be clearly seen in the Collect:

> Put forth, we beseech Thee, O Lord, Thy power and come, that under Thy protection and Thy liberating hand we may be happily saved from the dangers that threaten us because of our sins.

The Epistle emphasizes this idea in three sentences:

> Brethren, knowing that is now the hour for us to rise from sleep.
> For now our salvation is nearer than when we believed.
> The night is passed and the day is at hand.

The purpose is clear in this passage: it is to gain salvation. The Collect tells us in these words:

> ...that under Thy protection...we may be happily saved from the dangers that threaten us because of our sins, Who livest and reignest..."

And the Postcommunion almost at the end of the Mass repeats the idea:

> May we receive Thy mercy, O Lord, in the midst of Thy temple: that we may prepare with fitting honor for the approaching solemnities of our redemption. Through our Lord, etc.

The Mass opens with the note of trust in God: "To Thee have I lifted up my soul: in Thee O my God, I put my trust, let me not be ashamed: neither let my enemies laugh at me." This will save us from being ashamed or confounded. "We shall follow the ways of the Lord, we shall learn His paths."

The Gospel tells the story of the Second Coming of Christ—"coming in a cloud with great power and majesty." In the final judgment our redemption will be achieved.

Coming of Christ in Our Hearts. In the Introit we lift up our soul to God, and put our trust in Him. This idea is found again in the Gradual and the Offertory in the exact words of the Introit. There is the earnest longing of the soul in the words of the Psalmist:

> Show, O Lord, Thy ways to me, and teach me Thy paths.

And these words are repeated in the Gradual. In the Collect we pray to be delivered from the "dangers that threaten us because of our sins." And in the language of the Epistle we resolve to "cast off the works of darkness." Or more positively

> "to walk honestly"
> "to put on the armor of light"
> "to put on the Lord Jesus Christ"

In the Secret we pray that the Holy Mysteries will "cleanse" and purify us. And so the *Alleluia* cries out: "Show us, O Lord, Thy mercy: and grant us Thy salvation. *Alleluia.*" Then in the language of the Postcommunion we shall "prepare for the approaching solemnities of our redemption." And this is the note of hope!

Second Coming of Christ. The Gospel in the glorious language of St. Luke describes those signs and wonders, when we shall lift up our heads "because your redemption is at hand." The Gospel of the twenty-fourth Sunday after Pentecost, which tells more fully of the Second Coming of Christ, may be compared with St. Luke's account. As in the Church year, the beginning and the end tells of the last act of the Redemption, so in life, our last end must guide our actions.

Jesus Christ, the Saviour whom God promised, was born
of the Virgin Mary, on the first Christmas Day.

What We May Learn from the Mass.   The spirit of this Mass for the first Sunday in Advent is a spirit of petition and praise and adoration. We must begin as the Mass does to lift up our soul and put our trust in God. We must avoid sin and its "dangers," and unless the Lord come we shall not be delivered. We must keep alive the hope that He will come, if we are worthy. We must prepare for His Coming. If we have the right spirit, He will surely show His ways to us, and teach us His path. And when He comes in glory at the Second Coming we shall be ready and happy, for our redemption is at hand.

1. With what spirit should you enter the Church on the first Sunday of Advent?
2. Give in the words of the Collect the reason why we look forward to the coming of Christ.
3. How is this idea expressed in the Postcommunion?
4. What is the significance to you of the Gospel relating to the Second Coming of Christ in this 'first week of Advent— the beginning of the church year?
5. What does it mean "to put on the armor of light"?
6. What does this mean: "Let us work honestly as in the day"? Why is this appropriate for this Sunday?

Memorize:
   a) The Collect of this Sunday
   b) The Postcommunion
   c) "Show, O Lord, Thy ways to me: and teach me Thy paths." (From Introit and Gradual)

Poem:
Alice Meynell's, "I Am the Way."

Chapter XIX

FEAST OF THE IMMACULATE CONCEPTION OF THE BLESSED VIRGIN MARY

December 8. Holy day of Obligation

1. Part of the Sanctoral Cycle (not the Temporal Cycle).
2. Occurs during Season of Advent (though not part of it).
3. White vestments.

Immaculate Conception of Mary and the Virgin Birth of Christ. In this feast we commemorate the Immaculate Conception of the Blessed Virgin Mary—that is the fact that Mary, unlike us, was conceived without original sin. There was never the least stain of sin in her. How fitting this was for the Mother of Christ.

The Immaculate Conception of Mary must not be confused with the virgin birth. The doctrine of the virgin birth of Christ refers to the fact that Christ was born of the Virgin Mary. It was God's plan acting through the Holy Ghost that Christ should have no human father. Joseph was to be His foster father and take care of Him. The miracle of a virgin birth was part of God's plan of redemption.

Praise, Grace, and Glory of Mary. In this Mass we pay glorious tribute to the purity and beauty of Mary's soul. It was truly full of grace. It was without spot. The Mass is full of joy and praise of this handmaiden of the Lord. Well might we praise Mary in the words of one of the *Alleluia* verses:

> Thou art all fair, O Mary, and there is no spot in thee. *Alleluia.*

Mary, the most pure Mother of God, was free from sin
from the first moment of her life.
"Thou art all fair, O Mary, and there is no spot in thee."

The best statement of the reason for the feast is in the words of the Collect:

> O God who, by the Immaculate Conception of the Virgin, didst prepare a worthy dwelling place for Thy Son; we beg Thee, that as by the foreseen death of that same Son of Thine Thou didst preserve her from all stain, so Thou wouldst grant us also, by her intercession, to arrive unspotted in Thy sight.

Let us list the praises of Mary. From Isaias the Introit uses:

> He hath clothed me with the garments of salvation, and with the robe of justice He hath covered me, as a bride adorned with her jewels.

From Judith, the Gradual takes the praise of Mary:

> Blessed art thou, O Virgin Mary, by the Lord the Most High God above all women upon the earth. Thou art the glory of Jerusalem, thou art the joy of Israel, thou art the honor of our people.

In the *Alleluia* the praise of Mary is taken from the Song of Solomon, "Thou art all fair, O Mary." The Gospel uses the words of Gabriel at the Annunciation:

> Hail, full of grace, the Lord is with thee: blessed art thou among women.

The Offertory repeats this with an *Alleluia* added.

Meaning for Us. Mary is for us the greatest model of purity, sinlessness, and unspoiled or supernatural human nature, full of grace. In the Collect we pray that as "Thou didst preserve Mary unsullied by sin, so may we likewise come to Thee pure in heart." In the Secret we pray God to accept the "saving oblation" of the Mass "on the solemn festival of the Immaculate Conception of the Blessed Virgin Mary, that as we confess her free from all stain of sin, we may through her intercession be delivered from all our transgressions." And finally in the Postcommunion we pray:

> May the sacraments which we have received, O Lord our God, heal in us the wounds of that sin, from which Thou didst preserve the Immaculate Conception of Blessed Mary in a remarkable manner. Through our Lord...

THE CATECHISM

1. ON THE END OF MAN

1. Q. Who made the world?
A. God made the world.

2. Q. Who is God?
A. God is the Creator of heaven and earth and of all things.

3. Q. What is man?
A. Man is a creature composed of body and soul and made to the image and likeness of God.

4. Q. Is this likeness in the body or in the soul?
A. The likeness is chiefly in the soul.

5. Q. How is the soul like to God?
A. The soul is like to God because it is a *spirit* that will never die, and has *understanding* and free will.

6. Q. Why did God make you?
A. God made me to know Him, to love Him, and to serve Him in this world, and to be happy with Him forever in the next.

7. Q. Of which must we take more care, our soul or our body?
A. We must take more care of our soul than of our body.

8. Q. Why must we take more care of our soul than of our body?
A. We must take more care of our soul than of our body, because in losing our soul we lose God and everlasting happiness.

9. Q. What must we do to save our souls?

A. To save our souls we must worship God by *faith, hope,* and *charity;* that is, we must believe in Him, hope in Him, and love Him with all our heart.

10. Q. How shall we know the things which we are to believe?

A. We shall know the things which we are to believe from the Catholic Church, through which God speaks to us.

11. Q. Where shall we find the chief truths which the Church teaches?

A. We shall find the chief truths which the Church teaches in the Apostles' Creed.

12. Q. Say the Apostles' Creed.

A. I believe in God, the Father Almighty, Creator of heaven and earth; and in Jesus Christ, His only Son, our Lord; who was conceived by the Holy Ghost, born of the Virgin Mary, suffered under Pontius Pilate, was crucified; died, and was buried. He descended into hell; the third day He arose again from the dead; He ascended into heaven, and sitteth at the right hand of God, the Father Almighty; from thence He shall come to judge the living and the dead. I believe in the Holy Ghost, the Holy Catholic Church, the communion of Saints, the forgiveness of sins, the resurrection of the body, and the life everlasting. Amen.

2. ON GOD AND HIS PERFECTIONS

13. Q. What is God?

A. God is a spirit infinitely perfect.

14. Q. Had God a beginning?

A. God had no beginning; He always was and He always will be.

15. **Q. Where is God?**
    A. God is everywhere.

16. **Q. If God is everywhere, why do we not see Him?**
    A. We do not see Him, because He is a pure spirit and cannot be seen with bodily eyes.

17. **Q. Does God see us?**
    A. God sees us and watches over us.

18. **Q. Does God know all things?**
    A. God knows all things, even our most secret thoughts, words, and actions.

19. **Q. Can God do all things?**
    A. God can do all things, and nothing is hard or impossible to Him.

20. **Q. Is God just, holy, and merciful?**
    A. God is all just, all holy, all merciful, as He is infinitely perfect.

3. ON THE UNITY AND TRINITY OF GOD

21. **Q. Is there but one God?**
    A. Yes; there is but one God.

22. **Q. Why can there be but one God?**
    A. There can be but one God because God, being supreme and infinite, cannot have an equal.

23. **Q. How many persons are there in God?**
    A. In God there are three Divine Persons, really distinct, and equal in all things—the Father, the Son, and the Holy Ghost.

24. **Q. Is the Father God?**
    A. The Father is God and the first Person of the Blessed Trinity.

25. **Q. Is the Son God?**
    A. The Son is God and the second Person of the Blessed Trinity.

26. Q. Is the Holy Ghost God?
A. The Holy Ghost is God and the third Person of the Blessed Trinity.

27. Q. What do you mean by the Blessed Trinity?
A. By the Blessed Trinity I mean one God in three Divine Persons.

28. Q. Are the three Divine Persons equal in all things?
A. The three Divine Persons are equal in all things.

29. Q. Are the three Divine Persons one and the same God?
A. The three Divine Persons are one and the same God, having one and the same Divine nature and substance.

30. Q. Can we fully understand how the three Divine Persons are one and the same God?
A. We cannot fully understand how the three Divine Persons are one and the same God, because this is a mystery.

31. Q. What is a mystery?
A. A mystery is a truth which we cannot fully understand.

4. ON CREATION

32. Q. Who created heaven and earth, and all things?
A. God created heaven and earth, and all things.

33. Q. How did God create heaven and earth?
A. God created heaven and earth from nothing by His word only; that is, by a single act of His all-powerful will.

34. Q. Which are chief creatures of God?
A. The chief creatures of God are angels and men.

35. Q. What are angels?
A. Angels are pure spirits without a body, created to adore and enjoy God in heaven.

36. Q. Were the angels created for any other purpose?
A. The angels were also created to assist before the throne of God and to minister unto Him; they have often been sent as messengers from God to man; and are also appointed our guardians.

37. **Q. Were the angels, as God created them, good and happy?**

A. The angels, as God created them, were good and happy.

38. **Q. Did all the angels remain good and happy?**

A. All the angels did not remain good and happy; many of them sinned and were cast into hell, and these are called devils or bad angels.

5. ON OUR FIRST PARENTS AND THE FALL

39. **Q. Who were the first man and woman?**

A. The first man and woman were Adam and Eve.

40. **Q. Were Adam and Eve innocent and holy when they came from the hand of God?**

A. Adam and Eve were innocent and holy when they came from the hand of God.

41. **Q. Did God give any command to Adam and Eve?**

A. To try their obedience, God commanded Adam and Eve not to eat of a certain fruit which grew in the garden of Paradise.

42. **Q. Which were the chief blessings intended for Adam and Eve had they remained faithful to God?**

A. The chief blessings intended for Adam and Eve, had they remained faithful to God, were a constant state of happiness in this life and everlasting glory in the next.

43. **Q. Did Adam and Eve remain faithful to God?**

A. Adam and Eve did not remain faithful to God; but broke His command by eating the forbidden fruit.

44. **Q. What befell Adam and Eve on account of their sin?**

A. Adam and Eve on account of their sin lost innocence and holiness, and were doomed to sickness and death.

45. Q. What evil befell us on account of the disobedience of our first parents?

A. On account of the disobedience of our first parents, we all share in their sin and punishment, as we should have shared in their happiness if they had remained faithful.

46. Q. What other effects followed from the sin of our first parents?

A. By the sin of our first parents we lost sanctifying grace, faith, hope, love, and freedom from evil tendencies, and were made subject to death and the other miseries of this life.

47. Q. What is the sin called which we inherit from our first parents?

A. The sin which we inherit from our first parents is called original sin.

48. Q. Why is this sin called original?

A. This sin is called original because it comes down to us from our first parents, and we are brought into the world with its guilt on our soul.

49. Q. Do these effects remain in us after original sin is forgiven?

A. These effects remain in us after original sin is forgiven.

50. Q. Was anyone ever preserved from original sin?

A. The Blessed Virgin Mary, through the merits of her Divine Son, was preserved free from the guilt of original sin, and this privilege is called her Immaculate Conception.

6. ON SIN AND ITS KINDS

51. Q. Is original sin the only kind of sin?

A. Original sin is not the only kind of sin; there is another kind of sin, which we commit ourselves, called actual sin.

52. Q. What is actual sin?

    A. Actual sin is any willful thought, word, deed, or omission contrary to the law of God.

53. Q. How many kinds of actual sin are there?

    A. There are two kinds of actual sin—mortal and venial.

54. Q. What is mortal sin?

    A. Mortal sin is a grievous offense against the law of God.

55. Q. Why is this sin called mortal?

    A. This sin is called mortal because it deprives us of spiritual life, which is sanctifying grace, and brings everlasting death and damnation on the soul.

56. Q. How many things are necessary to make a sin mortal?

    A. To make a sin mortal three things are necessary: a grievous matter, sufficient reflection, and full consent of the will.

57. Q. What is a venial sin?

    A. Venial sin is a slight offense against the law of God in matters of less importance, or in matters of great importance it is an offense committed without sufficient reflection or full consent of the will.

58. Q. Which are the effects of venial sin?

    A. The effects of venial sin are the lessening of the love of God in our heart, the making us less worthy of His help, and the weakening of the power to resist mortal sin.

59. Q. Which are the chief sources of sin?

    A. The chief sources of sin are seven: Pride, Covetousness, Lust, Anger, Gluttony, Envy, and Sloth; and they are commonly called capital sins.

7. ON THE INCARNATION AND REDEMPTION

60. Q. Did God abandon man after he fell into sin?

    A. God did not abandon man after he fell into sin, but promised him a Redeemer, who was to satisfy for man's sin and reopen to him the gates of heaven.

61. Q. Who is the Redeemer?

A. Our Blessed Lord and Saviour Jesus Christ is the Redeemer of mankind.

62. Q. What do you believe of Jesus Christ?

A. I believe that Jesus Christ is the Son of God, the second Person of the Blessed Trinity, true God and true man.

63. Q. Why is Jesus Christ true God?

A. Jesus Christ is true God because He is the true and only Son of God the Father.

64. Q. Why is Jesus Christ true man?

A. Jesus Christ is true man because He is the Son of the Blessed Virgin Mary and has a body and soul like ours.

65. Q. How many natures are there in Jesus Christ?

A. In Jesus Christ there are two natures, the nature of God and the nature of man.

66. Q. Is Jesus Christ more than one person?

A. No, Jesus Christ is but one Divine Person.

67. Q. Was Jesus Christ always God?

A. Jesus Christ was always God, as He is the second Person of the Blessed Trinity equal to His Father from all eternity.

68. Q. Was Jesus Christ always man?

A. Jesus Christ was not always man, but became man at the time of His Incarnation.

69. Q. What do you mean by the Incarnation?

A. By the Incarnation I mean that the Son of God was made man.

70. Q. How was the Son of God made man?

A. The Son of God was conceived and made man by the power of the Holy Ghost, in the womb of the Blessed Virgin Mary.

71. Q. Is the Blessed Virgin Mary truly the Mother of God?

A. The Blessed Virgin Mary is truly the Mother of God, because the same Divine Person who is the Son of God is also the Son of the Blessed Virgin Mary.

72. Q. Did the Son of God become man immediately after the sin of our first parents?

A. The Son of God did not become man immediately after the sin of our first parents, but was promised to them as a Redeemer.

73. Q. How could they be saved who lived before the Son of God became man?

A. They who lived before the Son of God became man could be saved by believing in a Redeemer to come, and by keeping the Commandments.

74. Q. On what day was the Son of God conceived and made man?

A. The Son of God was conceived and made man on Annunciation day—the day on which the Angel Gabriel announced to the Blessed Virgin Mary that she was to be the Mother of God.

75. Q. On what day was Christ born?

A. Christ was born on Christmas day in a stable at Bethlehem, over nineteen hundred years ago.

76. Q. How long did Christ live on earth?

A. Christ lived on earth about thirty-three years, and led a most holy life in poverty and suffering.

77. Q. Why did Christ live so long on earth?

A. Christ lived so long on earth to show us the way to heaven by His teachings and example.

8. ON OUR LORD'S PASSION, DEATH, RESURRECTION, AND ASCENSION

78. Q. What did Jesus Christ suffer?

A. Jesus Christ suffered a bloody sweat, a cruel scourging, was crowned with thorns, and was crucified.

79. Q. On what day did Christ die?

A. Christ died on Good Friday.

80. Q. Why did you call that day "good" on which Christ died so sorrowful a death?

A. We call the day good on which Christ died, because by His death He showed His great love for man, and purchased for him every blessing.

81. Q. Where did Christ die?

A. Christ died on Mount Calvary.

82. Q. How did Christ die?

A. Christ was nailed to the Cross and died on it between two thieves.

83. Q. Why did Christ suffer and die?

A. Christ suffered and died for our sins.

84. Q. What lessons do we learn from the sufferings and death of Christ?

A. From the sufferings and death of Christ we learn the great evil of sin, the hatred God bears to it, and the necessity of satisfying for it.

85. Q. Whither did Christ's soul go after His death?

A. After Christ's death His soul descended into hell.

86. Q. Did Christ's soul descend into the hell of the damned?

A. The hell into which Christ's soul descended was not the hell of the damned, but a place or state of rest called Limbo, where the souls of the just were waiting for Him.

87. **Q. Why did Christ descend into Limbo?**

A. Christ descended into Limbo to preach to the souls who were in prison—that is to announce to them the joyful tidings of their redemption.

88. **Q. Where was Christ's body while His soul was in Limbo?**

A. While Christ's soul was in Limbo His body was in the holy sepulcher.

89. **Q. On what day did Christ rise from the dead?**

A. Christ rose from the dead, glorious and immortal, on Easter Sunday, the third day after His death.

90. **Q. How long did Christ stay on earth after His resurrection?**

A. Christ stayed on earth forty days after His resurrection to show that He was truly risen from the dead, and to instruct His Apostles.

91. **Q. After Christ had remained forty days on earth whither did He go?**

A. After forty days Christ ascended into heaven, and the day on which He ascended into heaven is called Ascension day.

92. **Q. Where is Christ in heaven?**

A. In heaven Christ sits at the right hand of God the Father Almighty.

93. **Q. What do you mean by saying that Christ sits at the right hand of God?**

A. When I say that Christ sits at the right hand of God I mean that Christ as God is equal to His Father in all things, and that as man He is in the highest place in heaven next to God.

9. ON THE HOLY GHOST AND HIS DESCENT UPON THE APOSTLES

94. Q. Who is the Holy Ghost?
   A. The Holy Ghost is the third Person of the Blessed Trinity.

95. Q. From whom does the Holy Ghost proceed?
   A. The Holy Ghost proceeds from the Father and the Son.

96. Q. Is the Holy Ghost equal to the Father and the Son?
   A. The Holy Ghost is equal to the Father and the Son, being the same Lord and God as they are.

97. Q. On what day did the Holy Ghost come down upon the Apostles?
   A. The Holy Ghost came down upon the Apostles ten days after the Ascension of our Lord; and the day on which He came down upon the Apostles is called Whitsunday, or Pentecost.

98. Q. How did the Holy Ghost come down upon the Apostles?
   A. The Holy Ghost came down upon the Apostles in the form of tongues of fire.

99. Q. Who sent the Holy Ghost upon the Apostles?
   A. Our Lord Jesus Christ sent the Holy Ghost upon the Apostles.

100. Q. Why did Christ send the Holy Ghost?
   A. Christ sent the Holy Ghost to sanctify His Church, to enlighten and strengthen the Apostles, and to enable them to preach the Gospel.

101. Q. Will the Holy Ghost abide with the Church forever?
   A. The Holy Ghost will abide with the Church forever, and guide it in the way of holiness and truth.

10. ON THE EFFECTS OF THE REDEMPTION

102. Q. Which are the chief effects of the Redemption?

A. The chief effects of the redemption are two: The satisfaction of God's justice by Christ's sufferings and death, and the gaining of grace for men.

103. Q. What do you mean by grace?

A. By grace I mean the supernatural gift of God bestowed on us, through the merits of Jesus Christ, for our salvation.

104. Q. How many kinds of grace are there?

A. There are two kinds of grace, sanctifying grace and actual grace.

105. Q. What is sanctifying grace?

A. Sanctifying grace is that grace which makes the soul holy and pleasing to God.

106. Q. What do you call those graces or gifts of God by which we believe in Him, hope in Him, and love Him?

A. Those graces or gifts of God by which we believe in Him, hope in Him, and love Him, are called the Divine virtues of Faith, Hope, and Charity.

107. Q. What is Faith?

A. Faith is a Divine virtue by which we firmly believe the truths which God has revealed.

108. Q. What is Hope?

A. Hope is a Divine virtue by which we firmly trust that God will give us eternal life and the means to obtain it.

109. Q. What is Charity?

A. Charity is a Divine virtue by which we love God above all things for His own sake, and our neighbor as ourselves for the love of God.

110. Q. What is actual grace?

A. Actual grace is that help of God which enlightens our mind and moves our will to shun evil and do good.

111. Q. Is grace necessary to salvation?
 A. Grace is necessary to salvation, because without grace we can do nothing to merit heaven.

112. Q. Can we resist the grace of God?
 A. We can, and unfortunately often do, resist the grace of God.

113. Q. What is the grace of perseverance?
 A. The grace of perseverance is a particular gift of God which enables us to continue in the state of grace till death.

11. ON THE CHURCH

114. Q. Which are the means instituted by our Lord to enable men at all times to share in the fruits of the Redemption?
 A. The means instituted by our Lord to enable men at all times to share in the fruits of the Redemption are the Church and the Sacraments.

115. Q. What is the Church?
 A. The Church is the congregation of all those who profess the faith of Christ, partake of the same Sacraments, and are governed by their lawful pastors under one visible Head.

116. Q. Who is the invisible Head of the Church?
 A. Jesus Christ is the invisible Head of the Church.

117. Q. Who is the visible Head of the Church?
 A. Our Holy Father the Pope, the Bishop of Rome, is the Vicar of Christ on earth and the visible Head of the Church.

118. Q. Why is the Pope, the Bishop of Rome, the visible Head of the Church?
 A. The Pope, the Bishop of Rome, is the visible Head of the Church, because he is the successor of St. Peter, whom Christ made the chief of the Apostles and the visible Head of the Church.

119. Q. Who are the successors of the other Apostles?
A. The successors of the other Apostles are the Bishops of the Holy Catholic Church.

120. Q. Why did Christ found the Church?
A. Christ founded the Church to teach, govern, sanctify, and save all men.

121. Q. Are all bound to belong to the Church?
A. All are bound to belong to the Church, and he who knows the Church to be the true Church and remains out of it cannot be saved.

12. ON THE ATTRIBUTES AND MARKS OF THE CHURCH

122. Q. Which are the attributes of the Church?
A. The attributes of the Church are three: authority, infallibility, and indefectibility.

123. Q. What do you mean by the authority of the Church?
A. By the authority of the Church I mean the right and power which the Pope and the Bishops, as the successors of the Apostles, have to teach and to govern the faithful.

124. Q. What do you mean by the infallibility of the Church?
A. By the infallibility of the Church I mean that the Church cannot err when it teaches a doctrine of faith or morals.

125. Q. When does the Church teach infallibly?
A. The Church teaches infallibly when it speaks through the Pope and Bishops united in general council, or through the Pope alone when he proclaims to all the faithful a doctrine of faith or morals.

126. Q. What do you mean by the indefectibility of the Church?
A. By the indefectibility of the Church I mean that the Church, as Christ founded it, will last till the end of time.

127. Q. In whom are these attributes found in their fullness?

A. These attributes are found in their fullness in the Pope, the visible Head of the Church, whose infallible authority to teach bishops, priests, and people in matters of faith or morals will last to the end of the world.

128. Q. Has the Church any marks by which it may be known?

A. The Church has four marks by which it may be known: it is One; it is Holy; it is Catholic; it is Apostolic.

129. Q. How is the Church One?

A. The Church is One because all its members agree in one faith, are all in one communion, and are all under one head.

130. Q. How is the Church Holy?

A. The Church is Holy because its founder, Jesus Christ, is holy; because it teaches a holy doctrine; invites all to a holy life, and because of the eminent holiness of so many thousands of its children.

131. How is the Church Catholic or universal?

A. The Church is Catholic or universal because it subsists in all ages, teaches all nations, and maintains all truth.

132. Q. How is the Church Apostolic?

A. The Church is Apostolic because it was founded by Christ on His Apostles, and is governed by their lawful successors, and because it has never ceased, and never will cease, to teach their doctrine.

133. Q. In which Church are these attributes and marks found?

A. These attributes and marks are found in the Holy Roman Catholic Church alone.

134. Q. From whom does the Church derive its undying life and infallible authority?

A. The Church derives its undying life and infallible authority from the Holy Ghost, the spirit of truth, who abides with it forever.

135. Q. By whom is the Church made and kept One, Holy, and Catholic?

A. The Church is made and kept One, Holy, and Catholic by the Holy Ghost, the spirit of love and holiness, who unites and sanctifies its members throughout the world.

13. ON THE SACRAMENTS IN GENERAL

136. Q. What is a Sacrament?

A. A Sacrament is an outward sign instituted by Christ to give grace.

137. Q. How many Sacraments are there?

A. There are seven Sacraments: Baptism, Confirmation, Holy Eucharist, Penance, Extreme Unction, Holy Orders, and Matrimony.

138. Q. Whence have the Sacraments the power of giving grace?

A. The Sacraments have the power of giving grace from the merits of Jesus Christ.

139. Q. What grace do the Sacraments give?

A. Some of the Sacraments give sanctifying grace, and others increase it in our souls.

140. Q. Which are the Sacraments that give sanctifying grace?

A. The Sacraments that give sanctifying grace are Baptism and Penance; and they are called Sacraments of the dead.

141. Q. Why are Baptism and Penance called Sacraments of the dead?

A. Baptism and Penance are called Sacraments of the dead, because they take away sin, which is the death of the soul, and give grace, which is its life.

142. Q. Which are the Sacraments that increase sanctifying grace in our soul?

A. The Sacraments that increase sanctifying grace in our souls are: Confirmation, Holy Eucharist, Extreme Unction, Holy Orders, and Matrimony; and they are called Sacraments of the living.

143. **Q. Why are Confirmation, Holy Eucharist, Extreme Unction, Holy Orders, and Matrimony called Sacraments of the living?**

A. Confirmation, Holy Eucharist, Extreme Unction, Holy Orders, and Matrimony, are called Sacraments of the living, because those who receive them worthily are already living the life of grace.

144. **Q. What sin does he commit who receives the Sacraments of the living in mortal sin?**

A. He who receives the Sacraments of the living in mortal sin commits a sacrilege, which is a great sin, because it is an abuse of a sacred thing.

145. **Q. Besides sanctifying grace do the Sacraments give any other grace?**

A. Besides sanctifying grace the Sacraments give another grace, called sacramental.

146. **Q. What is Sacramental grace?**

A. Sacramental grace is a special help which God gives, to attain the end for which He instituted each Sacrament.

147. **Q. Do the Sacraments always give grace?**

A. The Sacraments always give grace, if we receive them with the right dispositions.

148. **Q. Can we receive the Sacraments more than once?**

A. We can receive the Sacraments more than once, except Baptism, Confirmation, and Holy Orders.

149. **Q. Why can we not receive Baptism, Confirmation, and Holy Orders more than once?**

A. We cannot receive Baptism, Confirmation, and Holy Orders more than once, because they imprint a character in the soul.

150. **Q. What is the character which these Sacraments imprint in the soul?**

A. The character which these Sacraments imprint in the soul is a spiritual mark which remains forever.

151. Q. Does the character remain in the soul even after death?

A. This character remains in the soul even after death; for the honor and glory of those who are saved; for the shame and punishment of those who are lost.

14. ON BAPTISM

152. Q. What is Baptism?

A. Baptism is a Sacrament which cleanses us from original sin, makes us Christians, children of God, and heirs of heaven.

153. Q. Are actual sins ever remitted by Baptism?

A. Actual sins and all the punishment due to them are remitted by Baptism, if the person baptized be guilty of any.

154. Q. Is Baptism necessary to salvation?

A. Baptism is necessary to salvation, because without it, we cannot enter into the kingdom of heaven.

155. Q. Who can administer Baptism?

A. The priest is the ordinary minister of baptism; but in case of necessity anyone who has the use of reason may baptize.

156. Q. How is Baptism given?

A. Whoever baptizes should pour water on the head of the person to be baptized; and say, while pouring the water: *I baptize thee in the name of the Father, and of the Son, and of the Holy Ghost.*

157. Q. How many kinds of Baptism are there?

A. There are three kinds of Baptism: Baptism of water, of desire, and of blood.

158. Q. What is Baptism of water?

A. Baptism of water is that which is given by pouring water on the head of the person to be baptized, and saying at the same time, *I baptize thee in the name of the Father, and of the Son, and of the Holy Ghost.*

159. Q. What is Baptism of desire?

A. Baptism of desire is an ardent wish to receive Baptism, and to do all that God has ordained for our salvation.

160. Q. What is Baptism of blood?

A. Baptism of blood is the shedding of one's blood for the faith of Christ.

161. Q. Is Baptism of desire or of blood sufficient to produce the effects of Baptism of water?

A. Baptism of desire or of blood is sufficient to produce the effects of the Baptism of water, if it is impossible to receive the Baptism of water.

162. Q. What do we promise in Baptism?

A. In Baptism we promise to renounce the devil with all his works and pomps.

163. Q. Why is the name of a saint given in Baptism?

A. The name of a saint is given in Baptism in order that the person baptized may imitate his virtues and have him for a protector.

164. Q. Why are godfathers and godmothers given in Baptism?

A. Godfathers and godmothers are given in Baptism in order that they may promise, in the name of the child, what the child itself would promise if it had the use of reason.

165. Q. What is the obligation of a godfather and a godmother?

A. The obligation of a godfather and a godmother is to instruct the child in its religious duties, if the parents neglect to do so or die.

15. ON CONFIRMATION

166. Q. What is Confirmation?

A. Confirmation is a Sacrament through which we receive the Holy Ghost to make us strong and perfect Christians and soldiers of Jesus Christ.

167. Q. Who administers Confirmation?

A. The bishop is the ordinary minister of Confirmation.

168. Q. How does the bishop give Confirmation?

A. The bishop extends his hands over those who are to be confirmed, prays that they may receive the Holy Ghost, and anoints the forehead of each with holy chrism in the form of a cross.

169. Q. What is holy chrism?

A. Holy chrism is a mixture of olive oil and balm consecrated by the bishop.

170. Q. What does the bishop say in anointing the person he confirms?

A. In anointing the person he confirms the bishop says: *I sign thee with the sign of the cross, and I confirm thee with the chrism of salvation, in the name of the Father, and of the Son, and of the Holy Ghost.*

171. Q. What is meant by anointing the forehead with chrism in the form of a cross?

A. By anointing the forehead with chrism in the form of a cross is meant, that the Christian who is confirmed must openly profess and practice his faith, never be ashamed of it, and rather die than deny it.

172. Q. Why does the bishop give the person he confirms a slight blow on the cheek?

A. The bishop gives the person he confirms a slight blow on the cheek, to put him in mind that he must be ready to suffer everything, even death, for the sake of Christ.

173. Q. To receive Confirmation worthily is it necessary to be in the state of grace?

A. To receive Confirmation worthily it is necessary to be in the state of grace.

174. **Q. What special preparation should be made to receive Confirmation?**

A. Persons of an age to learn should know the chief mysteries of faith and the duties of a Christian, and be instructed in the nature and effects of this Sacrament.

175. **Q. Is it a sin to neglect Confirmation?**

A. It is a sin to neglect Confirmation, especially in these evil days when faith and morals are exposed to so many and such violent temptations.

16. ON THE GIFTS AND FRUITS OF THE HOLY GHOST

176. **Q. Which are the effects of Confirmation?**

A. The effects of Confirmation are an increase of sanctifying grace, the strengthening of our faith, and the gifts of the Holy Ghost.

177. **Q. Which are the gifts of the Holy Ghost?**

A. The gifts of the Holy Ghost are Wisdom, Understanding, Counsel, Fortitude, Knowledge, Piety, and Fear of the Lord.

178. **Q. Why do we receive the gift of Fear of the Lord?**

A. We receive the gift of Fear of the Lord to fill us with the dread of sin.

179. **Q. Why do we receive the gift of Piety?**

A. We receive the gift of Piety to make us love God as a Father and obey Him because we love Him.

180. **Q. Why do we receive the gift of Knowledge?**

A. We receive the gift of Knowledge to enable us to discover the will of God in all things.

181. **Q. Why do we receive the gift of Fortitude?**

A. We receive the gift of Fortitude to strengthen us to do the will of God in all things.

182. Q. Why do we receive the gift of Counsel?

A. We receive the gift of Counsel to warn us of the deceits of the devil, and of the dangers to salvation.

183. Q. Why do we receive the gift of Understanding?

A. We receive the gift of Understanding to enable us to know more clearly the mysteries of faith.

184. Q. Why do we receive the gift of Wisdom?

A. We receive the gift of Wisdom to give us a relish for the things of God, and to direct our whole life and all our actions to His honor and glory.

185. Q. Which are the Beatitudes?

A. The Beatitudes are:

1. Blessed are the poor in spirit, for theirs is the kingdom of heaven.
2. Blessed are the meek, for they shall possess the land.
3. Blessed are they that mourn, for they shall be comforted.
4. Blessed are they that hunger and thirst after justice, for they shall be filled.
5. Blessed are the merciful, for they shall obtain mercy.
6. Blessed are the clean of heart, for they shall see God.
7. Blessed are the peacemakers, for they shall be called the children of God.
8. Blessed are they that suffer persecution for justice' sake, for theirs is the kingdom of heaven.

186. Q. Which are the twelve fruits of the Holy Ghost?

A. The twelve fruits of the Holy Ghost are Charity, Joy, Peace, Patience, Benignity, Goodness, Long-Suffering, Mildness, Faith, Modesty, Continency, and Chastity.

17. ON THE SACRAMENT OF PENANCE

187. Q. What is the Sacrament of Penance?

A. Penance is a Sacrament in which the sins committed after Baptism are forgiven.

188. Q. How does the Sacrament of Penance remit sin, and restore to the soul the friendship of God?

A. The Sacrament of Penance remits sin and restores the friendship of God to the soul by means of the absolution of the priest.

189. Q. How do you know that the priest has the power of absolving from the sins committed after Baptism?

A. I know that the priest has the power of absolving from the sins committed after Baptism, because Jesus Christ granted that power to the priests of His Church when He said: *"Receive ye the Holy Ghost. Whose sins you shall forgive, they are forgiven them; whose sins you shall retain, they are retained "*

190. Q. How do the priests of the Church exercise the power of forgiving sins?

A. The priests of the Church exercise the power of forgiving sins by hearing the confession of sins, and granting pardon for them as ministers of God and in His name.

191. Q. What must we do to receive the Sacrament of Penance worthily?

A. To receive the Sacrament of Penance worthily we must do five things:

    1. We must examine our conscience.
    2. We must have sorrow for our sins.
    3. We must make a firm resolution never more to offend God.
    4. We must confess our sins to the priest.
    5. We must accept the penance which the priest gives us.

192. Q. What is the examination of conscience?

A. The examination of conscience is an earnest effort to recall to mind all the sins we have committed since our last worthy confession.

193. Q. How can we make a good examination of conscience?

    A. We can make a good examination of conscience by calling to memory the commandments of God, the precepts of the Church, the seven capital sins, and the particular duties of our state in life, to find out the sins we have committed.

194. Q. What should we do before beginning the examination of conscience?

    A. Before beginning the examination of conscience we should pray to God to give us light to know our sins and grace to detest them.

18. ON CONTRITION

195. Q. What is contrition, or sorrow for sin?

    A. Contrition, or sorrow for sin, is a hatred of sin and a true grief of the soul for having offended God, with a firm purpose of sinning no more.

196. Q. What kind of sorrow should we have for our sins?

    A. The sorrow we should have for our sins should be interior, supernatural, universal, and sovereign.

197. Q. What do you mean by saying that our sorrow should be interior?

    A. When I say that our sorrow should be interior, I mean that it should come from the heart, and not merely from the lips.

198. Q. What do you mean by saying that our sorrow should be supernatural?

    A. When I say that our sorrow should be supernatural, I mean that it should be prompted by the grace of God, and excited by motives which spring from faith, and not by merely natural motives.

199. Q. What do you mean by saying that our sorrow should be universal?

A. When I say that our sorrow should be universal, I mean that we should be sorry for all our mortal sins without exception.

200. Q. What do you mean when you say that our sorrows should be sovereign?

A. When I say that our sorrow should be sovereign, I mean that we should grieve more for having offended God than for any other evil that can befall us.

201. Q. Why should we be sorry for our sins?

A. We should be sorry for our sins, because sin is the greatest of evils and an offense against God our Creator, Preserver, and Redeemer, and because it shuts us out of heaven and condemns us to the eternal pains of hell.

202. Q. How many kinds of contrition are there?

A. There are two kinds of contrition; perfect contrition and imperfect contrition.

203. Q. What is perfect contrition?

A. Perfect contrition is that which fills us with sorrow and hatred for sin, because it offends God, who is infinitely good in Himself and worthy of all love.

204. Q. What is imperfect contrition?

A. Imperfect contrition is that by which we hate what offends God, because by it we lose heaven and deserve hell; or because sin is so hateful in itself.

205. Q. Is imperfect contrition sufficient for a worthy confession?

A. Imperfect contrition is sufficient for a worthy confession, but we should endeavor to have perfect contrition.

206. Q. What do you mean by a firm purpose of sinning no more?

A. By a firm purpose of sinning no more I mean a fixed resolve not only to avoid all mortal sin, but also its near occasions.

207. Q. What do you mean by the near occasions of sin?

A. By the near occasions of sin I mean all the persons, places, and things that may easily lead us into sin.

209. Q. What sins are we bound to confess?

A. We are bound to confess all our mortal sins, but it is well also to confess our venial sins.

210. Q. Which are the chief qualities of a good Confession?

A. The chief qualities of a good Confession are three; it must be humble, sincere, and entire.

211. Q. When is our Confession humble?

A. Our Confession is humble, when we accuse ourselves of our sin, with a deep sense of shame and sorrow for having offended God.

212. Q. When is our Confession sincere?

A. Our Confession is sincere, when we tell our sins honestly and truthfully, neither exaggerating nor excusing them.

213. Q. When is our Confession entire?

A. Our Confession is entire when we tell the number of kinds of our sins and the circumstances which change their nature.

214. Q. What should we do if we cannot remember the number of our sins?

A. If we cannot remember the number of our sins, we should tell the number as nearly as possible, and say how often we may have sinned in a day, a week, or a month, and how long the habit or practice has lasted.

215. Q. Is our Confession worthy if, without our fault, we forget to confess a mortal sin?

A. If without our fault we forget to confess a mortal sin, our Confession is worthy, and the sin is forgiven; but it must be told in Confession if it again comes to our mind.

216. Q. Is it a grievous offense willfully to conceal a mortal sin in Confession?

A. It is a grievous offense willfully to conceal a mortal sin in Confession, because we thereby tell a lie to the Holy Ghost, and make our Confession worthless.

217. Q. What must he do who has willfully concealed a mortal sin in Confession?

A. He who has willfully concealed a mortal sin in Confession must not only confess it, but must also repeat all the sins he has committed since his last worthy Confession.

218. Q. Why does the priest give us a penance after Confession?

A. The priest gives us a penance after Confession that we may satisfy God for the temporal punishment due to our sins.

219. Q. Does not the Sacrament of Penance remit all punishment due to sin?

A. The Sacrament of Penance remits the eternal punishment due to sin, but it does not always remit the temporal punishment which God requires as satisfaction for our sins.

220. Q. Why does God require a temporal punishment as a satisfaction for sin?

A. God requires a temporal punishment as a satisfaction for sin, to teach us the great evil of sin, and to prevent us from falling again.

221. Q. Which are the chief means by which we satisfy God for the temporal punishment due to sin?

A. The chief means by which we satisfy God for the temporal punishment due to sin are: Prayer, Fasting, Almsgiving, all spiritual and corporal works of mercy, and the patient suffering of the ills of life.

222. Q. Which are the chief spiritual works of mercy?

A. The chief spiritual works of mercy are seven: To admonish the sinner, to instruct the ignorant, to counsel the doubtful, to comfort the sorrowful, to bear wrongs patiently, to forgive all injuries, and to pray for the living and the dead.

223. Q. Which are the chief corporal works of mercy?

A. The chief corporal works of mercy are seven: To feed the hungry, to give drink to the thirsty, to clothe the naked, to ransom the captive, to harbor the harborless, to visit the sick, and to bury the dead.

225. Q. Which are the first things we should tell the priest in Confession?

A. The first things we should tell the priest in Confession are the time of our last Confession, and whether we said the penance and went to Holy Communion.

226. Q. After telling the time of our last Confession and Communion what should we do?

A. After telling the time of our last Confession and Communion we should confess all the mortal sins we have since committed, and all the venial sins we may wish to mention.

227. Q. What must we do when the confessor asks us questions?

A. When the confessor asks us questions we must answer them truthfully and clearly.

228. Q. What should we do after telling our sins?

A. After telling our sins we should listen with attention to the advice which the confessor may think proper to give.

229. Q. How should we end our Confession?

A. We should end our Confession by saying I also accuse myself of all the sins of my past life telling, if we choose, one or several of our past sins.

230. Q. What should we do while the priest is giving us absolution?

A. While the priest is giving us absolution we should from our hearts renew the Act of Contrition.

21. ON INDULGENCES

231. Q. What is an indulgence?

A. An Indulgence is the remission in whole or in part of the temporal punishment due to sin.

232. Q. Is an Indulgence a pardon of sin, or a license to commit sin?

A. An Indulgence is not a pardon of sin, nor a license to commit sin, and one who is in a state of mortal sin cannot gain an Indulgence.

233. Q. How many kinds of Indulgences are there?

A. There are two kinds of Indulgences—Plenary and Partial.

234. Q. What is a Plenary Indulgence?

A. A Plenary Indulgence is the full remission of the temporal punishment due to sin.

235. Q. What is a Partial Indulgence?

A. A Partial Indulgence is the remission of a part of the temporal punishment due to sin.

236. Q. How does the Church by means of Indulgences remit the temporal punishment due to sins?

A. The Church by means of Indulgences remits the temporal punishment due to sin by applying to us the merits of Jesus Christ, and the superabundant satisfactions of the Blessed Virgin Mary and of the saints; which merits and satisfactions are its spiritual treasury.

237. Q. What must we do to gain an Indulgence?

A. To gain an Indulgence we must be in the state of grace and perform the works enjoined.

22. ON THE HOLY EUCHARIST

238. Q. What is the Holy Eucharist?

A. The Holy Eucharist is the Sacrament which contains the body and blood, soul and divinity, of our Lord Jesus Christ under the appearances of bread and wine.

239. Q. When did Christ institute the Holy Eucharist?

A. Christ instituted the Holy Eucharist at the Last Supper, the night before He died.

240. Q. Who were present when our Lord instituted the Holy Eucharist?

A. When our Lord instituted the Holy Eucharist, the twelve Apostles were present.

241. Q. How did our Lord institute the Holy Eucharist?

A. Our Lord instituted the Holy Eucharist by taking bread, blessing, breaking, and giving to His Apostles, saying: *"Take ye and eat. This is My body";* and then by taking the cup of wine, blessing and giving it, saying to them: *"Drink ye all of this. This is My blood which shall be shed for the remission of sins. Do this for a commemoration of Me."*

242. Q. What happened when our Lord said, This is My body; This is My blood?

A. When our Lord said, *This is My body,* the substance of the bread was changed into the substance of His body; when He said, *This is My blood,* the substance of the wine was changed into the substance of His blood.

243. Q. Is Jesus Christ whole and entire both under the form of bread and under the form of wine?

A. Jesus Christ is whole and entire both under the form of bread and under the form of wine.

244. Q. Did anything remain of the bread and wine after their substance had been changed into the substance of the body and blood of our Lord?

A. After the substance of the bread and wine had been changed into the substance of the body and blood of our Lord there remained only the appearances of bread and wine.

245. Q. What do you mean by the appearances of bread and wine?

A. By the appearances of bread and wine I mean the figure, the color, the taste, and whatever appears to the senses.

246. Q. What is this change of the bread and wine into the body and blood of our Lord called?

A. This change of the bread and wine into the body and blood of our Lord is called Transubstantiation.

247. Q. How was the substance of the bread and wine changed into the substance of the body and blood of Christ?

A. The substance of the bread and wine was changed into the substance of the body and blood of Christ by His almighty power.

248. Q. Does this change of bread and wine into the body and blood of Christ continue to be made in the Church?

A. This change of bread and wine into the body and blood of Christ continues to be made in the Church by Jesus Christ through the ministry of His priests.

249. Q. When did Christ give His priests the power to change bread and wine into His body and blood?

A. Christ gave His priests the power to change bread and wine into His body and blood when He said to the Apostles, *Do this in commemoration of Me.*

250. Q. How do the priests exercise this power of changing bread and wine into the body and blood of Christ?

A. The priests exercise this power of changing bread and wine into the body and blood of Christ through the words of consecration in the Mass, which are the words of Christ: *This is My body; this is My blood.*

23. ON THE ENDS FOR WHICH THE HOLY EUCHARIST WAS INSTITUTED

251. Q. Why did Christ institute the Holy Eucharist?

A. Christ instituted the Holy Eucharist—
1. To unite us to Himself and to nourish our soul with His divine life.
2. To increase sanctifying grace and all virtues in our soul.
3. To lessen our evil inclinations.
4. To be a pledge of everlasting life.
5. To fit our bodies for a glorious resurrection.
6. To continue the sacrifice of the Cross in His Church.

252. Q. How are we united to Jesus Christ in the Holy Eucharist?

A. We are united to Jesus Christ in the Holy Eucharist by means of Holy Communion.

253. Q. What is Holy Communion?

A. Holy Communion is the receiving of the body and blood of Christ.

254. Q. What is necessary to make a good Communion?

A. To make a good Communion it is necessary to be in the state of sanctifying grace and to be fasting from midnight.

255. Q. Does he who receives Communion in mortal sin receive the body and blood of Christ?

A. He who receives Communion in mortal sin receives the body and blood of Christ, but does not receive His grace, and he commits a great sacrilege.

256. Q. Is it enough to be free from mortal sin to receive plentifully the graces of Holy Communion?

A. To receive plentifully the graces of Holy Communion it is not enough to be free from mortal sin, but we should be free from all affection to venial sin, and should make acts of lively faith, of firm hope, and ardent love.

257. Q. What is the fast necessary for Holy Communion?

A. The fast necessary for Holy Communion is the abstaining from midnight from everything which is taken as food or drink.

258. Q. Is anyone ever allowed to receive Holy Communion when not fasting?

A. Anyone in danger of death is allowed to receive Holy Communion when not fasting.

259. Q. When are we bound to receive Holy Communion?

A. We are bound to receive Holy Communion, under pain of mortal sin, during the Easter time and when in danger of death.

260. Q. Is it well to receive Holy Communion often?

A. It is well to receive Holy Communion often, as nothing is a greater aid to a holy life than often to receive the Author of all grace and the Source of all good.

261. Q. What should we do after Holy Communion?

A. After Holy Communion we should spend some time in adoring our Lord, in thanking Him for the grace we have received, and in asking Him for the blessings we need.

24. ON THE SACRIFICE OF THE MASS

262. Q. When and where are the bread and wine changed into the body and blood of Christ?

A. The bread and wine are changed into the body and blood of Christ at the Consecration in the Mass.

263. Q. What is the Mass?

A. The Mass is the unbloody sacrifice of the body and blood of Christ.

264. Q. What is a sacrifice?

A. A sacrifice is the offering of an object by a priest to God alone, and the consuming of it to acknowledge that He is the Creator and Lord of all things.

265. Q. Is the Mass the same sacrifice as that of the Cross?

A. The Mass is the same sacrifice as that of the Cross.

266. Q. How is the Mass the same sacrifice as that of the Cross?

A. The Mass is the same sacrifice as that of the Cross because the offering and the priest are the same— Christ our Blessed Lord; and the ends for which the sacrifice of the Mass is offered are the same as those of the sacrifice of the Cross.

267. Q. What were the ends for which the sacrifice of the Cross was offered?

A. The ends for which the sacrifice of the Cross was offered were: 1st, To honor and glorify God; 2nd, To thank Him for all the graces bestowed on the whole world; 3rd, To satisfy God's justice for the sins of men; 4th, To obtain all graces and blessings.

268. Q. Is there any difference between the sacrifice of the Cross and the sacrifice of the Mass?

A. Yes; the manner in which the sacrifice is offered is different. On the Cross Christ really shed His blood and was really slain; in the Mass there is no real shedding of blood nor real death, because Christ can die no more; but the sacrifice of the Mass, through the separate consecration of the bread and wine, represents His death on the Cross.

269. Q. How should we assist at Mass?

A. We should assist at Mass with great interior recollection and piety and with every outward mark of respect and devotion.

270. Q. Which is the best manner of hearing Mass?

A. The best manner of hearing Mass is to offer it to God with the priest for the same purpose for which it is said, to meditate on Christ's sufferings and death, and to go to Holy Communion.

25. ON EXTREME UNCTION AND HOLY ORDERS

271. Q. What is the Sacrament of Extreme Unction?

A. Extreme Unction is the Sacrament which, through the anointing and prayer of the priest, gives health and strength to the soul, and sometimes to the body, when we are in danger of death from sickness.

272. Q. When should we receive Extreme Unction?

A. We should receive Extreme Unction when we are in danger of death from sickness, or from a wound or accident.

273. Q. Should we wait until we are in extreme danger before we receive Extreme Unction?

A. We should not wait until we are in extreme danger before we receive Extreme Unction, but if possible we should receive it while we have the use of our senses.

274. Q. Which are the effects of the Sacrament of Extreme Unction?

A. The effects of Extreme Unction are: 1st, To comfort us in the pains of sickness and to strengthen us against temptations; 2nd, To remit venial sins and to cleanse our soul from the remains of sin; 3rd, To restore us to health, when God sees fit.

275. Q. What do you mean by the remains of sin?
  A. By the remains of sin I mean the inclination to evil and the weakness of the will which are the result of our sins, and which remain after our sins have been forgiven.

276. Q. How should we receive the Sacrament of Extreme Unction?
  A. We should receive the Sacrament of Extreme Unction in the state of grace, and with lively faith and resignation to the will of God.

277. Q. Who is the minister of the Sacrament of Extreme Unction?
  A. The priest is the minister of the Sacrament of Extreme Unction.

278. Q. What is the Sacrament of Holy Orders?
  A. Holy Orders is a Sacrament by which bishops, priests, and other ministers of the Church are ordained and receive the power and grace to perform their sacred duties.

279. Q. What is necessary to receive Holy Orders worthily?
  A. To receive Holy Orders worthily it is necessary to be in the state of grace, to have the necessary knowledge and a divine call to this sacred office.

280. Q. How should Christians look upon the priests of the Church?
  A. Christians should look upon the priests of the Church as the messengers of God and the dispensers of His mysteries.

281. Q. Who can confer the Sacrament of Holy Orders?
  A. Bishops can confer the Sacrament of Holy Orders.

26. ON MATRIMONY

282. Q. What is the Sacrament of Matrimony?
  A. The Sacrament of Matrimony is the Sacrament which unites a Christian man and woman in lawful marriage.

283. Q. Can a Christian man or woman be united in lawful marriage in any other way than by the Sacrament of Matrimony?

A. A Christian man and woman cannot be united in lawful marriage in any other way than by the Sacrament of Matrimony, because Christ raised marriage to the dignity of a Sacrament.

284. Q. Can the bond of Christian marriage be dissolved by any human power?

A. The bond of Christian marriage cannot be dissolved by any human power.

285. Q. Which are the effects of the Sacrament of Matrimony?

A. The effects of the Sacrament of Matrimony are, 1st, To sanctify the love of husband and wife; 2nd, To give them grace to bear with each other's weaknesses; 3rd, To enable them to bring up their children in the fear and love of God.

286. Q. To receive the Sacrament of Matrimony worthily is it necessary to be in the state of grace?

A. To receive the Sacrament of Matrimony worthily it is necessary to be in the state of grace, and it is necessary also to comply with the laws of the Church.

287. Q. Who has the right to make laws concerning the Sacrament of Marriage?

A. The Church alone has the right to make laws concerning the Sacrament of Marriage, though the state also has the right to make laws concerning the civil effects of the marriage contract.

288. Q. Does the Church forbid the marriage of Catholics with persons who have a different religion or no religion at all?

A. The Church does forbid the marriage of Catholics with persons who have a different religion or no religion at all.

289. Q. **Why does the Church forbid the marriage of Catholics with persons who have a different religion or no religion at all?**

A. The Church forbids the marriage of Catholics with persons who have a different religion or no religion at all, because such marriages generally lead to indifference, loss of faith, and to the neglect of the religious education of the children.

290. Q. **Why do many marriages prove unhappy?**

A. Many marriages prove unhappy because they are entered into hastily and without worthy motives.

291. Q. **How should Christians prepare for a holy and happy marriage?**

A. Christians should prepare for a holy and happy marriage by receiving the Sacraments of Penance and Holy Eucharist, by begging God to grant them a pure intention and to direct their choice; and by seeking the advice of their parents and the blessing of their pastors.

27. ON THE SACRAMENTALS

292. Q. **What is a sacramental?**

A. A sacramental is anything set apart or blessed by the Church to excite good thoughts, and to increase devotion, and through these movements of the heart to remit venial sin.

293. Q. **What is the difference between the Sacraments and the sacramentals?**

A. The difference between the Sacraments and the sacramentals is: 1st, The Sacraments were instituted by Jesus Christ and the sacramentals were instituted by the Church; 2nd, The Sacraments give grace of themselves when we place no obstacle in the way; the sacramentals excite in us pious dispositions, by means of which we may obtain grace.

294. Q. Which is the chief sacramental used in the Church?

A. The chief sacramental used in the Church is the sign of the cross.

295. Q. How do we make the sign of the cross?

A. We make the sign of the cross by putting the right hand to the forehead, then on the breast, and then to the left and right shoulders, saying, *In the name of the Father, and of the Son, and of the Holy Ghost. Amen.*

296. Q. Why do we make the sign of the cross?

A. We make the sign of the cross to show that we are Christians and to profess our belief in the chief mysteries of our religion.

297. Q. How is the sign of the cross a profession of faith in the chief mysteries of our religion?

A. The sign of the cross is a profession of faith in the chief mysteries of our religion because it expresses the mysteries of the Unity and Trinity of God and of the Incarnation and death of our Lord.

298. Q. How does the sign of the cross express the mystery of the Unity and Trinity of God?

A. The words, *in the name,* express the Unity of God; the words that follow, *of the Father, and of the Son, and of the Holy Ghost,* express the mystery of the Trinity.

299. Q. How does the sign of the cross express the mystery of the Incarnation and death of our Lord?

A. The sign of the cross expresses the mystery of the Incarnation by reminding us that the Son of God, having become man, suffered death on the cross.

300. Q. What other sacramental is in very frequent use?

A. Another sacramental in very frequent use is holy water.

301. Q. What is Holy Water?

    A. Holy water is water blessed by the priest with solemn prayer to beg God's blessing on those who use it, and protection from the powers of darkness.

302. Q. Are there other sacramentals besides the sign of the cross and holy water?

    A. Besides the sign of the cross and holy water there are many other sacramentals, such as blessed candles, ashes, palms, crucifixes, images of the Blessed Virgin and of the saints, rosaries, and scapulars.

28. ON PRAYER

303. Q. Is there any other means of obtaining God's grace than the Sacraments?

    A. There is another means of obtaining God's grace, and it is prayer.

304. Q. What is prayer?

    A. Prayer is the lifting up of our minds and hearts to God to adore Him, to thank Him for His benefits, to ask His forgiveness, and to beg of Him all the graces we need whether for soul or body.

305. Q. Is prayer necessary to salvation?

    A. Prayer is necessary to salvation, and without it no one having the use of reason can be saved.

306. Q. At what particular times should we pray?

    A. We should pray particularly on Sundays and holydays, every morning and night, in all dangers, temptations, and afflictions.

307. Q. How should we pray?

    A. We should pray: 1st, with attention; 2nd, With a sense of our own helplessness and dependence upon God; 3rd, With a great desire for the graces we beg of God; 4th, With trust in God's goodness; 5th, With perseverance.

308. Q. Which are the prayers most recommended to us?

A. The prayers most recommended to us are the Lord's Prayer, the Hail Mary, the Apostles' Creed, the Confiteor, and the Acts of Faith, Hope, Love, and Contrition.

309. Q. Are prayers said with distractions of any avail?

A. Prayers said with willful distractions are of no avail.

29. ON THE COMMANDMENTS OF GOD

310. Q. Is it enough to belong to God's Church in order to be saved?

A. It is not enough to belong to the Church in order to be saved, but we must also keep the Commandments of God and of the Church.

311. Q. Which are the Commandments that contain the whole law of God?

A. The Commandments which contain the whole law of God are these two: 1st, Thou shalt love the Lord thy God with thy whole heart, with thy whole soul, with thy whole strength, and with thy whole mind; 2nd, Thou shalt love thy neighbor as thyself.

312. Q. Why do these two Commandments of the love of God and of our neighbor contain the whole law of God?

A. These two Commandments of the love of God and of our neighbor contain the whole law of God because all the other Commandments are given either to help us to keep these two, or to direct us how to shun what is opposed to them.

313. Q. Which are the Commandments of God?
   A. The Commandments of God are these ten:
   1. I am the Lord thy God, who brought thee out of the land of Egypt, out of the house of bondage. Thou shalt not have strange gods before Me. Thou shalt not make to thyself a graven thing, nor the likeness of anything that is in heaven above, or in the earth beneath, nor of those things that are in the waters under the earth. Thou shalt not adore them, nor serve them.
   2. Thou shalt not take the name of the Lord thy God in vain.
   3. Remember thou keep holy the Sabbath day.
   4. Honor thy father and thy mother.
   5. Thou shalt not kill.
   6. Thou shalt not commit adultery.
   7. Thou shalt not steal.
   8. Thou shalt not bear false witness against thy neighbor.
   9. Thou shalt not covet thy neighbor's wife.
   10. Thou shalt not covet thy neighbor's goods.

314. Q. Who gave the Ten Commandments?
   A. God Himself gave the Ten Commandments to Moses on Mount Sinai, and Christ our Lord confirmed them.

30. ON THE FIRST COMMANDMENT

315. Q. What is the first Commandment?
   A. The first Commandment is: I am the Lord thy God; thou shalt not have strange gods before Me.

316. Q. How does the first Commandment help us to keep the great Commandment of the love of God?
   A. The first Commandment helps us to keep the great Commandment of the love of God because it commands us to adore God alone.

317. Q. How do we adore God?

A. We adore God by faith, hope, and charity, by prayer and sacrifice.

318. Q. How may the first Commandment be broken?

A. The first Commandment may be broken by giving to a creature the honor which belongs to God alone; by false worship; and by attributing to a creature a perfection which belongs to God alone.

319. Q. Do those who make use of spells and charms, or who believe in dreams, in mediums, spiritists, fortune tellers, and the like, sin against the first Commandment?

A. Those who make use of spells and charms, or who believe in dreams, in mediums, spiritists, fortune tellers, and the like, sin against the first Commandment, because they attribute to creatures perfections which belong to God alone.

320. Q. Are sins against faith, hope, and charity, also sins against the first Commandment?

A. Sins against faith, hope, and charity are also sins against the first Commandment.

321. Q. How does a person sin against faith?

A. A person sins against faith: 1st, By not trying to know what God has taught; 2nd, By refusing to believe all that God has taught; 3rd, By neglecting to profess his belief in what God has taught.

322. Q. How do we fail to try to know what God has taught?

A. We fail to try to know what God has taught by neglecting to learn the Christian doctrine.

323. Q. Who are they who do not believe all that God has taught?

A. They who do not believe all that God has taught are the heretics and infidels.

324. Q. Who are they who neglect to profess their belief in what God has taught?

A. They who neglect to profess their belief in what God has taught are all those who fail to acknowledge the true Church in which they really believe.

325. Q. Can they who fail to profess their faith in the true Church in which they believe expect to be saved while in that state?

A. They who fail to profess their faith in the true Church in which they believe cannot expect to be saved while in that state, for Christ has said: "Whoever shall deny Me before men, I will also deny him before My Father who is in heaven."

326. Q. Are we obliged to make open profession of our faith?

A. We are obliged to make open profession of our faith as often as God's honor, our neighbor's spiritual good, or our own requires it. "Whosoever," says Christ, "shall confess Me before men, I will also confess him before My Father who is in heaven."

327. Q. Which are the sins against hope?

A. The sins against hope are presumption and despair.

328. Q. What is presumption?

A. Presumption is a rash expectation of salvation without making proper use of the necessary means to obtain it.

329. Q. What is despair?

A. Despair is the loss of hope in God's mercy.

330. Q. How do we sin against the love of God?

A. We sin against the love of God by all sin, but particularly by mortal sin.

31. THE FIRST COMMANDMENT—ON THE HONOR AND INVOCATION OF SAINTS

331. Q. Does the first Commandment forbid the honoring of saints?

A. The first Commandment does not forbid the honoring of the saints, but rather approves of it; because by honoring the saints who are the chosen friends of God, we honor God Himself.

332. Q. Does the first Commandment forbid us to pray to the saints?

A. The first Commandment does not forbid us to pray to the saints.

333. Q. What do you mean by praying to the saints?

A. By praying to the saints we mean the asking of their help and prayers.

334. Q. How do we know that the saints hear us?

A. We know that the saints hear us; because they are with God, who makes our prayers known to them.

335. Q. Why do we believe that the saints will help us?

A. We believe that the saints will help us, because both they and we are members of the same Church, and they love us as their brethren.

336. Q. How are the saints and we members of the same Church?

A. The saints and we are members of the same Church, because the Church in heaven and the Church on earth are one and the same Church, and all its members are in communion with one another.

337. Q. What is the Communion of the members of the Church called?

A. The communion of the members of the Church is called the communion of saints.

338. Q. What does the communion of saints mean?

A. The communion of saints means the union which exists between the members of the Church on earth with one another, and with the blessed in Heaven, and with the suffering souls in Purgatory.

339. Q. What benefits are derived from the communion of saints?

A. The following benefits are derived from the communion of saints—the faithful on earth assist one another by their prayers and good works, and they are aided by the intercession of the saints in Heaven, while both the saints in Heaven and the faithful on earth help the souls in Purgatory.

340. Q. Does the first Commandment forbid us to honor relics?

A. The first Commandment does not forbid us to honor relics, because relics are the bodies of the saints or objects directly connected with them or with our Lord.

341. Q. Does the first Commandment forbid the making of images?

A. The first Commandment does forbid the making of images if they are made to be adored as gods, but it does not forbid the making of them to put us in mind of Jesus Christ, His Blessed Mother, and the saints.

342. Q. Is it right to show respect to the pictures and images of Christ and His saints?

A. It is right to show respect to the pictures and images of Christ and His saints, because they are the representations and memorials of them.

343. Q. Is it allowed to pray to the crucifix or to the images and relics of the saints?

A. It is not allowed to pray to the crucifix or images and relics of the saints, for they have no life, nor power to help us, nor sense to hear us.

344. Q. Why do we pray before the crucifix and the images and relics of the saints?

A. We pray before the crucifix and the images and relics of the saints because they enliven our devotion by exciting pious affections and desires, and by reminding us of Christ and of the saints, that we may imitate their virtues.

32. FROM THE SECOND TO THE FOURTH COMMANDMENT

345. Q. What is the second Commandment?

A. The second Commandment is: Thou shalt not take the name of the Lord thy God in vain.

346. Q. What are we commanded by the second Commandment?

A. We are commanded by the second Commandment to speak with reverence of God and of the saints, and of all holy things, and to keep our lawful oaths and vows.

347. Q. What is an oath?

A. An oath is the calling upon God to witness the truth of what we say.

348. Q. When may we take an oath?

A. We may take an oath when it is ordered by lawful authority or required for God's honor or for our own or our neighbor's good.

349. Q. What is necessary to make an oath lawful?

A. To make an oath lawful it is necessary that what we swear to be true, and that there be a sufficient cause for taking an oath.

350. Q. What is a vow?

A. A vow is a deliberate promise made to God to do something that is pleasing to Him.

351. Q. Is it a sin not to fulfill our vows?

A. Not to fulfill our vows is a sin, mortal or venial, according to the nature of the vow and the intention we had in making it.

352. Q. What is forbidden by the second Commandment?

A. The second Commandment forbids all false, rash, unjust, and unnecessary oaths, blasphemy, cursing, and profane words.

353. Q. What is the third Commandment?

A. The third Commandment is: Remember thou keep holy the Sabbath day.

354. Q. What are we commanded by the third Commandment?

A. By the third Commandment we are commanded to keep holy the Lord's day and holydays of obligation, on which we are to give our time to the service and worship of God.

355. Q. How are we to worship God on Sundays and holydays of obligation?

A. We are to worship God on Sundays and holydays of obligation by hearing Mass, by prayer, and by other good works.

356. Q. Are the Sabbath day and the Sunday the same?

A. The Sabbath day and the Sunday are not the same. The Sabbath is the seventh day of the week, and is the day which was kept holy in the old law; the Sunday is the first day of the week, and is the day which is kept holy in the new law.

357. Q. Why does the Church command us to keep the Sunday holy instead of the Sabbath?

A. The Church commands us to keep the Sunday holy instead of the Sabbath because on Sunday Christ rose from the dead, and on Sunday He sent the Holy Ghost upon the Apostles.

358. Q. What is forbidden by the third Commandment?

A. The third Commandment forbids all unnecessary servile work and whatever else may hinder the due observance of the Lord's day.

359. Q. What are servile works?

A. Servile works are those which require labor rather of body than of mind.

360. Q. Are servile works on Sunday ever lawful?

A. Servile works are lawful on Sunday when the honor of God, the good of our neighbor, or necessity requires them.

33. FROM THE FOURTH TO THE SEVENTH COMMANDMENT

361. Q. What is the fourth Commandment?

A. The fourth Commandment is: Honor thy father and thy mother.

362. Q. What are we commanded by the fourth Commandment?

A. We are commanded by the fourth Commandment to honor, love, and obey our parents in all that is not sin.

363. Q. Are we bound to honor and obey others than our parents?

A. We are also bound to honor and obey our bishops, pastors, magistrates, teachers, and other lawful superiors.

364. Q. Have parents and superiors any duties toward those who are under their charge?

A. It is the duty of parents and superiors to take good care of all under their charge and give them proper direction and example.

365. Q. What is forbidden by the fourth Commandment?

A. The fourth Commandment forbids all disobedience, contempt, and stubbornness toward our parents or lawful superiors.

366. Q. What is the fifth Commandment?
A. The fifth Commandment is: Thou shalt not kill.

367. Q. What are we commanded by the fifth Commandment?
A. We are commanded by the fifth Commandment to live in peace and union with our neighbor, to respect his rights, to seek his spiritual and bodily welfare, and to take proper care of our own life and health.

368. Q. What is forbidden by the fifth Commandment?
A. The fifth Commandment forbids all willful murder, fighting, anger, hatred, revenge, and bad example.

369. Q. What is the sixth Commandment?
A. The sixth Commandment is: Thou shalt not commit adultery.

370. Q. What are we commanded by the sixth Commandment?
A. We are commanded by the sixth Commandment to be pure in thought and modest in all our looks, words, and actions.

371. Q. What is forbidden by the sixth Commandment?
A. The sixth Commandment forbids all unchaste freedom with another's wife or husband; it forbids also immodesty with ourselves or others in looks, dress, words, or actions.

372. Q. Does the sixth Commandment forbid the reading of bad and immodest books and newspapers?
A. The sixth Commandment does forbid the reading of bad and immodest books and newspapers.

34. FROM THE SEVENTH TO THE END OF THE TENTH COMMANDMENT

373. Q. What is the seventh Commandment?
A. The seventh Commandment is: Thou shalt not steal.

374. Q. What are we commanded by the seventh Commandment?

A. By the seventh Commandment we are commanded to give to all men what belongs to them and to respect their property.

375. Q. What is forbidden by the seventh Commandment?

A. The seventh Commandment forbids all unjust taking or keeping what belongs to another.

376. Q. Are we bound to restore ill-gotten goods?

A. We are bound to restore ill-gotten goods, or the value of them, as far as we are able; otherwise we cannot be forgiven.

377. Q. Are we obliged to repair the damage we have unjustly caused?

A. We are bound to repair the damage we have unjustly caused.

378. Q. What is the eighth Commandment?

A. The eighth Commandment is: Thou shalt not bear false witness against thy neighbor.

379. Q. What are we commanded by the eighth Commandment?

A. We are commanded by the eighth Commandment to speak the truth in all things, and to be careful of the honor and reputation of everyone.

380. Q. What is forbidden by the eighth Commandment?

A. The eighth Commandment forbids all rash judgment, backbiting, slanders, and lies.

381. Q. What must they do who have lied about their neighbor and seriously injured his character?

A. They who have lied about their neighbor and seriously injured his character must repair the injury done as far as they are able, otherwise they will not be forgiven.

382. Q. What is the ninth Commandment?

A. The ninth Commandment is: Thou shalt not covet thy neighbor's wife.

383. Q. What are we commanded by the ninth Commandment?

A. We are commanded by the ninth Commandment to keep ourselves pure in thought and desire.

384. Q. What is forbidden by the ninth Commandment?

A. The ninth Commandment forbids unchaste thoughts, desires of another's wife or husband, and all other unlawful impure thoughts and desires.

385. Q. Are impure thoughts and desires always sins?

A. Impure thoughts and desires are always sins, unless they displease us and we try to banish them.

386. Q. What is the tenth Commandment?

A. The tenth Commandment is: Thou shalt not covet thy neighbor's goods.

387. Q. What are we commanded by the tenth Commandment?

A. By the tenth Commandment we are commanded to be content with what we have, and to rejoice in our neighbor's welfare.

388. Q. What is forbidden by the tenth Commandment?

A. The tenth Commandment forbids all desires to take or keep wrongfully what belongs to another.

35. ON THE FIRST AND SECOND COMMANDMENTS OF THE CHURCH

389. Q. Which are the chief Commandments of the Church?

A. The chief Commandments of the Church are six:

1. To hear Mass on Sundays and holydays of obligation.
2. To fast and abstain on the days appointed.
3. To confess at least once a year.
4. To receive the Holy Eucharist during the Easter time.
5. To contribute to the support of our pastors.
6. Not to marry persons who are not Catholics, or who are related to us within the third degree of kindred, nor privately without witnesses, nor to solemnize marriage at forbidden times.

390. Q. Is it a mortal sin not to hear Mass on a Sunday or holyday of obligation?

A. It is a mortal sin not to hear Mass on a Sunday or a holyday of obligation, unless we are excused for a serious reason. They also commit a mortal sin who, having others under their charge, hinder them from hearing Mass, without a sufficient reason.

391. Q. Why are holydays instituted by the Church?

A. Holydays were instituted by the Church to recall to our minds the great mysteries of religion and the virtues and rewards of the saints.

392. Q. How should we keep the holydays of obligation?

A. We should keep the holydays of obligation as we should keep the Sunday.

393. Q. What do you mean by fast days?

A. By fast days I mean days on which we are allowed but one full meal.

394. Q. What do you mean by days of abstinence?

A. By days of abstinence I mean days on which we are forbidden to eat flesh meat, but are allowed the usual number of meals.

395. Q. Why does the Church command us to fast and abstain?

A. The Church commands us to fast and abstain, in order that we may mortify our passions and satisfy for our sins.

396. Q. Why does the Church command us to abstain from flesh meat on Fridays?

A. The Church commands us to abstain from flesh meat on Fridays, in honor of the day on which our Saviour died.

36. ON THE THIRD, FOURTH, FIFTH, AND SIXTH COMMANDMENTS OF THE CHURCH

397. Q. What is meant by the command of confessing at least once a year?

A. By the command of confessing at least once a year is meant that we are obliged under pain of mortal sin, to go to confession within the year.

398. Q. Should we confess only once a year?

A. We should confess frequently, if we wish to lead a good life.

399. Q. Should children go to Confession?

A. Children should go to Confession when they are old enough to commit sin, which is commonly about the age of seven years.

400. Q. What sin does he commit who neglects to receive Communion during Easter time?

A. He who neglects to receive Communion during the Easter time commits a mortal sin.

401. Q. What is the Easter time?

A. The Easter time is, in this country, the time between the first Sunday of Lent and Trinity Sunday.

402. Q. Are we obliged to contribute to the support of our pastors?

A. We are obliged to contribute to the support of our pastors, and to bear our share in the expenses of the Church and school.

403. Q. What is the meaning of the commandment not to marry within the third degree of kindred?

A. The meaning of the commandment not to marry within the third degree of kindred is that no one is allowed to marry another within the third degree of blood relationship.

404. Q. What is the meaning of the command not to marry privately?

A. The command not to marry privately means that none should marry without the blessing of God's priests or without witnesses.

405. Q. What is the meaning of the precept not to solemnize marriage at forbidden times?

A. The meaning of the precept not to solemnize marriage at forbidden times is that during Lent and Advent the marriage ceremony should not be performed with pomp or a nuptial Mass.

406. What is nuptial Mass?

A. The nuptial Mass is a Mass appointed by the Church to invoke a special blessing upon the married couple.

407. Q. Should Catholics be married at a nuptial Mass?

A. Catholics should be married at a nuptial Mass, because they thereby show greater reverence for the holy Sacrament and bring richer blessings upon their wedded life.

37. ON THE LAST JUDGMENT AND THE RESURRECTION, HELL, PURGATORY, AND HEAVEN

408. Q. When will Christ judge us?

A. Christ will judge us immediately after our death, and on the last day.

409. Q. What is the judgment called which we have to undergo immediately after death?

A. The judgment we have to undergo immediately after death is called the Particular Judgment.

410. Q. What is the judgment called which all men have to undergo on the last day?

A. The judgment which all men have to undergo on the last day is called the General Judgment.

411. Q. Why does Christ judge men immediately after death?

A. Christ judges men immediately after death to reward or punish them according to their deeds.

412. Q. What are the rewards or punishments appointed for men's souls after the Particular Judgment?

A. The rewards or punishments appointed for men's souls after the Particular Judgment are Heaven, Purgatory, and Hell.

413. Q. What is Hell?

A. Hell is a state to which the wicked are condemned, and in which they are deprived of the sight of God for all eternity, and are in dreadful torments.

414. Q. What is Purgatory?

A. Purgatory is the state in which those suffer for a time who die guilty of venial sins, or without having satisfied for the punishment due to their sins.

415. Q. Can the faithful on earth help the souls in Purgatory?

A. The faithful on earth can help the souls in Purgatory by their prayers, fasts, almsdeeds; by indulgences, and by having Masses said for them.

416. Q. If everyone is judged immediately after death, what need is there of a general judgment?

A. There is need of a general judgment, though everyone is judged immediately after death, that the providence of God, which on earth, often permits the good to suffer and the wicked to prosper, may in the end appear just before all men.

417. Q. Will our bodies share in the reward or punishment of our souls?

A. Our bodies will share in the reward or punishment of our souls, because through the resurrection they will again be united to them.

418. Q. In what state will the bodies of the just rise?

A. The bodies of the just will rise glorious and immortal.

419. Q. Will the bodies of the damned also rise?

A. The bodies of the damned will also rise, but they will be condemned to eternal punishment.

420. Q. What is heaven?

A. Heaven is the state of everlasting life in which we see God face to face, are made like unto Him in glory, and enjoy eternal happiness.

421. Q. What words should we bear always in mind?

A. We should bear always in mind these words of our Lord and Saviour Jesus Christ: *"What doth it profit a man if he gain the whole world and suffer the loss of his own soul, or what exchange shall a man give for his soul? For the Son of man shall come in the glory of His Father with His angels; and then will He render to every man according to his works."*

Printed in the USA
CPSIA information can be obtained
at www.ICGtesting.com
JSHW011909260924
70275JS00008B/151

9 781640 510388